# EARTHQUAKES

OINK

GLENDOWER:
The frame and huge foundation of the earth
Shak'd like a coward....
I say the earth did shake when I was born....
The heavens were all on fire, the earth did tremble.
HOTSPUR:
Diseased Nature oftentimes breaks forth
In strange eruptions: oft the teeming earth
Is with a kind of colic pinch'd and vex'd
By the imprisoning of unruly wind
Within her womb; which, for enlargement striving,
Shakes the old beldam earth, and topples down
Steeples, and moss-grown towers. At your birth
Our granddam earth, having this distemperature,
In passion shook.

Shakespeare, *Henry IV, Pt. 1*

# EARTHQUAKES

## G A Eiby

**Heinemann**

**Heinemann Educational Books**
26 Kilham Avenue, Auckland 9, New Zealand
22 Bedford Square, London WC 1B 3HH, England
4 Front Street, Exeter, New Hampshire 03833, U.S.A.

Also at Edinburgh, Melbourne, Johannesburg, Ibadan,
Nairobi, Lusaka, New Delhi, Hong Kong, Singapore,
Kuala Lumpur, Kingston, Port of Spain

ISBN 0 86863 380 1
SBN 435 55076 4

© 1980 G. A. Eiby
First published 1980


Type set by Rennies Illustrations, Auckland
Printed by Bright Sun Printing Press Co. Ltd., Hong Kong

80 010082

# Contents

Preface    vi
Acknowledgements    vii
List of plates    ix
List of figures    xi

| | | |
|---|---|---:|
| 1 | By way of introduction | 1 |
| 2 | On feeling an earthquake | 3 |
| 3 | Recording an earthquake | 7 |
| 4 | Reading the records | 16 |
| 5 | Preliminary probing | 30 |
| 6 | Down to rock bottom | 38 |
| 7 | Inside the Earth | 44 |
| 8 | Continents and oceans | 54 |
| 9 | How earthquakes happen | 60 |
| 10 | Where earthquakes happen | 70 |
| 11 | Sizes and numbers | 78 |
| 12 | Earth waves and sea waves | 83 |
| 13 | Earthquakes and volcanoes | 89 |
| 14 | Earthquake prediction | 95 |
| 15 | Safe as houses | 106 |
| 16 | Zoning and insurance | 129 |
| 17 | Earthquakes and the bomb | 134 |
| 18 | Out of this world | 141 |
| 19 | More seismic geography | 146 |
| 20 | Some famous earthquakes | 164 |
| 21 | Some recent earthquakes | 172 |

| | |
|---|---:|
| Appendix | 182 |
| Facts and figures | 182 |
| The size of the Earth | 182 |
| The geological column | 183 |
| Felt intensity scales | 183 |
| Magnitudes and energies | 184 |
| Earthquake statistics | 186 |
| Historical earthquakes 1500-1902 | 187 |
| Important earthquakes since 1903 | 189 |
| New Zealand earthquakes | 193 |
| A short book-list | 196 |
| Index | 199 |

# Preface

*Earthquakes* began as a series of notes answering questions raised by the volunteers who operate many of New Zealand's seismograph stations. They were combined with a series of radio talks to become a small book published by Frederick Muller in 1957, which ran to two editions in Britain and one in the U.S.A. Although intended for the man in the street who wanted to know 'something about earthquakes' it was also well received in academic and technical circles and by engineers and architects who wanted background information.

Since the original book was written there has been something of a revolution in seismological thought and practice, and a new book rather than a revision seemed to be called for. With a change in publisher, this has become possible.

Readers familiar with it will find vestiges of the original version — some chapter headings, some illustrations, and here and there a whole paragraph — and it is hoped that something of the style and flavour that pleased its readers still remains, but much is new in both content and presentation. The new concepts of plate tectonics, and of the role of dilatancy in the mechanism of earthquakes have had to be explained, lunar seismology has become a reality, and earthquake prediction appears at last to be an attainable goal. The new book is therefore larger than the old. All the original figures have been redraughted, many new ones have been prepared, and there are additional photographs.

I must record my debt to all those seismologists, both of the present and of earlier generations, from whom I have learned. Chief among these is the late Mr R. C. Hayes, former Director of the Seismological Observatory in Wellington, who first introduced me to professional seismology, and whose long-neglected pioneering studies of the seismology of the south-west Pacific were belatedly recognized by the award to him in 1975 of the Royal Society of New Zealand's Hector Medal.

Thanks are also due to those colleagues who have pointed out errors and shortcomings of the earlier book, and offered criticisms of all or part of the new manuscript. Among these Mr M. A. Lowry, Dr M. J. Randall, Dr Warwick Smith, Dr John Latter, and Miss Diane Ware call for special mention. Their support and the encouragement of an even wider circle of colleagues and friends has added to the pleasure of the task.

G. A. Eiby

# Acknowledgements

The author wishes to record his indebtedness and to express his thanks to the seismologists in many lands, the scientists working in related disciplines, the international agencies, the prospecting companies, and the instrument manufacturers who have helped in innumerable ways with the preparation of this book. His gratitude towards those who have provided illustrations or granted permission for their use is particularly deep. This help has been extended at various times over a period of more than twenty years, since the first edition of the book was planned. It is possible that the passage of time has resulted in the omission of some desirable acknowledgement. If this is so, I hope the person overlooked will accept this expression of intent as the equivalent of the deed.

Thanks are due to the following for the specific assistance listed:

To Dr R. D. Adams, former Superintendent of the Seismological Observatory of the Geophysics Division of the New Zealand Department of Scientific and Industrial Research, for all seismograms reproduced, except those in Figure 64, which are printed with the permission of Dr Frank Press, and the lunar seismograms in Figure 68, which were supplied by Dr Nafi Toksöz, both of the Massachusetts Institute of Technology. Mention must be made of the help of Mr Brian Ferris of the Observatory staff in finding seismograms with suitable characteristics.

To the Director of the Geological Survey, D.S.I.R. for permission to use photographs from the Survey files, to Mr Lensen of his staff for help in choosing them, and to the photographers S. N. Beatus (Plate 17), D. L. Homer (Plates 18, 38, 65, 84 and 86), and B. D. Scott (Plate 40), also to Mr I. A. Nairn, District Geologist, Rotorua, for Plate 35.

To the Alexander Turnbull Library, Wellington, for Plates 2, 42, 43, 45, 58 and 85.

To Dr T. Hisada of the Building Research Institute of the Japanese Ministry of Construction, for Plates 50, 61 and 70; and for his considerable help in collecting photographs from other Japanese colleagues, to whom I extend individual thanks: Drs K. Muto (Plate 49), S. Omote (Plate 33), and K. Kishida (Plate 66).

To Dr N. Ambraseys, Dept. of Civil Engineering, Imperial College, London for Plates 25, 26, 27 and 28.

To Mr John Hollings of Wellington for Plates 52, 53 and 68.

To Mr Ray Rodley of Nelson, for Plate 1, and to Mr Albert Jones for related help.

To Dr George Pararas-Carayannis, Director of the International Tsunami Information Centre, Honolulu, for Plates 31 and 32.

To Professor T. Matsuda of the International Institute of Seismology and Earthquake Engineering, Tokyo, for Plate 78.

To Dr George Plafker of the U.S. Geological Survey for Plates 57 and 78 and the information on which Figure 80 is based.

To Mr R. G. Enticknap of the Lincoln Laboratories, Massachusetts Institute of Technology, for Figures 65 and 66.

To the late Mr B. W. Spooner, formerly Chief Engineer of the N.Z. Ministry of Works, Wellington, for Plates 62 and 88.

To Professor A. Heim, of Zurich, Switzerland, for Plate 23.

To Professor R. Shepherd of the School of Engineering, University of Auckland, for Plates 46 and 60.

To Mr R. Stanton of the Christchurch Civil Defence Organisation, for Plates 51, 90 and 91.

To Dr Ersin Arioğlu, Yapi Merkezi, Istanbul, Turkey, for Plates 29 and 30.

To Profesor B. A. Bolt, Department of Geology and Geophysics, University of California, Berkeley, for Plates 55, 56 and 69.

To Dr Mattsson, UNESCO Field Science Office for Southeast Asia, Djakarta, Indonesia, for Plates 34, 36 and 37.

To Dr Nafi Toksöz of the Massachusetts Institute of Technology and the U.S. National Aeronautics and Space Administration for Plate 60.

To the late Professor Beno Gutenberg, to Professor C. F. Richter, and to the Princeton University Press for Figures 50 and 51, which have been taken from their *Seismicity of the Earth*.

To Dr M. Barazangi, of Cornell University, Ithaca, New York, and to the editors of the *Bulletin of the Seismological Society of America* for permission to reproduce Figure 52.

To Prakla-Seismos GMBH, Hannover, Germany, for Plates 10, 12 and 13.

To the Seismograph Service Corporation, Tulsa, Oklahoma, for Plates 10, 11 and 15.

To the Geotechnical Corporation, Dallas, Texas, U.S.A., for Plates 4 and 5.

To the W. F. Sprengnether Instrument Co. Inc., Saint Louis, Missouri, U.S.A. for Plates 6 and 7.

To the Cambridge Scientific Instrument Co., Cambridge, England, for Plate 8.

To Hilger and Watts, Ltd, London, England, for Plate 9.

To the Director, U.S. National Centre for Earthquake Research, Menlo Park, California, for Figure 70.

To the U.S. National Earthquake Information Centre, Rockville, Maryland, for Plates 63, 75 and 83.

To the publishers of *Life* magazine for permission to reproduce Plate 24 (Photograph by David Scherman).

To the Director of the Institute of Engineering Mechanics, Harbin, China for Plates 41, 47, 48, 54, 71, 88 and 89, 103, 104, and to Dr R. D. Adams for related help.

To Asahi Shimbun for permission to reproduce Plates 59, 64, 67, 87 and 92.

The picture of faulting in the Mino-Owari earthquake (Plate 22) is a detail from a Collotype by K. Ogawa.

All figures not otherwise acknowledged, and Plates 16, 19 and 21 are the work of the author.

Finally, the help of Messrs E. Thornley, S. N. Beatus, and J. Whalan of the Science Information Division of the N.Z. Department of Scientific and Industrial Research in copying seismograms and other material, and in preparing Figure 3 calls for special mention and thanks.

# List of plates

| | | |
|---|---|---|
| **1** | Felt intensity scales | *page* 4 |
| **2** | Felt intensity scales | 5 |
| **3** | Mechanical seismographs | 9 |
| **4** | Benioff vertical seismometer | 12 |
| **5** | Benioff horizontal seismometer | 13 |
| **6** | A vertical pendulum | 14 |
| **7** | A horizontal pendulum | 14 |
| **8** | Galitzin seismograph | 15 |
| **9** | Willmore seismometer | 15 |
| **10** | Artificial earthquakes | 33 |
| **11** | A drilling rig | 34 |
| **12** | Seismic recording truck | 35 |
| **13** | Seismic prospecting | 35 |
| **14** | Seismic work at sea | 37 |
| **15** | Prospecting in shallow water | 37 |
| **16** | Sedimentary rocks | 39 |
| **17** | The geological column | 39 |
| **18** | Fossils | 40 |
| **19** | The geological column disrupted | 43 |
| **20** | Gravity measurements | 55 |
| **21** | Geological faulting | 60 |
| **22** | Vertical faulting | 61 |
| **23** | Vertical faulting | 62 |
| **24** | Transcurrent faulting | 62 |
| **25** | Transcurrent faulting | 62 |
| **26** | Mole tracks | 63 |
| **27** | Faulting and topography | 63 |
| **28** | The stronger wins | 63 |
| **29** | Weak buildings | 70 |
| **30** | Weak buildings | 71 |
| **31** | Tsunami damage | 85 |
| **32** | Tsunami damage | 86 |
| **33** | A tsunami wave | 87 |
| **34** | An andesitic cone | 90 |
| **35** | A vulcanian eruption | 90 |
| **36** | A nuée ardente | 91 |
| **37** | A nuée ardente | 91 |
| **38** | A lahar | 92 |
| **39** | Regional strain | 96 |
| **40** | A laser geodimeter | 97 |
| **41** | Earthquake prediction | 100, 101 |
| **42** | Inadequate cross-bracing | 106 |
| **43** | Chimneys | 107 |
| **44** | Bricks and tiles | 108 |
| **45** | Differences in natural period | 109 |
| **46** | Inertia | 110 |
| **47** | Chimneys | 111 |
| **48** | Inverted pendulum | 111 |
| **49** | Framed masonry panels | 112 |
| **50** | Unreinforced brick | 112 |

| 51 | Complete collapse | *page* 113 |
| 52 | Look both ways | 113 |
| 53 | Traditional and modern | 114 |
| 54 | Lateral movement | 115 |
| 55 | Poor bracing | 115 |
| 56 | Frame distortion | 116 |
| 57 | Wooden houses | 116 |
| 58 | Fires follow earthquakes | 117 |
| 59 | Rival neighbours | 117 |
| 60 | A building vibrator | 118 |
| 61 | A large shaking-table | 120 |
| 62 | Liquefaction of subsoil | 121 |
| 63 | Sand craters | 122 |
| 64 | Ground water | 123 |
| 65 | Broken communications | 124 |
| 66 | Bridge piers | 125 |
| 67 | Bridge approach | 126 |
| 68 | The weakest link | 127 |
| 69 | Temporary diversion | 127 |
| 70 | Poor foundations | 128 |
| 71 | Soil creep | 128 |
| 72 | An array seismograph | 138 |
| 73 | Data centre | 140 |
| 74 | Lunar seismology | 142 |
| 75 | San Andreas fault | 146 |
| 76 | The Alpine fault | 149 |
| 77 | Regional uplift | 155 |
| 78 | Faulting and uplift | 156 |
| 79 | Transcurrent faulting | 156 |
| 80 | Kwanto earthquake, 1923 | 157 |
| 81 | The ruins of Tokyo | 158 |
| 82 | Refugees | 158 |
| 83 | San Francisco earthquake, 1906 | 162 |
| 84 | Raised beach terraces | 166 |
| 85 | Marlborough earthquake, 1848 | 168 |
| 86 | Landslide | 170 |
| 87 | Superficial slumping | 175 |
| 88 | Improvisation | 177 |
| 89 | Restoration | 177 |
| 90 | The Huascarán avalanche | 178 |
| 91 | Lahar debris | 179 |
| 92 | What now? | 180 |

# List of figures

| | | |
|---|---|---|
| 1 | An isoseismal map | *page* 5 |
| 2 | Effect of focal depth on felt intensity | 6 |
| 3 | Response of a simple pendulum | 7 |
| 4 | Magnification of a seismograph | 8 |
| 5 | Common types of seismograph pendulum | 10,11 |
| 6 | Benioff vertical seismometer | 12 |
| 7 | Wood-Anderson torsion seismometer | 13 |
| 8 | Longitudinal and transverse waves | 16 |
| 9 | Finding the distance | 17 |
| 10 | Locating an epicentre | 18 |
| 11 | Focus and epicentre | 19 |
| 12 | Locating a deep earthquake | 19 |
| 13 | The shadow zone | 20 |
| 14 | Reflections from the core | 22 |
| 15 | Reflections at the Earth's surface | 22 |
| 16 | Core phases | 23 |
| 17 | A travel-time curve | 23 |
| 18 | A Love wave | 24 |
| 19 | A Rayleigh wave | 24 |
| 20 | Particle motion in a Rayleigh wave | 25 |
| 21 | Depth phases | 25 |
| 22 | Seismogram of a near earthquake | 27 |
| 23 | Distant earthquake record | 28 |
| 24 | Distant earthquake record | 28 |
| 25 | Distant earthquake record | 28 |
| 26 | A complex record | 29 |
| 27 | Deep and shallow earthquakes | 29 |
| 28 | Origin of crustal pulses | 31 |
| 29 | Travel-times of crustal pulses | 31 |
| 30 | Crustal pulses in a near earthquake | 32 |
| 31 | Reflection prospecting | 36 |
| 32 | The geological column | 41 |
| 33 | Mountain-building | 42 |
| 34 | Cross-sections of the crust | 46 |
| 35 | Wave motion | 47 |
| 36 | Dispersion of surface-waves | 48 |
| 37 | The crustal low-velocity channel | 50 |
| 38 | Density and seismic velocity inside the Earth | 51 |
| 39 | The Earth's interior | 52 |
| 40 | Free oscillations of the Earth | 53 |
| 41 | The principle of isostasy | 54 |
| 42 | Deflection of the plumb-line | 54 |
| 43 | Continental drift | 56 |
| 44 | Magnetic striping of the sea floor | 58 |
| 45 | Geological faulting | 61 |
| 46 | Elastic rebound | 64 |
| 47 | Elastic rebound | 65 |
| 48 | First-motion studies | 67 |
| 49 | First motions at Wellington | 68 |
| 50 | Seismicity of the Earth (shallow shocks) | 72 |

| | | |
|---|---|---|
| 51 | Seismicity of the Earth (deep shocks) | *page* 73 |
| 52 | Seismic geography | 74 |
| 53 | Plate tectonics | 75 |
| 54 | A spreading ridge | 76 |
| 55 | Attenuation in a subduction zone | 76 |
| 56 | Subduction beneath an island arc | 77 |
| 57 | Elastic creep | 81 |
| 58 | An aftershock sequence | 82 |
| 59 | A microseism storm | 84 |
| 60 | Volcanic tremor | 93 |
| 61 | Premonitory changes in velocity | 99 |
| 62 | Dilatancy and earthquake mechanism | 102 |
| 63 | A building vibrator | 119 |
| 64 | Which is the bomb? | 135 |
| 65 | A seismic array | 137 |
| 66 | A bore-hole seismometer | 139 |
| 67 | Lunar seismograph stations and moonquakes | 141 |
| 68 | Moonquake records | 144 |
| 69 | Internal structure of the Moon | 145 |
| 70 | Earthquakes in California | 147 |
| 71 | Faults in California | 148 |
| 72 | Large earthquakes in New Zealand | 150 |
| 73 | Shallow earthquakes in New Zealand | 151 |
| 74 | Deep earthquakes in New Zealand | 152 |
| 75 | Deep earthquakes in New Zealand | 153 |
| 76 | Seismotectonic features of New Zealand | 154 |
| 77 | Japanese deep earthquakes | 157 |
| 78 | Ground displacement in the Kwanto earthquake | 160 |
| 79 | Transform faulting | 161 |
| 80 | Uplift and subsidence in Alaska | 173 |
| 81 | New Zealand place-names | 194 |

# 1 By way of introduction

THIRD AVOCATORE: I've an earthquake in me!
Ben Jonson, *Volpone*

The study of earthquakes is neither a matter of compiling ancient tales of desolation and destruction, nor one of exploiting recent human misfortune for journalistic sensation. Earthquakes are an important part of man's environment, and no part of the globe can claim to be completely immune from them. Seismologists will be found at work in every civilized country, and in many that are not. They are in the first place concerned with why and how earthquakes occur, but this is far from being the whole of seismology. No part of the globe is more inaccessible than that lying directly beneath our feet, but by studying the earthquake-waves that have passed through it, the scientist is able to build up a picture of its internal structure in considerable detail. The methods he devised for doing so have turned out to be of equal value in the search for oil and minerals. In countries where earthquakes are frequent, they pose social and economic questions of great importance, and present special problems to the architect and the engineer. Seismology, then, has something to offer both the practical man and the seeker for fundamental truths of nature.

Scientific seismology is among the younger sciences. It is less than a century since the first satisfactory records of ground movement were made, and a much shorter time from the beginnings of an effective world network of seismograph stations. Serious gaps remain even today, and there are only a few regions in which detailed study of the smaller shocks is possible. One of these regions is New Zealand and because the author is a New Zealander many of the examples discussed in this book will be New Zealand ones, but other countries have not been neglected. The wise reader will keep an atlas handy, preferably one that shows the height of the land and the depth of the sea clearly. There is a map of New Zealand, including most of the place-names used, to be found in the Appendix (Figure 81). Seismology is an international science, and the whole Earth is its field. It is all too easy to assume that one's tribal customs are universal laws.

Seismology is part of the larger science called geophysics, which overlaps and bridges the gap between the older sciences of geology and physics. In its widest sense, geology concerns itself with the complete study of the Earth, but today the term is more usually applied to the largely descriptive study of the nature and history of rocks and the fossils they contain, and the transformation of the Earth's surface at the hand of nature. Physics is concerned with matter in all its forms, and the way it behaves under the influence of heat, pressure, electricity, and other forces. Geophysics, then, takes as its province all those parts of geology that involve physical measurement and calculation, and those parts of physics that concern the Earth and its atmosphere.

Observatories, perhaps to a greater degree than other scientific institutions, tend to attract visitors; but at first many of them find the seismologist's headquarters a disappointment. Because the instruments are sensitive to vibration, only the most favoured callers are allowed to visit the instrument cellars. When they get there, they find that everything is hidden inside heavy draught covers, and that because the charts are made photographically the recorders must be kept in a dim red light, and it is not possible to see much happening. In the offices above, the staff are surrounded by piles of charts covered with wiggly lines. They seem to spend their time putting marks on the charts, making entries in ledgers, and preparing computer tapes. It hardly seems a fitting manner to treat so momentous an affair as an earthquake. It's not the instruments or the charts that are exciting, it's what they mean. After a talk with the staff, most visitors are satisfied.

In writing this book, I have kept in mind the kind of ordinary citizen who calls at the observatory. Most of them want to know more about an earthquake they have felt, about their local earthquake risks, or the earthquakes of the past. I have also had in mind those hundreds of volunteer observers who help us by reporting the times and intensities of the shocks they feel. These people should find the book an understandable account of what happens to their observations, and how they fit in with other types of earthquake research. I hope there will also be readers who have never felt and never expect to feel the slightest of seismic tremors. The nature and causes of earthquakes, the structure of the interior of the globe on which we live, and the behaviour of buildings when shaken are matters that should interest anyone endowed with normal human curiosity.

This is not a technical book, but I have done my best to see that the statements stand up to technical scrutiny. I have tried to distinguish opinion from fact, but the parts of the subject where the experts differ have not been avoided. To leave those out would be to deprive the reader of just the things that make men become seismologists.

# 2 On feeling an earthquake

The tott'ring China shook without a wind
Alexander Pope, *The Rape of the Lock*

Some people insist that they never feel earthquakes. It all depends: where they are, what they are doing, and what kind of earthquake. In some parts of the world tremors are frequent; in others they occur almost never. At their mildest, earthquakes can be taken for the passing of a truck or the effects of a gust of wind; at their most severe they can destroy buildings, roads and bridges, move hillsides, and cause the sea to rise in huge waves that sweep inland from the coast and complete the destruction that the shaking began.

As long ago as the eighteenth century, John Michell realized that the shaking in an earthquake was due to the passage of elastic waves through the Earth. If they could be traced back to their origin, it might be possible to find the cause of the disturbance. The obvious way to do this was to visit the region affected, examine the damage, and talk to the people who felt it, but nearly two centuries were to pass before there was a serious attempt to follow up Michell's ideas.

Modern seismology dates from the appearance in 1862 of two beautifully illustrated volumes bearing the title *The Great Neapolitan Earthquake of 1857: the first Principles of Observational Seismology*. They were the work of Robert Mallet, an Irish engineer, who had obtained the support of the Royal Society for his expedition to Italy. Mallet drew a map of the affected region, which he divided into four zones. In the first, whole towns had been destroyed; in the second, large buildings were thrown down and people killed; in the third, there was only minor damage and no casualties; and in the fourth, although the shock was felt, no damage was reported. Mallet's four categories constitute a primitive form of earthquake intensity scale.

A classification of this kind was certainly necessary. A year or two before his trip to Italy Mallet had received a letter. It came from a professional colleague in New Zealand and described the south-west Wairarapa earthquake of 1855:

The house . . . gave a very extraordinary shake, which seemed to continue, and was accompanied by a fearful noise. I at once jumped up, rushed, as well as the violent motion would permit me, into the front garden, the motion increasing in violence, accompanied by a roaring as if a large number of cannon were being fired near together, and by a great dust caused by the falling chimneys. The motion at first was a sharp jerk back and forwards in an N. E. and S. W. direction, increasing in extent and rapidity, until I got into the garden — say 25 seconds; it was then succeeded by a shorter and quicker motion at right angles, for nearly the same time, still increasing, but appearing to be perfectly in the plane of the horizon. This was followed by a continuation of both, a sort of vorticose motion, exactly like the motion felt in an ill-adjusted railway carriage on a badly-laid railway at a very high speed, where one is swayed rapidly from side to side. This was accompanied by a sensible elevatory impulse . . .

There is a great deal more, giving evidence of the observational and analytical powers of a writer whose refusal to panic seems exemplary.

Earthquake motions are complex, but they can be classified, and it is not difficult to make more subtle estimates of intensity than the four degrees of shaking mapped by Mallet. Much ingenuity has been expended in drawing up intensity scales. One of the earliest to come into wide use was that of Rossi and Forel, devised in Switzerland and Italy at the end of last century, and describing ten degrees of shaking. Most modern scales have twelve, which seems to be the greatest number of categories that can be adequately distinguished from one another. The scale in most common use in English-speaking countries today is the Modified Mercalli scale. It extends from MM I, a barely perceptible shock, to MM XII, a truly awesome state of destruction, and lists the effects in homely terms that even untrained observers have little difficulty in distinguishing from one another. (Details are set out in the Appendix, page 183.)

Recently there have been attempts to introduce an international scale, the one proposed being known as the MSK scale, after its sponsors Medvedev, Sponheuer and Karnık. The scale is a good one, but as soon as several tests of a single intensity are given, it becomes necessary to establish that they are truly equivalent. The observatory in Australia that gives as one of the degrees on its scale 'like a horse rubbing itself against the veranda post' would have little use for the description 'sets church bells ringing', which is common in scales used in Europe. Europeans in turn would find it difficult to decide whether the shock they had felt could have overthrown one of the stone lanterns that appear in Japanese scales, and the ideas of 'an ordinary well-constructed building' held in San Francisco are not the same as those held in rural Iran.

It must be emphasized that intensity scales have nothing to do with instruments. They provide a convenient way for an observer to summarize what happened to him and to his surroundings, so that it can be compared with the happenings in other places or in other earthquakes. It would be a mistake to think that they are just an historical curiosity. No observatory could afford to scatter instruments as widely as human observers and buildings, and the relationship of the position of the shock worked out by the seismologist in his observatory to its effects can be checked only by observations on the spot.

Because the felt area of even a moderate earthquake can be a hundred kilometres across, and big ones can be felt for a thousand kilometres or more, field studies are usually supplemented by issuing postal questionnaires. They ask for the date and time of the shock, an estimate of the duration and direction of the movement, details of sounds heard, and particulars of objects moved and of any damage, so that the intensity can be rated. This task is usually left to the observatory staff, who can ensure that it is done in a consistent way. The accuracy of the information gathered is rather variable. In particular, few people have an accurate idea of the length of a second, and shocks lasting less than a minute are sometimes said to go on for ten minutes or more. The Jesuit missionary who described a shock as being 'as long as a *Paternoster* or a little longer' must be regarded as an exceptionally good observer.

*Plate 1: Felt intensity scales. The fall of these groceries from the shelves of a Nelson warehouse indicates an intensity of about MM VI.*

Where shocks are frequent, it becomes worthwhile to organize permanent observers. New Zealand, for example, has a network of volunteers spaced about 40 to 50 km apart over the whole country, and in some of the islands of the South Pacific. These volunteers include postal officials, lighthouse keepers, park rangers and private citizens, and they report about two earthquakes a week to the Seismological Observatory in Wellington.

When the reports of a shock have been collected, the intensities are assessed and plotted on a map. Lines are then drawn in such a way as to enclose areas of the same intensity. These lines are known as *isoseismals*. Figure 1 shows such a map.

If the Earth was of exactly the same constitution in all places, we would expect the energy to spread out evenly in all directions from the origin of the earthquake (a region known as the *focus*), and that the most severely shaken spot would be at the *epicentre*, the point on the Earth's surface vertically above it. The isoseismals would be a set of concentric circles around the epicentre, with the intensity falling off gradually and evenly as we went away from it. Sometimes this is the case, and the position of the epicentre can also be confirmed by the direction in which objects have been moved, and by the pattern of cracks in the damaged buildings. More usually the existence of areas of weak ground and of peculiarities in the geological structure beneath the surface introduces complications.

On unconsolidated materials like loose gravels the intensity is increased, and we shall return to this topic when we deal with engineering seismology. The deeper geology often has the effect of making the isoseismals elliptical rather than circular. Sometimes this is because the structure influences the mechanism of the earthquake, so that more energy is sent out in some directions than in others, but it is more often because the elastic waves are more readily transmitted along the axis of the structural folds and faults than across them.

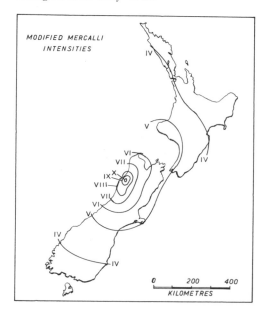

*Fig. 1: An isoseismal map. These isoseismals show the distribution of felt intensity in the large shallow earthquake at Inangahua in May 1968.*

*Plate 2: Felt intensity scales. Ruins of the nurses' home in Napier after the earthquake in 1931. Complete structural collapse indicates an intensity of at least MM X.*

A major factor affecting the isoseismal pattern of an earthquake is the depth of its focus. A shallow shock may be felt heavily over a small area, but the effects do not extend very far. A deep shock gives a more moderate shaking to a much greater area. Figure 2 makes clear why this should be so. In the case of shallow shocks, estimates of focal depth based on isoseismals may sometimes be better than those made instrumentally, particularly when there are few close recording stations. The isoseismal patterns for very deep shocks, however, are usually very distorted for reasons we shall explain in a later chapter, and they may be so far displaced sideways that the epicentre lies right outside the felt area.

Earthquakes can be felt on ships at sea, as well as on dry land, but the effect is rather different. As a rule, there is just a single upward jolt, as if the ship had struck a submerged obstacle. This is a result of the fact that liquids can transmit only some of the waves that can travel through the solid Earth, and these waves are bent sharply upwards as they leave the Earth for the water at the ocean bottom. These different wave-types will be discussed later. Seismic sea-waves, which are discussed in Chapter 12, are not usually noticeable on the high seas, but in coastal waters or in harbours their effects can be serious.

Much useful information about earthquakes is still to be gathered from felt observations and inspection of damage, but for the accurate location of the origin and an understanding of the mechanism of the shock, instruments are clearly needed. For half a century after Mallet, therefore, the history of earthquake study became largely the story of the search for a suitable recorder, and the efforts to understand the records it produced.

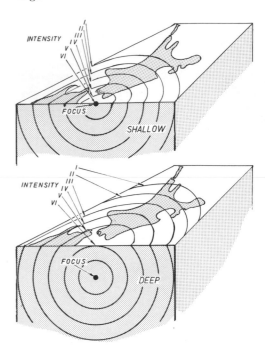

*Fig. 2: Effect of focal depth on felt intensity. The two earthquakes shown have the same epicentre and the same maximum felt intensity, but the isoseismals of the deeper shock are more widely spaced and the whole felt area is larger.*

# 3 Recording an earthquake

The moving finger writes; and having writ
Moves on:

    Fitzgerald, *Rubaiyat of Omar Khayyam*

Recording the motion of the ground during an earthquake is not an easy matter. The difficulty when everything fixed to the Earth is moving with it is to obtain some stationary point to start from. The method the seismologist adopts is to make use of *inertia*, the tendency a heavy body has to 'stay put'. A weight hanging from a flexible support tends to lag behind when the support is moved. If some method of recording the relative movement of the weight and the support is provided we have a primitive form of seismograph. The main defect of the arrangement is that once the support is moved, the weight will eventually follow, and it will tend to go on swinging after the support has come to rest. Quite a simple movement of the support becomes a most complicated movement of the weight, and it needs skill and experience to say exactly what the record indicates. When complicated movements are given to the support, it becomes almost impossible.

Science progresses by a combination of theory and experiment, and it will be easier to understand how a seismograph works if we perform a simple experiment ourselves. Get a piece of string about a metre long, and tie a small but reasonably heavy weight to one end. Hold on to the other end, and lift the weight just clear of the floor. Move your hand very slowly backwards and forwards. The weight will follow without any tendency to swing, so that there is no relative

*Fig. 3: Response of a simple pendulum. Time-exposure photographs showing the three stages of the experiment described here: (a) Movement slower than natural period; (b) Movement coincides with natural period; (c) Movement faster than natural period.*

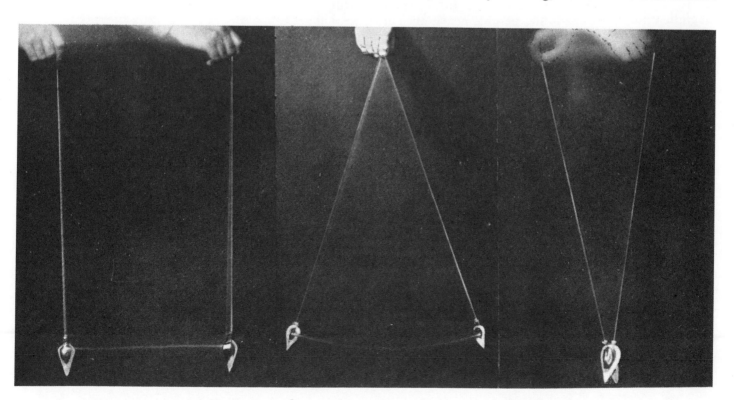

movement between the hand and the weight. If you increase the speed of the to-and-fro movement, the weight will begin to swing more and more vigorously. When you change the direction of movement of your hand about once a second, the swings of the weight will get very big, even if the movements of your hand are quite small. This occurs when the natural period of swing of the pendulum and the period of movement of your hand are the same. Under these conditions, you are obviously getting a big magnification of the movement of your hand, but when you stop, the pendulum will go on swinging, and give a spurious record. Stop the weight, and then try a sudden rapid to-and-fro movement of your hand. The weight remains almost stationary, whilst your hand moves relative to it. In this case we have just about reached the condition we need for recording the movement of the support in an earthquake. There are two disadvantages. There is very little magnification; and if we are going to measure the slower earthquake waves, we will need a pendulum which has a very long time of swing. Figure 3 shows photographs of an experiment of this kind, but the wise reader will repeat it for himself.

During an earthquake, buildings and other structures fixed to the Earth respond in a rather similar way, so the results are important. To sum up:

(1) When the period of movement of the support is much longer than the natural period of the pendulum, the weight just follows the support, and the magnification is zero. (2) When the period of the support movement is the same as the natural period of the pendulum, the magnification is very large. (3) When the period of the support movement is short compared with the natural period of the pendulum magnification is nearly one.

Let us try to apply these results to the design of a simple seismograph. The first problem is to choose a suitable period for the instrument. If we choose one that is long compared with that of the ground movements we want to record, we will get a very faithful record of the ground movement, but there will be hardly any magnification. If we make the periods nearly the same, we will get more magnification, but once the earthquake sets the instrument swinging, the later part of the record will depend more upon the instrument than upon the behaviour of the ground.

It becomes much easier to reach a useful compromise if we provide our pendulum with some form of *damping*. Damping is the drag that eventually brings any swinging object to rest, and usually results from air resistance and friction at the support. As our instrument must come to rest quickly, we shall have to increase the natural damping. This can be done by attaching a vane, which can either be arranged to increase the air resistance, or to trail in a bath of oil.

In more elaborate instruments, the vane is made of copper or aluminium and moves between the poles of a strong magnet. The eddy currents that are generated when it moves also have a damping effect, which cannot be upset by changes in temperature, air pressure, or humidity. The amount of damping is often arranged to be *critical*, that is to say, when the pendulum has been displaced, it will just return to the zero position without additional swings. Figure 4 shows how the magnification is affected by altering the amount of damping. A critically damped pendulum gives a fairly faithful picture of the ground movement over quite a wide range of periods, and by choosing the proper damping and pendulum period, it is possible to design a seismograph suitable for studying most of the problems in which we are interested.

*Fig. 4: Magnification of a seismograph. This graph shows how seismographs with a natural period of one second and different degrees of damping will amplify ground movements of differing periods.*

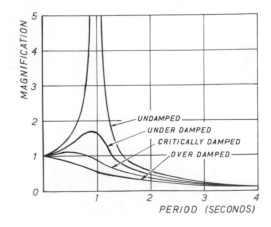

Since faithful recording has to be obtained at the expense of magnification, a seismograph is usually provided with some mechanism for enlarging the pendulum movement before it is recorded. In early instruments, levers were used, and the permanent record was made by a stylus fixed on the end of the last lever, which scratched a mark on a drum covered with smoked paper. These records could be made permanent and clean to handle by fixing them in a solution of shellac in methylated spirit. Instruments of this kind are still used for recording strong earthquakes, but they are not very suitable for large magnifications. The friction at the point of the stylus is transmitted back to the weight by the levers, and interferes with its movement unless the weight is made very large. In Europe, seismographs were built with suspended weights as large as twenty tons (Plate 3). At least one of these is still in use, but they are naturally expensive to house and install. There are also mechanical difficulties in making the magnifying levers themselves both strong and light, and in avoiding backlash and 'lost motion' at the pivots.

More present-day instruments use photographic recording, either directly or indirectly. The direct method is to fix a small mirror to the pendulum, and to reflect a beam of light from it on to a sheet of light-sensitive paper wrapped about a recording drum. Every schoolboy who has played with a piece of mirror on a sunny day will know that a very small movement of the mirror produces a very large movement of the reflected light spot. In this way, the pendulum movement can be magnified and recorded without introducing any friction or interference from the levers. When the paper is developed, the movements of the spot will appear as black lines on a white background.

The indirect method is perhaps the most commonly used today, although direct types are far from being out of date. Instruments which use indirect recording are called electromagnetic seismographs. In these the pendulum carries a small pick-up coil, which can swing between the poles of a magnet mounted on the frame of the instrument. Whenever it moves, an electric current is generated, and this is fed to a galvanometer, a sensitive meter with a mirror instead of a pointer. The movements of the galvanometer mirror are then recorded on photographic paper just as those of the pendulum were in the direct method. At first sight, the extra instrument might seem to be an unnecessary complication, but it has a number of advantages. First, the part of the instrument which is sensitive to ground movement can be placed some distance from the recording drum, and is consequently less likely to be disturbed by the visits of the operator. Secondly, electric currents are very simple to control, and they can be amplified, reduced, or modifed in a great number of ways for special purposes. Electromagnetic seismographs have the further advantages that they can be operated in daylight, and that they are unaffected by ground tilt. When mechanical or direct recording seismographs are used, slow tilting of the ground causes the zero position of the spot to wander, and the lines on the chart become unevenly spaced. When the tilting is severe, the lines overlap and make the record difficult to read. In an electromagnetic instrument, the size of the current generated depends upon the speed at which the coil moves and not upon the distance it travels, so that these slow movements do not have any appreciable effect.

Until quite recently observatory seismologists tended to avoid electronic equipment. A simple galvanometer coupled directly to the seismometer would give enough magnification for most purposes.

*Plate 3: Mechanical seismographs. The Omori seismograph is a classical horizontal pendulum with a mass of a few kilograms, a period of several seconds, and a magnification of about a hundred.*

*In the Wiechert instrument shown below, which can record both horizontal components, the mass is a great tank filled with 17 tons of iron ore. It has a period of about a second and a magnification of two thousand.*

Valve amplifiers were erratic and unreliable devices, difficult to calibrate, and needing large amounts of electric power. The advent of the transistor and the printed circuit quickly changed all this. Seismometers have become smaller, as an amplifier needs less input power than a galvanometer, and can produce enough output to drive a pen or stylus against quite heavy paper friction. This has brought smoked paper records back into favour, as they produce a very fine even trace. They are particularly useful for portable equipment, for photographic processing under field conditions is never very satisfactory. In fixed observatories, recorders using a heated stylus marking a heat-sensitive paper, or writing with ink fed through a fine capillary tube are used to make records that are produced in daylight, and available for tsunami warning or press and radio information services without further processing. Power requirements are surprisingly small, and battery operation is feasible.

Another possibility is the use of a radio link to increase the separation between the seismometer and the recorder. Distances of several tens of kilometres are easily obtained, and operators need no longer be inconvenienced by the fact that the quietest sites are usually in the least accessible places. It is possible to link a whole network of seismometers to a single recording point, simplifying timing problems, and cutting down the number of operators required. Networks of this kind are in use in California, and in New Zealand, and are becoming increasingly common.

Before I describe some actual observatory seismographs, a more unassuming part of the equipment must be mentioned — the recording drum. A complete seismograph consists of two equally important parts — the seismometer, which is sensitive to ground movements, and the recorder which makes its indications permanent. The recorder may seem so simple as to be unworthy of discussion. It consists of a drum, 30 centimetres or so in diameter and the same in length, with a motor to turn it round, usually either twice or four times in an hour, and a screw arrangement to move it slowly sideways so that the successive traces do not overlap. The slow speed is very difficult to keep constant. Small irregularities in the gears are serious, and if the drum is not perfectly balanced it will run ahead at times and then wait for the motor to catch up. Since the seismologist often wants to measure the time of arrival of a wave with an accuracy of a tenth of a second, ordinary clockwork cannot be used for the motor. Clock escapements drive the hands in a series of jerks which may be a fifth or even half a second apart.

The steadiest drive is a synchronous motor driven by an electric current whose frequency is very carefully controlled. Sometimes the mains are used, but most stations today are equipped with very accurate electronic clocks for timing purposes, and from these an even more stable current can be derived and used to turn the drums.

When the recording is photographic there will also be a recording lamp. An arrangement of lenses concentrates its light upon the seismometer mirror and ensures that the reflected ray is focused on the surface of the drum as a tiny but sharply defined spot. If this spot is not clear and sharp the timing accuracy will suffer and very fast movements cannot be seen clearly.

Somewhere in the path of the light beam there is a shutter which is closed for an instant once a minute by an accurate clock, leaving a brief gap in the trace. In many instruments, instead of a shutter, a glass prism is used, and the trace is moved sideways instead of being blacked out. In this way none of the record is lost, but if the

*Fig. 5: Common types of seismograph pendulum. A. Horizontal Pendulum (Omori, Milne-Shaw, Press-Ewing). B. Horizontal Pendulum with Zöllner Suspension (Galitzin). C. Inverted Pendulum (Wiechert 1 000 kg, 10 sec. period). D. Torsion Seismograph (Wood-Anderson). E. Vertical Pendulum (Galitzin, Press-Ewing). F. Vertical Seismograph (Benioff, Wilson-Lamison).*

*Recording arrangements are not shown. This diagram illustrates the principles involved, not the physical arrangement of the parts in the actual instruments.*

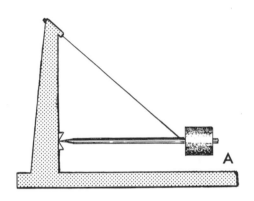

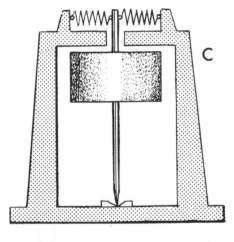

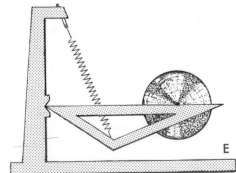

movements of the earthquake are large, the timing marks may be hard to see.

Many different kinds of pendulum have successfully been used as the basis of a seismograph, but not the simple pendulum we have been discussing so far. The reason is size. A pendulum designed to swing once a second is about a metre long, which is already a little large for convenience. It might be made to serve for local earthquakes, but if we wanted a simple pendulum to record the surface-waves from distant shocks, which have periods from 20 to 100 seconds or more, we should need the Eiffel tower to hang it from.

Figure 5 shows some of the arrangements that have been used to produce a more compact pendulum of the right period. The first four are sensitive to horizontal ground movements, and the last two to vertical ones. It will occur to some readers that arrangements like those shown at A, B and D will respond quite readily to movements at right angles to the plane of the paper, but that movements along the line joining the centre of the suspended weight to the hinges will have no effect on them at all. This is really an advantage, as it allows the seismologist to analyse the nature of an approaching wave, and to find what direction it is coming from. Seismographs often come in sets of three — two horizontal ones mounted at right angles (one usually north and south, and the other east and west, but not always), and a vertical one.

The elastic waves that an earthquake sets up have a very wide range of natural periods, and most observatories try to record those in the range between about a tenth of a second and a hundred seconds. It is possible to detect waves of even longer periods, but recording them is generally considered to be a special research project.

The limit to the magnification that we can use at any particular period is set by small movements of the ground called *microseisms*. They go on all the time, even when there are no earthquakes, and once a seismograph is sensitive enough to show them, an increase in the magnification only makes the recording more and more confused. The most common types of microseism have periods between two and six seconds, and it is therefore usual to install two sets of seismographs, one to cover the movements of shorter periods than the microseisms, and one for the longer periods. On a very quiet site short-period instruments can be operated with magnifications as great as a few hundred thousand, but the magnifications of long-period ones seldom go beyond a few thousand, and are often very much less. Strangely enough, it is the long-period instruments that are most useful for recording distant earthquakes. This is because short-period vibrations are more readily absorbed as they pass through the Earth, so that at great distances only the waves of longer periods are still strong enough to be detected.

At first, seismologists concentrated upon making their instruments as sensitive as possible, but less sensitive ones also have important uses. Engineers are particularly interested in the big waves close to the epicentres of destructive earthquakes. Even if these waves do not damage a sensitive instrument, they will give so confused a record that it is impossible to interpret it. Strong-motion instruments for engineering periods often have magnifications from one to about ten. A well-equipped observatory therefore has instruments with a very great range of periods and magnifications. At Wellington, for example, there are seventeen different samples of the ground movement being made continously.

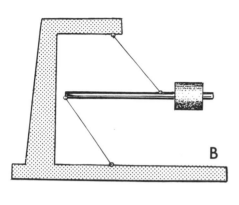

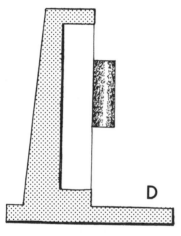

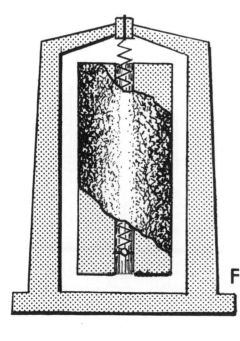

For the mechanically-inclined seismologist, seismographs exert all the fascination of a vintage car. The temptation to describe more than a representative selection of the more important must therefore be resisted.

When a station has only one instrument, it is usually a short-period vertical component. This will produce good records of local shocks, and of the first wave to arrive from more distant ones. Nowadays it will be an electromagnetic instrument, probably recording photographically, but possibly connected to an amplifier driving a pen-and-ink or heated stylus recorder.

In 1930, Dr Hugo Benioff produced the first seismometer to provide magnifications of a hundred thousand or more in the short-period range. The vertical instrument is shown in Figure 6 and Plate 4. A cylindrical mass of 100 kg is suspended from a framework about a metre in height by a spring that is housed in a hole passing along its axis. Flat metal guide-ribbons above and below the mass allow it to move freely up and down, but restrain it horizontally. Below the mass is the *transducer*, which converts its movements into electrical currents. It consists of a set of coils wound on soft-iron armatures that move with the mass, and a strong permanent magnet that is fixed to the frame. Relative movement between the two varies the magnetic flux through the coil, and generates the currents, which are fed to the galvanometer. Often there are two of these, one with a natural period of about a quarter of a second, and the other with a period of 90 seconds or more, coupled to separate coils, and recording on different drums.

In the horizontal instrument, the mass is divided into two parts, one placed on either side of the transducer (Plate 5). The guide ribbons provide sufficient restoring force to bring the mass back to the central position, so there is no central spring. The high sensitivity, simplicity and reliability of the Benioff instruments brought them into wide use, and they retain their popularity, but attempts were soon being made to retain their advantages in seismometers that were lighter and more compact.

Among the most successful of these is the one designed by Dr P. L. Willmore at Cambridge (Plate 9). In it, the transducer magnet also serves as the mass. It is supported on flat springs that can be disconnected if it is desired to record the horizontal movements, and induces currents in a coil fixed to the frame. The whole arrangement fits in a watertight cylindrical case 16 cm in diameter and 33 cm high, and its weight is less than 5 kg. It can easily be housed in a shallow concrete-lined pit, or even buried, greatly reducing the costs of housing and installation.

Both the Canadian and the New Zealand networks make extensive use of Willmore instruments, and they are in wide demand for field studies of volcanic tremor and aftershocks, but the earliest instrument to be really suitable for recording local earthquakes was a mechanical one, the Wood-Anderson torsion seismometer, developed in California in the late 1920s. The records of these intruments formed the basis of Professor Richter's magnitude scale (Chapter 11). The way they work can be seen in Figure 7.

The 'heavy' weight is a tiny cylinder of copper, only about 25 millimetres long, and not as thick as a piece of fencing wire. Since we do not ask it to drive anything, we can make it small and convenient. At the top end of the cylinder, a mirror is fixed, and the whole arrangement is carried on a thin tungsten wire about 20 cm long. Just above and below the weight, the wire passes through two small holes,

*Plate 4: Benioff variable-reluctance seismometer. This is the vertical component instrument shown diagrammatically in Figure 6. The coils of these instruments can be connected independently to short- and long-period galvanometers, but at stations of the World-Wide Standard Network only the short period is used.*

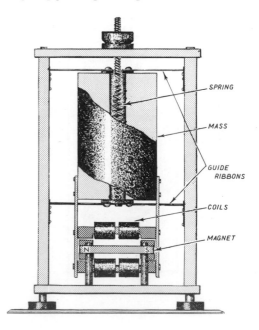

*Fig. 6: Benioff vertical seismometer. In this seismometer the magnet is fixed to the frame of the instrument, and the pick-up coils are carried by the moving mass. The cylindrical mass is constrained by tensioned guide-ribbons and supported by a spring passing through a central hole.*

SPRING

MASS

GUIDE RIBBONS

COILS

MAGNET

*Plate 5: Benioff variable-reluctance seismometer. In the horizontal instrument the mass is divided into two parts and the pick-up·assembly placed between them. The central spring found in the vertical instrument is unnecessary.*

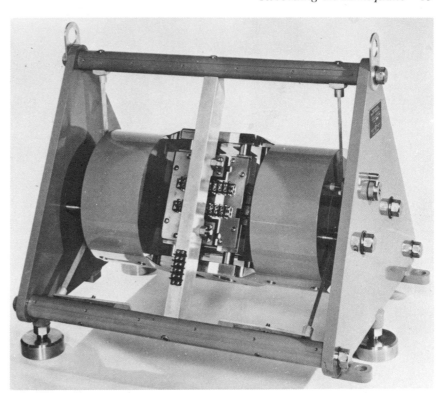

*Fig. 7: Wood-Anderson torsion seismometer. This mechanical-optical instrument was the first really satisfactory seismograph for recording near earthquakes.*

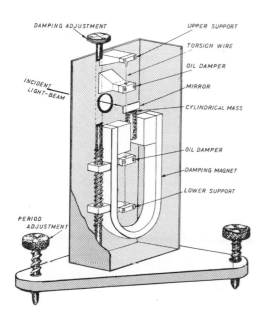

each holding a single drop of castor oil. This stops any tendency the wire might have to vibrate like the string of a violin, so that all the weight can do is to twist back and forth around the wire. On either side of the weight, the poles of a magnet provide eddy-current damping. This magnet is somewhat differently arranged in different models of the instrument, but it can always be moved up and down, and by arranging just the right length of the cylinder to come between the poles the damping can be adjusted to critical. This seismograph has a magnification of nearly three thousand, and a period of just over three-quarters of a second.

Historically, good short-period seismographs are comparative latecomers. This is partly because they are a little more difficult to design, and partly because the countries that had established schools of geophysics in the early part of the century were not the countries troubled by destructive earthquakes; but in 1889 a Japanese earthquake was recorded by von Rebeur-Paschwitz at Potsdam in Germany, on a pendulum intended for gravity studies, and the scientific uses of such records were at once realized. By 1900 several good horizontal pendulum instruments had been designed, and the British Association for the Advancement of Science had taken active steps towards setting up a world-wide network of earthquake recorders.

Some of the early instruments used photographic recording, but most of them produced a record on smoked paper. The Omori seismograph (Plate 3) is typical of these instruments, which did not develop greatly. Photographic intruments, on the other hand, were greatly improved, and the introduction of electromagnetic seismometers recording through a galvanometer made photographic recording the preferred method until the development of reliable amplifiers made a return to various forms of pen writing practicable.

*Plate 6: A vertical pendulum. The boom of the vertical Press-Ewing instrument is a horizontal framework pivoted at the left. At the right is the mass, divided into two parts and supported by the diagonal spring. The framework also carries the perforated pillar carrying the pick-up coils. The magnets are fixed to the frame of the instrument and placed above the spring. The movement of the boom is conveyed to the pick-up coils by the perforated pillar just behind the centre of the mass. Like the horizontal instruments, the vertical Press-Ewings can be operated at periods of 15 to 30 seconds.*

*Plate 7: A horizontal pendulum. In this Press-Ewing long-period seismometer the mass is carried on the end of a pivoted boom and supported by wires connected to a rigid upright. The pick-up and calibration coils move between the poles of cylindrical magnets attached to the base and placed on either side of the mass. When in operation the instrument is protected from barometric changes by a strong airtight metal case, and from temperature changes by an outer cover of polystyrene. These instruments and their vertical counterpart are used in the World-Wide Standard Network and are usually operated at periods of either 15 or 30 seconds.*

*Plate 8: Galitzin seismograph. This is the classical form of the electromagnetic instrument. The boom is pivoted at the right, and the copper damping vane moves between the poles of the outer set of magnets at the left. The pick-up coil moves between those of the inner set.*

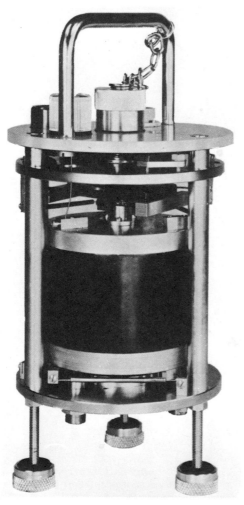

*Plate 9: Willmore seismometer, with its cover removed. In this very compact instrument, widely used for recording near earthquakes, the magnet is suspended from leaf-springs and acts as the mass. The springs can be detached to allow its use as a horizontal component. The geophones used in seismic prospecting are similar in construction but smaller and lighter.*

The first electromagnetic seismographs were produced in 1906 by the Russian Prince Boris Galitzin (Golitsyn in modern translitterations). A big attraction of the Galitzin instruments was that it was possible to make a homogeneous set in which the vertical instrument could be given the same period, damping, and magnification as the horizontal ones. Vertical seismographs have always been troublesome to design and operate. The only way to make the mass free to move up and down is to suspend it directly or indirectly from a spring, and springs do not behave conveniently. They change in length and elasticity when the temperature changes, and the metal of which they are made 'creeps' as it becomes fatigued. Special alloys and temperature-compensating devices have been used, but they add to the complexity, and the best seismographs have always been simple.

A classical Galitzin seismograph is shown in Plate 8. The mass is fixed to a boom, which takes the form of a triangular girder pivoted on flat springs at one end, and kept horizontal by the tension of a vertical coiled spring. The pick-up coil and a copper damping vane move between two sets of magnets mounted at the other end of the boom. By altering their position, the damping and sensitivity can be varied. They are usually operated with periods of twelve or twenty-four seconds, and magnifications of a few hundred.

The use of very long-period galvanometers in conjunction with Benioff seismometers led to a decline in the popularity of Galitzin-type instruments, but with the development of Press-Ewing seismometers at Lamont Observatory in the 1950s and their use in the American-sponsored world network of standardized stations, they have enjoyed a return to favour. The Press-Ewing instruments (Plates 6 and 7) are similar in principle and general mechanical arrangement to Galitzins, but special attention has been paid to their stability at long periods, and to the elimination of false resonances caused by the spring of the vertical component, and the pick-up coils are of a more efficient type. On suitable sites the pendulum can be made stable at periods as long as thirty seconds, and used to drive a galvanometer with a period of one hundred seconds or more.

# 4 Reading the records

The record of a distant earthquake (Figure 23) looks quite different from that of a near one (Figure 22). Can we use this difference to tell us the distance? If we can, it should be possible to locate the centre of the disturbance more accurately than we can by using isoseismals.

It is clear from the appearance of the records that the movement of the ground during the earthquake is a kind of wave. For a long time physicists have been interested in waves, and they have sorted out a great number of different kinds. There are about four or five possible ways in which the Earth could vibrate, and, if we are to understand the records, it is necessary to find out which types are actually involved.

Two kinds are of the greatest importance in earthquake study, and the seismologist has to refer to them so often that he has given them

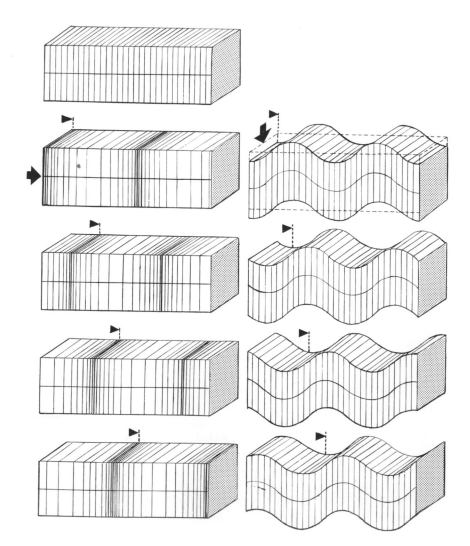

Fig. 8: Longitudinal and transverse waves. If the bar shown at the top left is given a sharp blow on its left-hand end a compressional wave will be sent along it towards the right. The particles move to and fro in the same direction as the wave is travelling and the wave is said to be longitudinal. A downwards blow, as shown on the right, starts a transverse wave like the one in a rope shaken at one end. Earthquakes send both kinds of wave through the Earth.

one-letter names, *P* and *S*. The letters really stand for 'primary' and 'secondary' in order of arrival; but it is easier to remember which is which if you think of them as 'push' and 'shake'. The physicist, who likes his names to give a mathematically exact description of what is happening, calls them 'longitudinal' and 'transverse' or 'compressional' and 'shear' respectively.

A longitudinal, or *P*-wave, is really a sound wave through the Earth, and is the fastest kind. As the wave passes, each particle of the rock moves to and fro in the same direction as the wave is travelling. The material therefore experiences a series of compressions and rarefactions. This is not the simplest kind of wave to picture, but Figure 8 will probably help. Imagine that the bar is given a sharp tap with a hammer at the left-hand end. Each particle hit by the hammer will move away for an instant and then spring back. When it moves away, it will transmit the force to its neighbour and cause a pulse to travel to the right. When the pulse gets to the other end, a ball resting against the rod would bounce away to show that it had arrived. In the transverse, or *S*-wave, the particles move at right angles to the direction in which the wave is travelling, exactly like they do in a rope which is fixed at one end and shaken at the other (Figure 8).

These waves do not travel at the same speed. The *P*-wave goes about eight kilometres in a second, and the *S*-wave only about four and a half kilometres. (Readers not yet used to the metric system may like to recall that a kilometre is about five eighths of a mile.)

This means that the *P*-wave always arrives first, and *S* lags behind. The farther the recorder is from the origin of the earthquake, the bigger the time interval between the arrival of the two waves. If we can identify them on the records and measure the time-interval between their arrivals we can work out how distant the origin was. The farther away an earthquake is, the deeper the waves will penetrate into the body of the Earth. The deeper they penetrate, the faster they travel, so a simple calculation based on the figures I have just quoted would not be accurate enough. Tables have been drawn up to show the amount of this change, or it can be shown in the form of a graph (Figure 9), so that in practice we can get the answer quite quickly.

If we have a three-component record, it is possible to work out the direction from which a wave has come, but several factors operate to make estimates of direction less reliable than estimates of distance. The more distant an earthquake is, the greater will be the effect that a small error in direction has upon the estimated position of the origin. It is therefore more usual to find earthquake origins by using distances from a number of stations that have recorded the shock. For this reason seismologists like to exchange readings with their colleagues in neighbouring countries as soon as possible.

Let us look at a practical case. We will forget for the present that the actual origin of the shock is at a focus some distance below the surface of the Earth, and concentrate upon the epicentre, the point on the surface vertically above it. This is convenient, because at some stage we will probably want to show our results on a map.

The Wellington record of a shock on 13th February, 1973 showed an earthquake with 17 seconds between the arrival of the *P* and the *S*. This indicates a distance of 149 km, so that the epicentre must lie somewhere on a circle with a radius of 149 km and its centre at Wellington (WEL). On the Tarata (TNZ) record the *S - P* interval was 14 seconds, making the radius of the corresponding circle 119

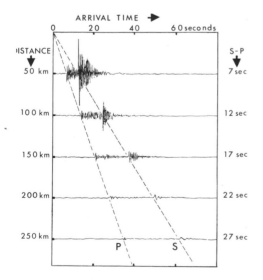

*Fig. 9: Finding the distance. The time interval between the arrival of the longitudinal* P-*wave and the slower transverse* S-*wave increases with increasing distance from the origin of the shock.*

km. If we draw these two circles on a map (Figure 10) we find that they cut in two points, and one of these must be the epicentre. One is near the coast, and the other some distance out to sea. Both these places have had earthquakes in the past, so we can't say that one answer is more likely than the other. We need a third station. The one at Taradale (TRZ) gave an interval of 16 seconds and a distance of 139 km. This lets us draw a third circle, which shows that the position near the coast is the correct one. The fact that the shock was felt quite strongly in the Wanganui district but not at all in the South Island makes it even more certain that we have the right answer.

We can use other stations to make absolutely sure, but if we do, we find that they don't all cut exactly in a single point, for the records are not perfect, and there are small local differences in the travel-times over different parts of the country. In spite of these difficulties a well-recorded shock can normally be located to within about five or ten kilometres, and by making lengthier calculations that allow for the regional variations important earthquakes can be located with even greater accuracy.

Instead of drawing circles most of the larger observatories now feed their readings to electronic computers in which details of the station positions and the travel-time tables have been stored. The computer goes about the job a little differently. First the seismologist has to guess roughly where the earthquake is, and tell the computer. It doesn't have to be a very good guess, but the computer has to start somewhere. From its tables it works out the times that *P* and *S* waves

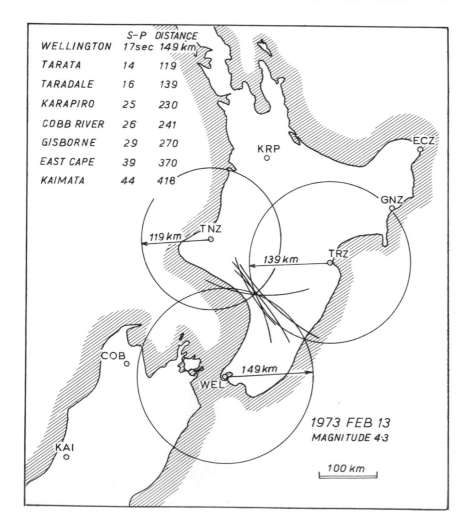

| | S–P | DISTANCE |
|---|---|---|
| WELLINGTON | 17sec | 149 km |
| TARATA | 14 | 119 |
| TARADALE | 16 | 139 |
| KARAPIRO | 25 | 230 |
| COBB RIVER | 26 | 241 |
| GISBORNE | 29 | 270 |
| EAST CAPE | 39 | 370 |
| KAIMATA | 44 | 418 |

1973 FEB 13
MAGNITUDE 4·3

100 km

*Fig. 10: Locating an epicentre. The time between the arrival of* P *and* S *at each station is used to find the distance of the origin. An arc with this distance as radius is then drawn round each station. The arcs intersect at the epicentre.*

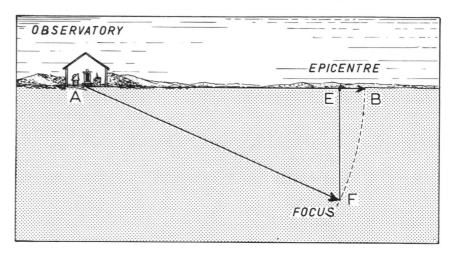

*Fig. 11: Focus and epicentre. The epicentre is the point on the Earth's surface directly above the focus, where shock originates. The length AE from the recording station to the epicentre is known as the epicentral distance △. Distances found from S - P intervals are not △, but AF, the distance to the focus. For shallow shocks this does not matter, but if the shock is deep a circle drawn on a map with centre A and radius AF will be much too big, and go through the point B instead of through the epicentre.*

from a shock in the position it was given should have arrived at the different recording stations, and compares them with the times of arrival that were actually recorded. If the trial position is too near the station, the calculated time will be too early; if it is too far away, it will be too late. The computer can now move the trial position a little in the direction indicated, and try again. This time the differences between the calculated arrival times and the real ones will be smaller, but the computer will go on moving the origin about until either it finds that further shifting gives bigger differences, or until the seismologist tells it that the fit is near enough. Three or four shifts are usually enough to give a satisfactory position, but there is one important kind of earthquake that seems never to give a good fit.

When we look at one of these problem shocks graphically, we find that the third circle does not go through either of the intersections of the other two. If we can be quite certain that the trouble does not lie in a poor record from one of the stations, or in something wrong with the timing, this is an indication that the focus of the earthquakes lies farther beneath the surface of the earth than usual; that is to say, we are dealing with a 'deep-focus' earthquake. The distances obtained from *S-P* intervals are of course distances between the focus and the recording station, not those between the station and the epicentre (Figure 11). It is not difficult to calculate the depth at which the focus must lie to make the circles meet in a point. Figure 12 shows the circles for a shock with an origin 160 kilometres below the central North Island, first assuming that it has a normal shallow focus, and then using tables worked out for the correct focal depth. The nearer a station is to the epicentre, the greater the effect changes in depth will have on the radius of the circle. To make good measurements of depth, we need a recording station as close to the epicentre as the shock is deep. This leads to the slightly surprising result that large depths are often more reliably known than small ones.

The records our seismographs produce give us a convenient method of locating the origin of an earthquake shock; and they tell us something about the way in which the ground at the recording station moved during the earthquake. This is important enough, but the geophysicist has found a use for earthquake waves which is of even greater interest to him. All of my country readers must at some time or other have tried to see how full the water tank is by thumping the outside, and listening to the way the sound changes when you thump above and below the water level. Town readers who have not will probably remember the proverb about empty vessels. The Earth is

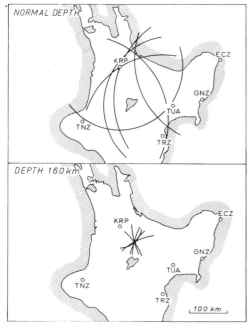

*Fig. 12: Locating a deep earthquake. The arcs in the upper figure were drawn on the supposition that the earthquake was of normal focal depth. When appropriate corrections for depth are applied the satisfactory cut shown in the lower figure is obtained.*

even harder to see inside than a water tank, and we have to look for equally indirect ways of working out what lies inside it. The principle used is almost the same, with earthquakes to do the thumping, and seismographs to listen. Since the *P*-wave is a sound wave, the analogy is quite a close one. An earthquake wave is the only thing we know of which can be sent to explore the very centre of the Earth.

Let us suppose that we have collected together all the records of a big earthquake. There will be a very big pile of them – perhaps five or six hundred, even if we don't count all three components at every recording station. Let us carefully measure each record, and find the time at which the first movement arrives. If we list the stations in order of their distance from the epicentre, we can see that there is a gradual change in the speed of the journey, and that it increases as the path lies deeper and deeper in the Earth. We should expect this to happen, because waves travel more rapidly in more rigid material, and the material deep in the Earth will be firmly packed together by the weight of the material on top of it.

This is a convenient place to note that when the seismologist deals with distances, he often states them in degrees, rather than in kilometres. This is like looking at the angle between two lines, one from the station and one from the epicentre, meeting at the centre of the Earth. There are 360° right round the Earth, and two points 180° apart are exactly opposite one another. A degree is about 111 km. There is a table in the Appendix to help you convert from one system to the other if you wish. The advantage of this system of measurement is that it reminds us that the Earth is a ball, and avoids any ambiguity between distances measured around the surface and through the middle.

But let us get back to our pile of records. As the distance between the station and the epicentre gets bigger, the size and clarity of the *P* movement gets rather worse, until at about 103°, the beginning of the record becomes indistinct. Something is happening to the wave in its

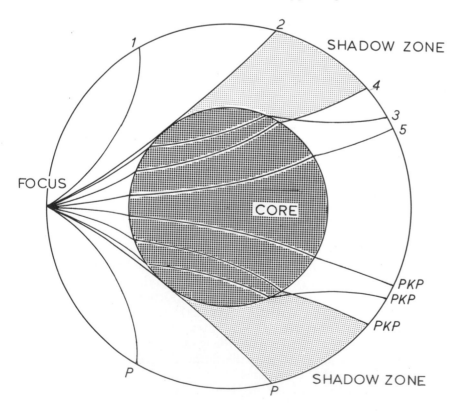

*Fig. 13: The shadow zone. When P-waves cross the boundary between the mantle and the core they are sharply bent. This creates a shadow zone for P at distances between 103° and 142° from the focus.*

travels. This something continues to happen until about 142°, when the movement again becomes sharp, but shows by its time of travel that it is not the same wave we started with. The region in between, where the wave is indistinct, is called the 'shadow zone for *P*' (Figure 13).

The reason the shadow zone exists is that at about half way to the centre the Earth's composition suddenly changes. The region above this boundary is known as the Earth's *mantle*, and the region below it is known as the *core*. Once a wave from an earthquake penetrates so deeply that it must pass through the core it is sharply bent, and emerges at a much greater distance that it otherwise would, creating the shadow zone. It was first observed by R. D. Oldham in 1906, and gave one of the earliest indications of the great part seismology would play in exploring the Earth's interior. With modern sensitive seismographs the core might have been harder to find, for the shadow zone is not one of complete darkness. In it are to be found waves that have taken rather less direct paths, but they are weaker than either the *P*-wave at 103°, or the wave through the core that re-appears at 142°, which can be very sharp and prominent. We shall discuss some of these other waves in due course.

The depth to the boundary between the mantle and the core is about 2 900 kilometres, and was first found by Professor Beno Gutenberg in 1913, using carefully measured travel-times. Although he believed that his estimate could be out by as much as fifty or a hundred kilometres, modern measurements have reduced it by less than twenty at the most. Because of his work the boundary is known as the *Gutenberg Discontinuity*.

Everyone is familiar with echoes. When a sound-wave meets an obstacle part of it is reflected, and we hear it as if there were another source behind the reflector. Sound-waves can also be *refracted,* or bent, whenever they pass from one medium to another in which their speed is different. Earthquake waves of both *P*- and *S*-type can also be both reflected and refracted, and we have already seen how the refraction of *P*-waves by the core creates a shadow zone. There are other boundaries inside the Earth at which reflection or refraction can occur, and waves can change type or meet a boundary more than once. As a result earthquake records become very complicated, but the complications are clues to the internal structure of the Earth.

Records of near earthquakes (within about 10° of the recording station) give information about layers near the surface, but first of all we shall look at the simpler construction of the deeper parts, which can be deduced from distant records.

The core is much denser than the mantle, and its surface reflects waves and sends them back like echoes. A reflected *P*-wave is called *PcP*, and a reflected *S*-wave *ScS*. The small *c* denotes a wave that reaches the core, but does not penetrate it. The time that the reflected wave takes to travel is naturally longer than that for the direct wave, for it has farther to go, and it appears as a distinct pulse on the records. But there is a complication here. When a wave is reflected or refracted at a boundary it can change type, from a *P*-wave to an *S*-wave or *vice-versa*. This means that instead of just two reflected waves there are four — *PcP, ScS, PcS* and *ScP*.

For *PcP* and *ScS*, in which there is no change of wave-type, the reflection takes place at the mid-point of the path, but when there is a change the two sections of the path are of unequal length, and the point of reflection is displaced to one side.

This means that *PcS* and *ScP* follow different paths, but have exactly the same time of travel (Figure 14).

In order to keep track of the different kinds of wave, the seismologist draws what is known as a *travel-time curve*. This is a graph which shows how long it will take a wave to travel by each of the possible routes, and there is a line on it for each separate kind of wave. Figure 14 shows the routes that the *P*- and *S*-waves and the core reflections take, and the corresponding travel-time for these phases. If the distance of the earthquake is read off along the horizontal line, the time at which the different pulses will arrive can be read off vertically.

A real seismogram shows many more phases than the half-dozen I have mentioned. In order to see what other kinds there are, I shall treat them in 'family groups'.

The first set are the surface reflections. There is a big difference in density between the air and the rocks of the Earth, and conditions are very favourable for reflecting a wave that comes up to the surface from the interior. If a *P*-wave is reflected at a point midway between the recording station and the epicentre, it gives rise to a wave called *PP*, and of course, there is an *SS*, following the same route. Once again, there can be a change of type on reflection, and there are also waves called *PS* and *SP*; but in this case, as with *PcS* and *ScP*, the point of reflection is not half way, though the waves again have the same travel-time. The paths of these phases are shown in Figure 15.

The number of possible internal reflections is not limited to one. Two reflections are quite common, and there is a whole series of this kind — *PPP, SSS, PPS, SPP, SSP, SPS,* and *PSP*. In the case of a very large earthquake, it is even possible to record *PPPP*, since the only limit to the complications is the amount of energy available. The energy is not of course divided equally between all the possible phases, and generally speaking, the simpler combinations are the most prominent in the records; but there are some striking exceptions, as the curved layers of the Earth can result in focusing effects for certain phases at some particular distances.

The next family of waves is the core refractions. We noticed earlier that beyond about 103° the direct *P*-wave cannot be recorded on account of the shadow effect of the core. Beyond this distance the first wave to appear on long-period instruments is often *PP*, which does not penetrate so deeply, and so is able to avoid the obstacle. Short-period ones often show a refracted wave arising from complexities within the core, but it is nothing like so prominent as *P* when it makes its re-appearance at 142°. Because it was deflected from its path, and disappeared altogether for nearly 40°, we give it a new name, and call it *PKP*. The *K* stands for *Kern*, the German word for core.

What are the other members of the family? If we look for an *S*-wave by the same route we find a surprise waiting, it seems to be much too early. In order to get through the core, it has had to change type and travel as a *P*. The core will not transmit transverse waves. We shall see why in Chapter 7. Since all waves through the core are longitudinal like *P*, the one letter *K* is the only symbol we need. The main core refractions are therefore written *PKS, SKP,* and *SKS*. There are also some rather more distant but not unimportant relatives that have been reflected inside the core itself. The main ones are *PKKP* and *SKKS*, and there are also some like *PKPPKP* that have been able to pass right through the core in order to be reflected back from the surface of the Earth on the opposite side of the globe (Figure 16).

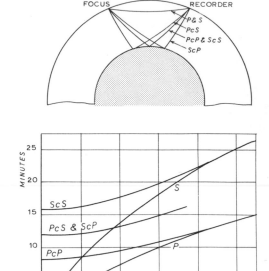

*Fig. 14: Reflections from the core. The upper part of the diagram shows the paths of waves reflected from the boundary between the mantle and the core, and the graph below shows their times of travel.*

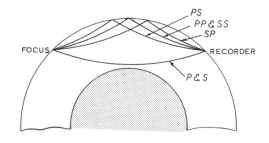

*Fig. 15: Single and multiple reflections at the Earth's surface. The upper diagram shows the paths of waves reflected once only, with and without change of type. Below are the paths of singly and doubly reflected P-waves.*

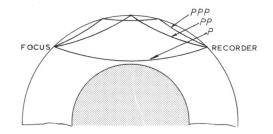

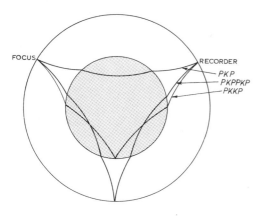

*Fig. 16: Core phases. The phase* PKP *arises from simple refraction by the cores.* PKKP *is internally relected within it, while* PKPPKP *emerges to undergo internal reflection at the surface on the far side of the Earth.*

Because it has had so far to travel, *PKPPKP* arrives a long time after most of the other phases, and it is not difficult to mistake it for the *P* of a new shock. If you trace out these paths on the different diagrams, you will not find it hard to work out how the different phases are named, and to imagine the paths of some of the more unusual ones like *PKPPKPPKP* and *PKSP*.

It should be mentioned that seismologists in a hurry sometimes write *P'* as a shorthand for *PKP*, so that *PKPPKP* becomes *P'P'* and so on, but we shall not use this notation again in this book.

We have already looked at a simple travel-time curve showing the direct waves and the core reflections. Figure 17 is a much more complete diagram, including most of the commonly recorded phases. In a large earthquake many more are possible, and at some distances they can appear quite prominent.

There is still one important class of wave to be considered. These are the surface waves, which are often the most prominent part of a record. They are often called *L*, or 'long' waves, since they oscillate more slowly than either the *P* or the *S* type, and they travel round the outside of the Earth instead of passing through the interior. Closer study shows that they are a mixture of two different kinds of wave — Love waves and Rayleigh waves, named after their respective discoverers. Both of these men showed mathematically that waves of this kind could exist before they were identified on seismograms. Love waves are a transverse movement, rather like *S*, but moving only in a horizontal plane. They are guided around the outside of the

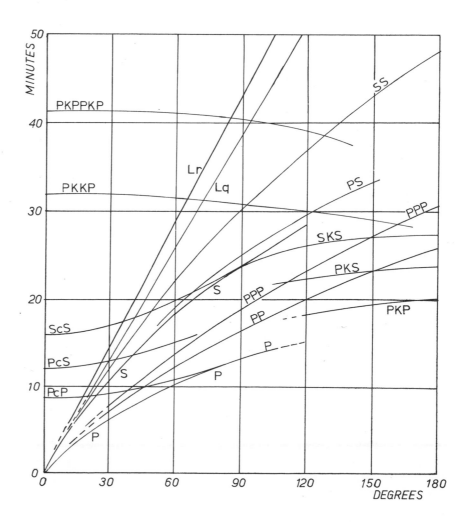

*Fig. 17: A travel-time curve. Seismologists use charts like this to help them identify the waves that appear on their records. These curves are for a shallow earthquake, and only the more common arrivals are shown.*

Earth by continuous reflection between the upper and lower boundaries of the surface layers. They have no vertical component at all (Figure 18).

Rayleigh waves, on the other hand, have quite a prominent vertical component, and are a kind of 'up and over backwards roll', which starts with a push in the direction of travel, then up, back, down, and push again (Figures 19 and 20). Both of these waves travel rather more slowly than $S$, and the Rayleigh wave is slower than the Love wave. When we need to distinguish them, we call the Love waves $L_Q$, from the German *Querwellen*, cross-waves, and the Rayleigh waves $L_R$.

Something has already been said about deep-focus earthquakes. More than half the world's earthquakes occure within the crust, that is to say, within 30 or 40 kilometres of the surface. In 1922 Professor F. J. Turner, who was then in charge of the *International Seismological Summary*, reported that some of the readings being sent to him would make sense only if it were assumed that the origins of these shocks were several hundred kilometres deeper than the normal ones.

For a number of reasons, seismologists were reluctant to believe this. It conflicted with what they thought they knew about the condition of the material below the crust, and Turner had also reported instances of 'high focus', so high indeed that on any reasonable assumption about the normal depth of earthquakes they would have been up in the air. Part of the difficulty was that there are no deep earthquakes in the parts of the world then covered closely with recording stations. It was not until 1928 that Professor Wadati showed that the waves from certain Japanese earthquakes arrived almost simultaneously at all the near stations, and put the reality of deep shocks beyond question. The deepest shocks so far recorded occur near the Tonga-Kermadec Trench to the north-east of New Zealand, and in the region south of Sulawesi in Indonesia. Their foci are almost 700 km below the surface.

This is a convenient place to mention that the focus is sometimes called the *hypocentre*. The term was used by early seismologists to distinguish the true origin below the ground from the centre of shaking on the surface. Since it means 'beneath the centre' it does not fit easily into modern thinking and is hard to reconcile with *epicentre* which is quite correctly 'upon the centre'. At the present time hypocentre is enjoying a vogue among American seismologists. The reason for it is obscure.

Records of deep-focus shocks look very different from those of shallow ones. To begin with there are few surface-waves, and the seismograms are complicated by the appearance of a new set of reflected phases. It will be recalled that a $P$- or an $S$-wave can be reflected near the mid-point of its path to produce the phases $PP$ and $SS$. When the shock originates below the surface, there is also a reflection very close to the epicentre. Because its path from the focus to the surface is so short, we denote this first leg of the journey by a small letter, so that the phases are called $pP$ (read as 'little pP'), $sP$, $pS$, $sS$, and so on. A glance at Figure 21 will show that the time of travel for $pP$ or $sS$ will not be very different from that of $P$ or $S$. Each phase in the record can therefore appear double or triple, and the inexperienced observer can mistake the record for that of two earthquakes which have become superimposed because they happened within a few seconds of one another. These phases give us one convenient method of working out the focal depth. Core

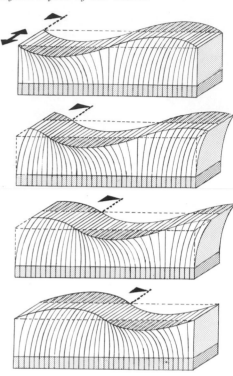

Fig. 18: *A Love wave. Love waves are one kind of surface wave. The particles have a transverse motion, rather like S, but they can move only in a horizontal plane and the waves are confined to the surface layers of the Earth.*

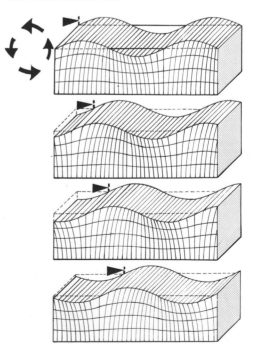

Fig. 19: *A Rayleigh wave. Rayleigh waves can travel only on the surface of the Earth. The particles move in ellipses, rolling over and over backwards as the wave moves on.*

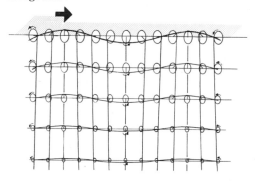

*Fig. 20: Particle motion in a Rayleigh wave. Below the Earth's surface the displacement of the particles becomes less and less until the movement dies out altogether.*

reflections such as *ScS* are also helpful, and in New Zealand the phase *sScS* has been used. New Zealand seismologists are very grateful for the good network of stations at the antipodes, in Europe. The phase *PKP* is often very well recorded in Sweden and gives a valuable check on the depth of New Zealand shocks.

With so many waves to be expected in an earthquake record, how does the seismologist sort them out? Fortunately it is often possible to pick the *P* and *S* waves just by looking at the record. This tells how far away the shock is, and reference to tables of travel-times helps to fit in the rest of the picture. The method of working most seismologists use is to draw out the tables of travel-times in the form of a graph, with the time scale the same as that of their records; that is to say, if the seismograph drum turns through 30 millimetres a minute, then 30 mm are made to represent a minute on the graph. He takes a narrow strip of paper as long as the record of the earthquakes he wishes to interpret, and makes a pencil mark on it opposite the beginning of every prominent phase. He can then lay the tape on top of the curves, keeping the first mark on *P* (or perhaps *PP* or *PKP* if it is a very distant earthquake) and moving it about until the other phases give the best possible fit.

When the phases have been identified, their times of arrival must be measured. If the arrivals are sharp and clear, this is done to a tenth of a second; but if the movement is very small, or there is a heavy background of microseisms, it is not always possible to be quite sure of the point on the record at which a movement begins, particularly for the waves of longer period.

In all record interpretation experience plays a big part, and in difficult cases it is often wiser to wait for information from other stations before attempting a final measurement of the records. Most observatories work in two stages. The first step is to select the well-recorded shocks and to read the time of the first arrival, which is usually *P*, or *PKP* if the shock is very distant. Some stations also read *S*, and *pP* if the shock is deep. The readings are sent as quickly as possible to a regional or an international centre that will undertake the determination of a preliminary epicentre. The most important of these international centres is the National Earthquake Information Service of the United States Geological Survey, and has offices near Denver in Colorado.

The NEIS now carries on a service started by the U.S. Coast and Geodetic Survey early in World War II. Large observatories in many countries send in their readings daily by urgent cable, and the NEIS works out approximate origin times, epicentres, and focal depths, the accuracy of which is astonishingly high. About twice a week lists of the epicentres and the data on which they are based are prepared and sent back to the contributing observatories by airmail. Once a month, they are arranged in chronological order and printed, thus becoming available to anyone interested in earthquakes at a very modest charge.

In most seismic countries, the headquarters of the national recording network arranges to provide very rapid information about large local shocks to the civil defence authorities, and many of them are also the centres of regional groupings providing less speedy but often more accurate determinations for shocks within their region.

European data are handled by the Bureau Central International de Séismologie in Strasbourg, and UNESCO has sponsored the organization of Regional Centres in Lima and Manila. In New Zealand and Japan, where the major networks are under government

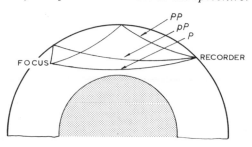

*Fig. 21: Depth phases. In deep-focus earthquakes additional phases like* pP *arise from internal reflections at the surface of the Earth close to the epicentre.*

control, the stations in Wellington and Tokyo carry out most of the functions of a regional centre, and in the vast territory of the U.S.S.R. there are centres that look after Central Asia and the Far East as well as the central station in Moscow.

International cooperation is not limited to producing preliminary epicentres. The International Seismological Centre, with its headquarters at Newbury in Berkshire, England, attempts a final summary of all the world's earthquakes. It is financed by contributions from more than twenty countries, and collects not only the preliminary epicentre information from the other services, but station readings from the many stations that do not contribute to the rapid services. The *Monthly Bulletin* of the I.S.C., which appears about two years after the earthquakes, lists all of the readings, and a new set of epicentres worked out in a standard manner. In keeping with its international character, the Centre has much of the computing and typesetting done in England, and then sends the *Bulletin* to Bangkok for printing. From time to time, the Centre also produces regional catalogues, maps, and a bibliography.

Although it was not set up until 1964, the Centre had had a distinguished predecessor, the *International Seismological Summary*, which had been doing similar work since 1923, but had run into financial trouble after the war, and needed reorganizing to take advantage of electronic computing methods. Even that was not the beginning, for the origins of the *I.S.S.* can be traced to the information of an International Seismological Association at a meeting in Strasbourg in 1903, and earlier still John Milne, who had returned from Japan in 1895 to settle in the Isle of Wight, began at once to collect the station registers from a world-wide network of stations sponsored by the British Association for the Advancement of Science, and to publish summaries of their readings.

The *International Seismological Summary* and the *Bulletins* of the I.S.C. contain a mountain of data, but many stations still find it useful to publish monthly or annual bulletins of their own containing more detail than it would be practicable to include in the *Summary*. A typical listing in such a bulletin looks something like this:

|  |  | h | m | s | μ | sec |  |
|---|---|---|---|---|---|---|---|
| 1953 Aug. 15 | iP! | 17 | 32 | 06 | 50 | 3 | △=83° *h*=N |
|  | PP |  | 34 | 17 | 10 | 7 | *M*=7·4 |
|  | PcP |  | 35 | 51 |  |  |  |
|  | eS |  | 40 | 33 | 75 | 5 |  |
|  | (SS) |  | 42 | 04 | 20 | 8 |  |
|  | L$_Q$ |  | 46·3 |  |  |  |  |
|  | L$_R$ |  | 47·1 |  |  |  |  |
|  | Max |  | 53 |  | 250 | 18 |  |

In it, there are some symbols that have not yet been explained.

When a phase has a sharp beginning, we prefix its symbol with an *i*, which stands for impulsive; and if it is very sharp indeed, we may even follow it with an exclamation mark. On the other hand, a movement may be so small, or the background of microseisms so heavy, that it is not easy to judge just what particular instant is the true beginning of the particular phase. Such a reading is labelled *e*, for emergent. Sometimes a sharp *P*-phase appears to be preceded by a slight 'curtsey', or small movement of the trace beforehand. In such a case the phase is written *ei*.

All phases will not agree precisely with a set of theoretical travel-time curves, and even a good seismologist is frequently uncertain of the true identity of some of the phases on his records. If he is not sure of the interpretation, he puts the name of the phase in brackets. On the other hand, a question mark means that the movement may not have anything to do with the earthquake at all, and could just as well be a prominent microseism, somebody working the cellar, or an insect in the works. The column headed $\mu$ (the Greek letter *mu*) is a measurement of how much the ground moved when that particular phase arrived. $\mu$ stands for microns, or thousandths of a millimetre, so it is obvious that the movements are not as a rule very big. The column headed 'sec' is the period, or time of swing of the ground movement. The final column gives the estimated distance ($\triangle$) in degrees, the depth of focus ($h$) in kilometres, or 'N' for normal depth; and the instrumental magnitude ($M$) of the shock which is explained in Chapter 11. Individual stations vary their procedures slightly, but the main pattern is always very similar, and there is no difficulty in following bulletins in Greek, Russian, Turkish, or Japanese!

To conclude the chapter, which is already a long one, let us review the characteristics of some typical records at different distances (Figures 22 - 27). Up to about 5°, the main phases are $P$ and $S$, the periods are short, and there are no obvious surface waves. From 20° to 40° $P$, $S$, and $L$ can be clearly picked out, and the reflected phases $PP$ and $SS$, are usually present. The main $S$-phase remains prominent in records up to 90° or 100°, but round about 80° there is a certain complication of the record resulting from the almost simultaneous arrival of $SKS$, $S$, and $ScS$, so that wrong identification is only too easy. Beyond this distance $PS$ and $PSP$ begin to show quite clearly. Records in the shadow zone (103° to 142°) present quite a changed appearance. Unless the earthquake is large, there will be gaps between the phases in which little but microseisms can be distinguished. The first phase is generally $PP$, followed by $PPP$, or $PKS$; and $PS$ and $PSP$ are prominent $SKKS$ is stronger than $SKS$. At very great distances 'textbook' records are seldom obtained, but $PKP$ is well established as the first movement. The records are also complicated by phases which have gone the long way round, and traversed more than half the Earth.

*Fig. 22: Seismogram of a near earthquake. These are the three components of the record of an aftershock of the Inangahua earthquake in May 1968 made on short-period Benioff instruments at Wellington. The distance of the epicentre was 2°·2, and the magnitude of the shock 4·3.*

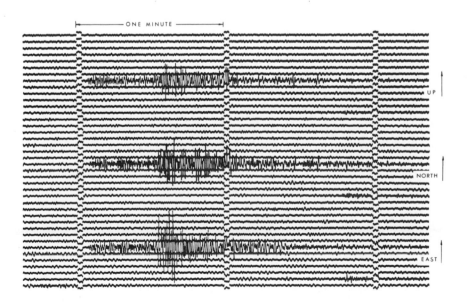

*Distant earthquake records. Records of three shallow earthquakes at increasing distances. All three were made on Press-Ewing instruments, the first two at Wellington, and the third at Scott Base. Only the vertical component is shown for the two more distant shocks. Note that the time-scales differ, to allow reproduction as large as possible.*

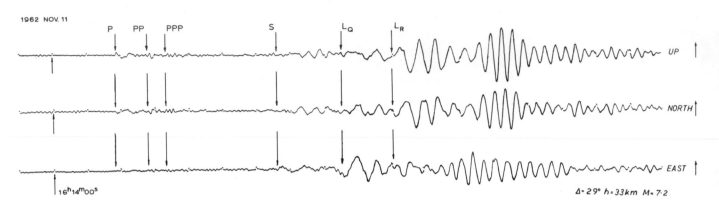

*Fig. 23. Santa Cruz Islands, 1962 Nov. 11.*

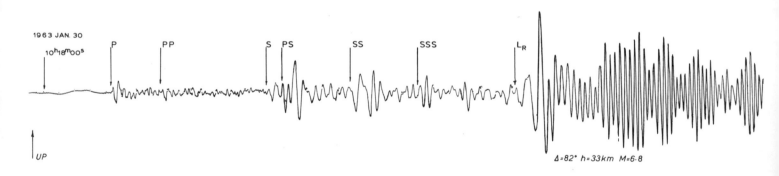

*Fig. 24. South Sandwich Islands, 1963 Jan. 30.*

*Fig. 25. Taiwan, 1972 Sept. 22. Scott Base lies just within the shadow zone, and* P *is not recorded.*

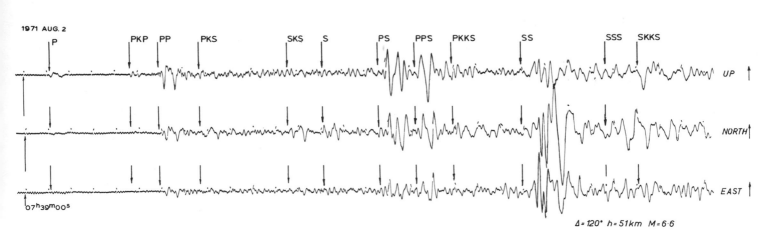

Fig. 26. A complex record showing the many phases that can be identified in the seismograms of earthquakes at great distances. The record was made at Scott Base, of a shock in Hokkaido, 1971 Aug. 2.

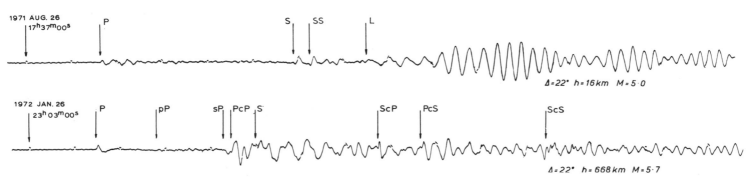

Fig. 27. Deep and shallow earthquakes. Both these vertical component records were made on Press-Ewing instruments at Wellington. The upper one is a shallow shock in the Loyalty Islands, and the lower one a deep shock near Fiji. The shallow shock has produced more surface waves, but the record of the deep one shows additional phases.

# 5 Preliminary probing

PROSPERO: Deeper than did ever plummet sound,
I'll drown my book.
Shakespeare, *The Tempest*

There is a story told about Sir J. J. Thomson, the discoverer of the electron, which should be more widely known. He was being asked, as many scientists are, what use could be made of his discoveries. 'Let us suppose,' he said, 'that at the time of the Franco-Prussian war, the nations had become alarmed at the great number of wounds in which pieces of bullet were still lodged, and could not be located; and that when the peace treaties were signed, the nations had agreed to offer a large premium to be paid to the man who could devise the most efficient method of finding these foreign bodies. What would have happened? Probing would have become a fine art, and the human body a pincushion — but we should not have discovered X-rays.'

The history of science offers many examples of discoveries that have found important applications in quite unrelated fields, and of the problems that have been solved by men who were looking for something quite different. If the early seismologists had worked in countries where earthquakes were a serious social problem, and had been dependent upon 'practical' politicians for their money, the effort that went into the study of the structure of the Earth could easily have been diverted to premature searches for a method of earthquake prediction, or to designing the details of earthquake-resistant buildings soon to be outdated by changing fashion and developments in structural engineering. If that had happened, we might still be without the most directly useful technique that seismology has developed — that of seismic prospecting. But this is to begin the story in the middle.

In 1910, there was published the study of an earthquake in Kulpa Valley, Croatia, in October of the previous year. The author, a geologist named Andrija Mohorovičić, noticed the records made at stations close to the epicentre did not show simple *P*- and *S*-phases, but had in addition a secondary movement following each of them. This, he suggested, could be explained if the outermost portion of the Earth were supposed to consist of a crust some 60 km in thickness, resting on top of the mantle. As we shall see, there have been great arguments about this figure, and seismologists are still discussing the nature of the outer portion of the Earth; but Mohorovičić had shown them a method of using local earthquakes to explore it. How does the method work?

Suppose that we have a series of seismographs spread out along a line from the origin of an earthquake, assumed to be at the surface of the Earth (Figure 28) and that the Earth has a crust about 30 km thick. (This is a better estimate for most big land areas than Mohorovičić's 60 km.) Let us further suppose that in the crust a *P*-wave travels at a speed of 6 km/sec, and in the mantle immediately beneath it at 8 km/sec. At a station within about 100 km of the epicentre, the first wave to arrive will be the slow one travelling directly along the path between the focus and the station. Simple

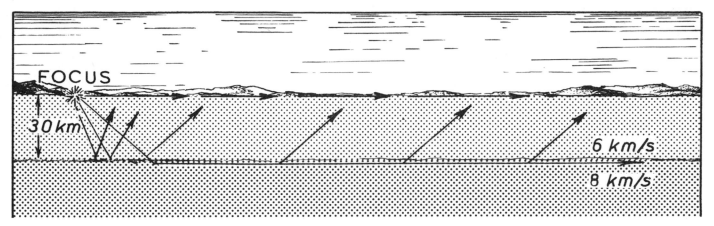

Fig. 28: *The origin of crustal pulses in the records of near earthquakes.*

arithmetic tells us that if the station is 50 km away the wave will take a little over 8 seconds for the trip; for 100 km between 16 and 17 sec; and for 300 km, 50 sec. We call this phase *Pg*, and if we draw a graph for it like the ones we drew for waves in the deeper parts of the Earth, we find that it is a simple straight line (Figure 29).

In addition to *Pg* there will be a second wave recorded. This has travelled by a less direct path, first going down to the base of the crust at 6 km/sec, and then travelling in the mantle at the faster 8 km/sec. Finally it must come up again at the slower speed to reach the recorder. This wave is called *Pn*, and is really the same wave that we called *P* when talking about distant earthquakes.

Because of its indirect route, the travel-time of *Pn* is a little harder to work out. It goes down a slanting path to the base of the crust, at an angle that depends upon the ratio of the speeds above and below the boundary, and comes up to the recorder again at exactly the same angle. At stations close to the origin *Pn* is later to arrive than *Pg*, as it has farther to go, but at greater distances its higher speed in the mantle enables it to overtake and become the first wave to arrive. At very short distances, where there is not room for a wave to go up and down at the correct angle, *Pn* is not recorded at all. Instead there is a reflection from the base of the crust, the reflected wave going up and down more steeply until right at the origin it goes straight down and straight up, taking 10 seconds for the double trip.

Fig. 29: *The travel-time of crustal pulses. These times assume a model crust 30 km thick in which the velocity of* P-*waves is 6 km/sec, overlying a mantle in which the velocity is 8 km/sec.*

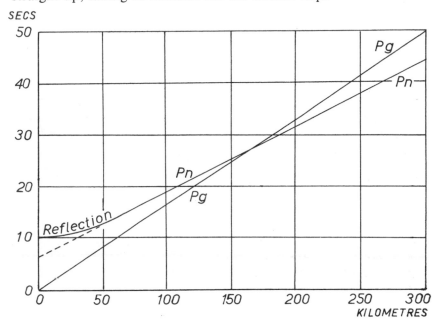

The travel-times of *Pn* and *Pg* in our imaginary crust can be summed up in a little table:

|        | *Pg*     | *Pn*      |
|--------|----------|-----------|
| 50 km  | 8·3 sec  | 12·8 sec  |
| 100    | 16·6     | 19·1      |
| 150    | 25·0     | 25·3      |
| 200    | 33·3     | 31·6      |
| 250    | 41·6     | 37·8      |
| 300    | 50·0     | 44·1      |

These values are not exactly the same as those in the real Earth, but they are approximately right and make our sums a little easier. With this model, a proper *Pn* could not be recorded at distances much less 70 km, and it would overtake *Pg* between 155 and 160 km.

Mohorovičić had to look at this problem the other way round, as he did not know either the speeds of the waves or the thickness of the crust to begin with. Let us look at it from his point of view. First he would have to work out where the earthquake was, and find the distances to his various recording stations. Then he could plot the arrival times on a graph like Figure 29. The slopes of the two lines would then give him the speeds of the two waves, and the distance at which the lines intersected would enable him to work out the thickness of the crust.

The base of the crust is now known as the *Mohorovičić Discontinuity*, or to those with less flexible tongues as the Moho. Seismologists everywhere were anxious to obtain better measurements of crustal thickness, but it proved unexpectedly difficult. There were not enough recording stations, the timing was not good enough, and the phases were not sharp enough to be measured accurately. A further complication made its appearance. In most parts of the world more than two pulses were recorded, suggesting that there were more than two layers (Figure 30). Not only was this so, but the variations in wave-speed that were reported made it obvious that different seismologists were not all measuring the same thing. In spite of this, most of them wanted to claim world significance for their results, and for a brief time of madness new layers were being added to the Earth's crust at a rate of about one a month!

An obvious solution to the problem was to use artificial explosions instead of earthquakes. They could be accurately timed and located,

*Fig. 30: Crustal pulses in the record of a near earthquake. The upper record shows the multiple phases due to the layering of the crust that are found in records of shallow earthquakes. The lower seismogram is one of a deep shock, and shows only simple P and S arrivals.*

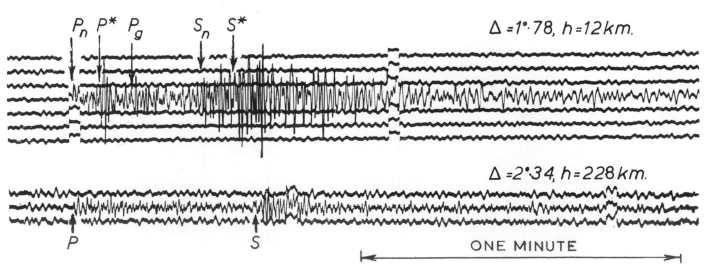

$P_n$  $P^*$  $P_g$       $S_n$  $S^*$          $\Delta = 1°\cdot78, h = 12\,km.$

$\Delta = 2°\cdot34, h = 228\,km.$

P          S                    ONE MINUTE

and they could be recorded on a special network of stations set up beforehand in the best places. At this point practical men began to take notice. Other hidden layers beneath the Earth's surface might be discovered by searching for them with seismic waves. The big oil companies were particularly interested in a method that could check the geologists' guesses about the way the strata they mapped at the surface of the Earth behaved at greater depths, without the costly trouble of drilling through hundreds of metres of rock to see whether some fold in the strata had trapped oil. The answer could now be obtained with a small explosive charge and a couple of dozen portable seismographs. Soon the big oil companies were providing money for geophysical research and the development of more convenient instruments.

The seismometers used by the modern oil prospector are known as *geophones*, and are smaller and more rugged than the ones used in observatories. Two factors make this possible. First of all, they can have short periods, as they are to be used close to the source of the vibrations, and secondly, they need have only a moderate output as they are almost always used with electronic amplifiers.

*Plate 10: Artificial earthquakes. When a seismic shot is fired, a little of the energy is usually wasted in blowing ground-water from the drill-hole. In desert conditions, where conventional drilling is not possible, many shallow charges may be placed in a regular pattern and exploded together, with even more spectacular results. For very shallow surveys, and in places where the use of explosives would be undesirable it is sometimes possible to get enough energy by dropping a heavy weight.*

*Plate 11: A drilling rig. In order to make the most efficient use of the explosive charge it is usual to drill through the surface material into more solid rock.*

Seismic prospecting has often to be carried out in undeveloped countries, in conditions varying from tropical deserts or jungles to the Arctic, and the equipment must be both rugged and self-contained. It is usual to mount it in a convoy of trucks, which may include servicing workshops and living quarters for the operators.

Under normal conditions the explosion is generated by a small plug of gelignite lowered down a hole about ten metres deep (Plate 10). This hole is necessary to get below the soil and weathered rock at the surface, so that the force of the explosion can be communicated to the ground as efficiently as possible. The convoy therefore includes drilling equipment and water-tanks to supply 'lubrication' to the point of the drill (Plate 11). When it is not possible to drill a suitable hole, elaborate patterns of small charges may be used instead of a single shot (Plate 10). At the other extreme, a sufficiently large shock may be obtained by dropping a large weight (Plate 10) or even tapping the ground with a hammer!

In a simple recording truck, of the kind that is still widely in use for scientific purposes, there is provision for recording the outputs from up to twenty-four geophones, which can be connected at intervals of about 30 metres to a cable run out from a drum at the rear. The amplifiers and filters can be so arranged as to turn each geophone into a pick-up of almost any characteristic likely to be useful. Twenty-four light-beams from the twenty-four galvanometers record side by side of a strip of photographic paper about ten centimetres wide. The truck carries facilities for developing the records, and radio equipment both enables the operator to keep in touch with the shot-firer, and automatically records the instant of the shot on the photographic paper along with the galvanometer traces. A built-in electronic clock puts precise timing-marks on the paper at intervals of 0·01 sec.

*Plate 12: A modern seismic recording truck.*

Equipment in the most modern trucks has become very elaborate (Plates 12 and 13), and in a large convoy things like the radio and photographic equipment acquire whole trucks of their own. Records are now very often made on magnetic tape, or in more complicated patterns than the old wavy line on a strip of paper. There is often a computer and an associated cathode-ray tube display. The magnetic tape record can be played back through a series of different filters, so that the best combination can be chosen, and the waves being looked for are not lost among confusing background movements.

Although oil companies have been responsible for much of the expenditure which has been needed for developing modern prospecting equipment, there are many other uses to which it can be put. In New Zealand, seismic surveys have been used to examine the dam-sites for our hydro-electric power stations, in connection with the search for geothermal power at Wairakei, and in the exploration of coal and other mineral resources. In this way, seismology is giving the answers to many problems which can scarcely have occurred to the early pioneers of earthquake study.

*Plate 13: Seismic prospecting. Inside the recording cabin. The outputs from as many as 48 geophones can be recorded either on paper or on magnetic tape. The equipment includes a computer and a cathode-ray tube display for use in the field.*

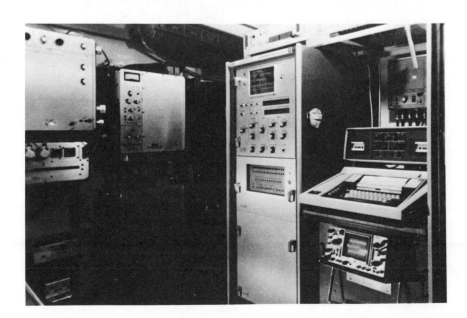

The technique I have described is known to the prospector as *refraction shooting*. In recent years it has been supplanted to a large extent by the reflection method, which is in many ways more straightforward, since it uses a direct record of the echoes from the boundaries between the rock strata beneath the surface. The geophones used to record reflections can be placed nearer to the shot-point than those used in refraction measurements, and this saves a great deal of time in laying cable for the geophone spread. Early seismic prospectors were forced to use the refraction method, because their geophones and amplifiers were able to record only the time of arrival of the first impulse with any clarity. By using modern geophones in conjunction with amplifiers and filters of known frequency characteristics, and automatic volume control to limit the effect of the first movement, the arrival of subsequent reflections can be clearly identified on the record (Figure 31).

Geophysical methods of prospecting for oil have perhaps been too successful, leading to the premature depletion of a limited resource. During the 1950s, when the possibility of shortages first became apparent, methods were developed for undertaking seismic surveys at sea (Plates 14 and 15). These have resulted in the exploitation of a number of previously unknown submarine oil and gas fields, first in the shallow waters of the Gulf of Mexico, later in the North Sea, off the coasts of North Africa and New Zealand, and in many other parts of the world.

We shall not end the chapter on a note of big business. Hydrographers have used seismic methods to obtain needed information about the sediments on the sea-bottom, and geologists use them for a multitude of purposes that have little to do with the

*Fig. 31: Reflection prospecting. This is a portion of a record made on Farewell Spit by a seismic unit of the Geophysics Division of the New Zealand Department of Scientific and Industrial Research. The shot was fired at the centre of a spread of 24 geophones. After the arrival of the direct wave (on the left) the traces are confused for a short time, but the ground is relatively steady again by the time the waves reflected from the solid bedrock under the less consolidated material of the Spit arrive. The instant of firing the shot is marked by a deflection of the third and fourth traces from the top, and the numbered timing-lines are a tenth of a second apart. The section of record reproduced here occupied less than a second.*

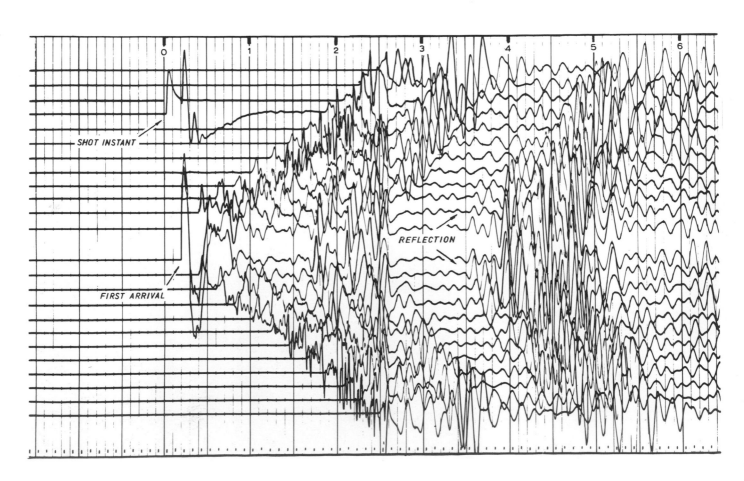

*Plate 14: Seismic work at sea. The research vessel* Explora, *intended for seismic, magnetic, and gravity measurements at sea.*

economic exploitation of minerals. Less expected was their value to the archaeologist.

Ground that has been dug over in the past does not transmit seismic waves so readily as ground that has not been touched, and buried masonry behaves differently from its surroundings. Readers who may fear the seismologists will establish another powder-magazine in the Parthenon can rest assured that for work on this small scale no explosives are needed. The necessary shock is produced by dropping a weight. By using a combination of geophysical methods, it has now been made reasonably certain that there are no undiscovered chambers concealed within the Great Pyramid, but the most celebrated occasion on which seismic exploration was used in archaeology was in 1951 when Father Daniel Linehan, a Jesuit seismologist, disposed his geophones about the church of Saint Peter in Rome. He was able to avoid a great deal of fruitless digging that might have endangered the structure, and lead the archaeologists to an ancient tomb that could contain the bones of Saint Peter himself.

*Plate 15: Prospecting in shallow water. This is a sea-going version of the seismic truck, intended for use close to the coast. Cable for the geophones is carried on the large drum aft of the recording cabin.*

# 6 Down to rock bottom

The Earth doth like a snake renew
Her winter weeds outworn
            Shelley, *Hellas*

What we have learned of seismology so far does nothing to explain why there should be earthquakes at all. If we set aside the small tremors that result from landslides, collapsing caverns, erupting volcanoes, and a few other minor sources of vibration, we find that nearly all earthquakes are the result of the geological forces that build mountains and shape the other major features of the Earth's surface. The study of these forces and their effects is called *tectonics*, from the Greek *tekton*, a builder, and the kind of shocks with which we shall in the main be dealing are called tectonic earthquakes. To understand their nature and their consequences we must learn both the source of the forces responsible, and about the material they act upon.

Judging from all the things we can find on its surface, the Earth is made of rock. Huge masses of rock stretch upwards to form mountain ranges; there is rock beneath the ooze of the ocean floor; the beds of our rivers are strewn with rocky boulders; and the sands of our beaches are ground-up rock. The lava that flows from volcanoes cools to form rock, and the material that is drilled from tunnels, mines, and wells is once again rock.

There are many different kinds of rock, and everyone is familiar with the names of some of them — granite, basalt, limestone, and so on. Geologists have grouped them into three main classes — *sedimentary*, *igneous*, and *metamorphic*. At the surface of the Earth, sedimentary rocks are by far the most plentiful, covering about three quarters of the total land area. The average depth to which they extend has been estimated at about a kilometre or two. They are not original features of the Earth's surface, but the product of an important process that is still going on.

It would be wrong to think of a geologist as a man who is concerned only with long-dead fossils and things that happened millions of years ago. He is probably more aware of the constant change and renewal of his surroundings than other people. Every rock that is exposed at the surface of the Earth, or *outcrops* as we say, is subjected to weathering, which gradually breaks it up into small fragments. In high mountain regions, alternate freezing and thawing makes the process a comparatively rapid one; but the chemical action of water on the material of the rock, the blasting of wind-driven sand, and grinding by glacier ice all play a part in the process of disintegration.

Once the rock mass has been reduced to small enough fragments, it is carried away and sorted by wind and water. Sometimes, the material can be moved bodily by the current, and in times of flood the amount of material shifted can be very great; sometimes the process is the gentle one of solution, but in the end the result is the same — the rocks of the mountain ranges are moved gradually to the coast. Material carried along rivers and watercourses enlarges the channel by scouring the bed and eroding the banks. Every year the Mississippi River moves more than four hundred million tons of material.

*Plate 16: Sedimentary rocks. Regular annual floods have built up layer upon layer of material that has become compressed and hardened to form this sandstone at Roche Percée, near Bourail in New Caledonia.*

During transportation further breaking up occurs, and the angular chips that make up the mountain shingle-slides become rounded gravel in the beds of the rivers of the plains. At the coast, the waves take a hand, adding material from the coastal cliffs to that brought down by the rivers, and depositing the broken and pulverized material on the sea bottom, where it is able to consolidate under the pressure of the superimposed material to form new rocks.

The nature of the new rock that is formed will depend upon the type of material that is being deposited. For example, very fine particles cannot come to rest in water that is running swiftly, or is churned up by breaking waves. The details of the process of deposition have been very carefully studied, but for our purposes it is sufficient to notice its importance. As time goes on, and more and more material accumulates, the distribution of currents alters, the depth of the sea changes and the supply of weathered material may now come from a different part of the mountain range and be different in texture or chemical compositon from that originally deposited. The rocks formed on the sea floor consequently lie in a series of superimposed layers (Plates 16 and 17).

*Plate 17: The geological column. These cliffs near Cape Kidnappers, south of Hawke Bay, show alternating beds of sandstone and pumiceous material. Some slight tilting has occurred, but the oldest rocks still remain at the bottom, and the most recent at the top.*

Material brought down by the rivers is not the only possible source of the sediment needed for rock formation. Limestone, for example, is a most important exception, although it is still a sedimentary rock. In this case, the material deposited originates in the sea itself, particularly where it is warm and shallow, and consists mainly of the shells and skeletons of dead sea creatures, which sink to the sea floor. When there is no admixture of other material we get a pure chalk or limestone; but under certain conditions they may serve merely as a kind of natural cement to bind material brought down by the rivers, or transported along the coast by ocean currents.

The superimposed layers of rock that result from the process of sedimentation are called *strata*. They have roughly parallel surfaces, and vary in thickness according to the rate at which the material accumulated and the time for which the deposition continued. In a series of undisturbed strata, the oldest rocks will lie at the bottom, and the youngest at the top. Sedimentary rocks often surround the shells or skeletons of animals and plants, which become buried in the sediments when they are being accumulated. These remains are known as *fossils* (Plate 18); and if they are well enough preserved to let us identify them, they give an important clue to the age of the rock. The types of creature living together have changed throughout geological history, so that if we find a similar set of fossils in two different rocks we can be fairly sure that they were laid down at about the same time. For example, a South Australian sandstone might contain the same fossils as those in a dissimilar rock from New Guinea, showing us how to piece together the sequences of strata in the two places. The complete sequence from the very oldest to the most recent is known as the *geological column*. The problem of dating a given geological event thus becomes the same thing as finding its correct place in the column (Figure 32).

It is not easy to determine how long the different geological periods lasted, but good estimates can now be made by using measurements

*Plate 18: Fossils. The remains of dead plants and animals become incorporated in the rocks, and help the geologist to assign them a date. These scallop-like* Monotis *shells lived in the Triassic period, some 200 million years ago. They measure about 30 to 40mm across.*

of the amount of radioactive material in the rocks. A schoolboy who knows the names of England's kings and queens in their right order knows that something which happened in the reign of Charles II took place before something in the reign of George IV, even if he doesn't know the dates of each reign. If he had a rough idea of the average length of a reign, he could make a good guess at the number of years involved. In the same way, a geologist knows that a Cambrian rock is older than a Jurassic one, and that he has got his events in the right order, even if he is uncertain of the speed of the complete process.

It is seldom that more than a limited section of the geological column is to be found in one place, so that the deciphering of the whole story of the Earth is a laborious process. Profesor Cotton has likened it to an attempt to assemble a complete book from a great pile of damaged copies which have been torn into groups of a few pages. A list of the geologist's periods with recent estimates of their lengths is given in the Appendix.

In many parts of the world, the volcanoes have long ceased to be active. We could not surprise the ordinary dweller in Indonesia, Japan, or Hawaii by telling him that the rocks on the nearby hillside had once been molten lava, and the soil of his fields hot ash, but it might surprise the people in parts of Scotland, the United States, or France of which our statement would be equally true. The second important type of rock is to be found in these places, as well as in places where volcanoes are still active. Such rocks are called *igneous*, a name which indicates their fiery origin. Sometimes they actually

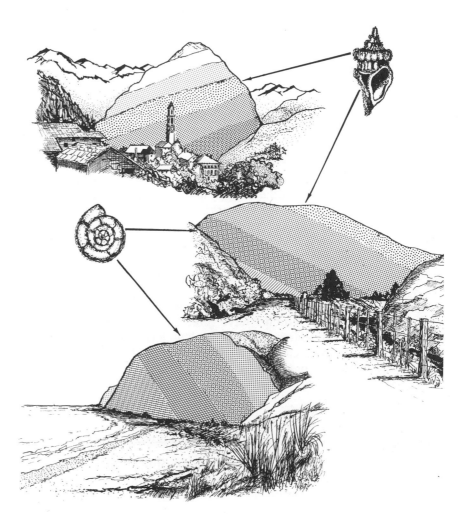

*Fig. 32: The geological column. The complete geological column must be pieced together by comparing the fossil sequences in the strata of many separate localities. Remember that the fossils determine the age of the rocks and not their composition. A limestone may have been formed in one place at the same time as a sandstone was forming somewhere else.*

came to the surface of the Earth in their hot condition, and flowed as lava from some volcanic vent; in other cases they have forced their way upwards through the underground strata, only to solidify and remain buried until erosion exposed them at the surface. In either case, they were once hot enough to flow with a greater or less degree of freedom, until they cooled or crystallized into their present form. Since they must once have been deep in the Earth, they are of great interest to the geophysicist, as they help to confirm his deductions about the nature of the Earth's interior.

The third main class, the *metamorphic* rocks, occupies an intermediate position between the other two classes. In its original form, a metamorphic rock may have belonged to either, but deep burial and subjection to heat and pressure, the behaviour during cooling and crystallization, or the heat from a nearby igneous intrusion have so changed its characteristics that it is necessary to describe it as a new kind of rock. The divisions between the three classes are not quite clear cut, but they are nevertheless very useful distinctions.

Changes of the Earth's surface are not a one-way process. The rocks of our land areas, igneous, metamorphic, and sedimentary, would seem from the account I have given to be alike destined to erosion, transportation by rivers, and deposition on some distant sea floor. This is only half the story. Since three-quarters of the land area is composed of sedimentary rocks, it is obvious that at some stage some of the sea-bed must once again become dry land. This is mainly the result of the process known as *orogenesis*, or mountain-building. The details of this process are still very speculative, and we shall have to return to them again.

It seems probable that the building of a mountain range begins with the filling of a shallow basin with a great mass of sediment (Figure 33). As the sediment accumulates, the supporting floor of the basin is further deformed and depressed. This structure is called a *geosyncline*. Because the floor of the geosyncline is forced to a greater depth than its original one, it is weakened by the higher temperature. Under the influence of compressional forces in the Earth's crust, the prism of sediment is folded and buckled, and dry land appears in the form of a new mountain range. By this time, the old continent which was the source of the sediment will have been largely eroded away, and the new mountain range will greatly alter the drainage pattern. Erosion will proceed as before, possibly contributing to the formation of a new geosyncline and a further period of mountain building. In this way a cyclic process comes into action, affording some justification for the claim of an early geologist that there is 'no trace of a beginning, and no prospect of an end'.

One result of mountain building is the widespread disruption of the geological column to which I have referred. Although we can find fairly extended sequences of strata, they have to be looked for carefully, and the rocks are often found bent and folded into strange shapes, cracked and shattered by the magnitude of the forces at work upon them (Plate 19). The process is a slow one, but the results are far-reaching.

Throughout geological history, periods of active mountain-building have alternated with periods of comparative calm during which major sedimentation proceeds. These orogenies have been sufficiently widespread for the major divisions of the geological column to be traced over large stretches of the globe. It is therefore possible to use the same broad time-scale everywhere, making only

*Fig. 33: Mountain-building. A: Sediment from the land is deposited in a shallow sea. B: A geosyncline is formed. C: Compression of the crust raises a chain of fold mountains.*

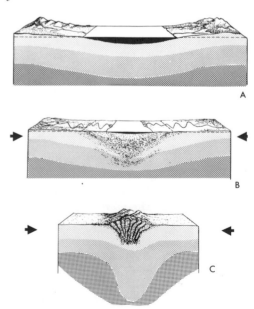

*Plate 19: The geological column disrupted. This contorted and fractured limestone at White Rock, in the eastern Wairarapa, shows how rock can behave under sufficient heat and pressure. It would be difficult to work out in detail all that has happened to this formation.*

minor changes to allow for local peculiarities, though it is possible that stratigraphers will protest at this summary treatment of their problems.

The story of mountain-building as we have just outlined it is unsatisfactory in a number of ways. Great compressional forces are needed to fold the geosynclinal sediments, but we have not explained where they come from. The geologist can tell us what has happened, but he cannot tell us why. The reason is probably that the cause lies too deep in the Earth to have left clues in the surface rocks. In the next chapter we shall see how physics can probe a little deeper.

# 7 Inside the Earth

Our souls, whose faculties can comprehend
The wondrous Architecture of the world.
    Christopher Marlowe, *Tamburlaine*

The Earth is a ball 12 700 kilometres in diameter, revolving about the Sun at a distance of nearly 150 million kilometres. By drilling we have been able to pierce less than ten of the six and a half thousand kilometres that lie between us and its centre and even these drill-holes provide a most inadequate sample of the outer parts. The rest of our knowledge has been laboriously pieced together from indirect evidence, the greater part of which has come from seismology, but astronomy and the other fields of geophysics have also played an important part.

As the Earth spins on its axis and journeys about the Sun; the Sun, the Moon and the other planets lie sometimes on one side of its equatorial bulge, and sometimes on the other. As a result, their gravitational pull gives the Earth a wobble. This wobble is called *nutation,* and it can be measured by taking accurate sightings on distant stars. The amount of wobble to be expected depends upon the way the internal mass of the Earth is distributed. If all the heavy parts were concentrated near the outside like the rim of a fly-wheel, for example, it would be much harder to disturb than if it had a uniform structure all the way through. By the end of last century astronomers were fairly sure that there was a heavy lump in the centre, and we have already seen how Oldham was able to use seismic waves to prove it in 1906, and Gutenberg to make an accurate measurement of its size a few years later.

Until a few years ago most scientists believed that the Earth began as a very hot body, and that most of its subsequent behaviour could be explained on the assumption that it had been cooling down ever since. Recently these ideas have undergone many changes. Some astronomers still think that the material of the Earth was once ejected from the Sun or torn from it by the gravitational pull of some passing star, but most now believe that it was formed from cooler matter, gathered from space by the Sun's attraction, or as part of the process that formed the Sun itself.

There is little doubt that the interior of the Earth is hot. Measurements in mines and deep drill holes show that for every kilometre we go down the temperature rises about 25° C, so that at no great depth we should expect to reach a point at which all rocks of the kind we meet at the surface would melt and become something like the lava that flows out of volcanoes. Some people, like the characters in Georg Büchner's play, have found this alarming:

FIRST CITIZEN: You're not frightened, surely?
SECOND CITIZEN: Well you see, sir, the Earth has a very thin crust — very thin, sir, very thin. I always fancy you might drop right through if you stepped into a hole like that. One has to tread very carefully indeed, sir, very carefully indeed. You might break through . . .

A little reflection should convince us that the rapid rise in temperature we observe at the surface cannot continue, for if it did, the material at the Earth's centre would be hotter than the Sun itself. Most of the Earth's heat seems to be due to its present radioactivity, rather than a relic of its past history. There is more than enough radioactive material in the crust alone to account for the whole of the measured outward heat-flow through the surface. It seems quite clear that if the Earth was not originally molten, it must soon have become so when sufficient material had concentrated about its original nucleus. The big problem for the geophysicist is whether it is at present heating or cooling.

The three main divisions of the Earth — the crust, the mantle, and the core — must have formed quite early. Gravitational attraction would concentrate the heavier elements in the central core, and help the lighter constituents of the mantle to separate out and form the crust. In 1799 Henry Cavendish carried out his famous measurement of the mass of the Earth, and found that the planet as a whole had a mean density that is almost twice as great as the average of the surface rocks. It is natural to ask what other materials are present in the deeper interior.

One line of argument has been based upon the chemical analysis of meteorites, which are generally supposed either to be the remnants of a disrupted planet, or to be surplus material left over when the formation of the major planets was complete. It is hard to know how far the meteorites reaching the Earth's surface are a representative sample, but there are two main groups, the *stones,* which have a predominantly silicate composition, and the *irons* which are metallic. The two types can not unreasonably be considered to parallel the existence of the core and the mantle of the Earth.

We shall now see how far these deductions are borne out by the behaviour of seismic waves, beginning with the crust, which behaves in a more familiar way than the deeper parts of the Earth, and work our way downwards to the centre.

In the previous chapter we saw how refracted waves can be used to measure the layers that make up the crust. In the upper part of it where geological processes have free reign, the situation, if not exactly chaotic, is at least complex. The speed of a *P*-wave can be as low as two kilometres per second, or it may reach six or more according to the nature of the rocks, but in most regions the base of the crust is marked by a sharp rise in velocity. The level at which this takes place is the Mohorovičić discontinuity, and just beneath it the velocity is nearly always a little above 8 km/sec.

The thickness of the crust is very variable. Beneath the continents, it is usually about thirty to thirty-five kilometres, but whenever there are great mountains standing far above the average level of the surface, there is nearly always a corresponding 'root' underneath. Measurements in Tibet have disclosed thicknesses of more than seventy kilometres.

Just as high mountains mean thick crusts, deep oceans mean thin ones, and there are differences in the structure of continental and oceanic crusts. A selection of cross-sections is shown in Figure 34. In the continents the basement material beneath the cover of surface sediments is usually hard crystalline rock, chemically acidic, and of a kind that the seismologist usually calls granitic, though geologists will hasten to insist that they are not always granite. Beneath the granitic layer is a second one of more basic rocks, usually described as basaltic but sometimes called 'intermediate'. There is often a sharp change in velocity between the two layers, at a boundary known as the Conrad discontinuity, but in some places there is a more gradual transition distributed throughout the crust.

In the thinner oceanic crusts the granitic layer is missing, and it used to be said that under the deepest oceans all we could expect to find above the Mohorovičić discontinuity was a few hundred metres of ooze and five or six kilometres of sea water, but more recent measurements show that there is nearly always several kilometres of basaltic material, with the base of the crust about ten kilometres below sea level.

The waves from near earthquakes and explosions are not the only source of information about the nature and thickness of the crust. Another powerful technique uses the records of surface-waves. The method depends not upon their time of arrival, but upon details of their structure that will be easier to understand if we begin by clearing up the meanings of some of the terms that seismologists use when talking about waves.

Figure 35 shows an ordinary enough wave of the kind that mathematicians call a *sine wave*. One of the most important things about sine waves is that you can build up waves of any other shape at all (including ones with sharp corners) by adding together a sufficient

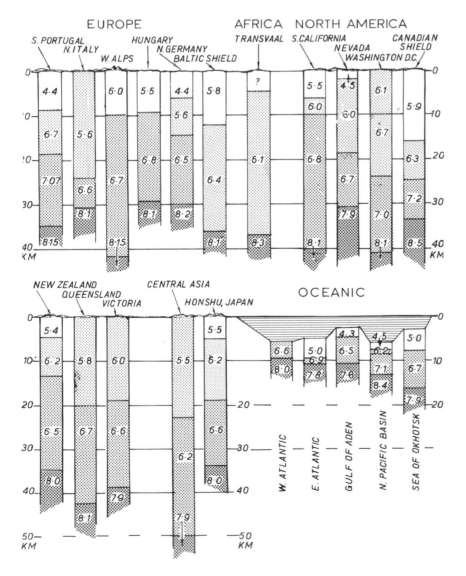

Fig. 34: Typical cross-sections of the crust.
The depth of the Mohorovičić Discontinuity is much greater in continental than in oceanic regions. It is usually marked by a sharp rise in the velocity of P-waves to about 8·1 km/sec. The continental crust is often divided into an upper granitic and a lower basaltic layer, and may be overlain by widely varying thicknesses of sediment.

number of sine waves of different sizes. In this simple kind of wave, if B, F, and J are successive crests, and D, H, and L successive troughs, the distance from B to F, F to J, D to H, or H to L is the same. This distance between corresponding points is called the *wave-length,* and is often represented just by the Greek letter λ (lambda).

The difference in height between the crests and the troughs, PQ, is sometimes called the *amplitude,* but that name is more usually given to PA, the maximum swing in one direction. When I use the word 'amplitude' I shall mean PA.

If the wave is moving, a certain number of crests will pass a fixed point every second. This number is called the *frequency* of the wave. The frequency, velocity, and wavelength are connected in a very simple way:

Velocity = frequency times wavelength $v = n\lambda$,
Frequency = velocity divided by wavelength $n = v/\lambda$

Since the frequencies in which a seismologist is most interested are generally less than one a second, he more often refers to the *period.* This is the time interval between the arrival of two successive crests, and is the reciprocal of the frequency. That means, a frequency of half a cycle per second is a period of two seconds, one third of a cycle a period of three seconds, and so on. A frequency of one cycle per second is often called one Hertz.

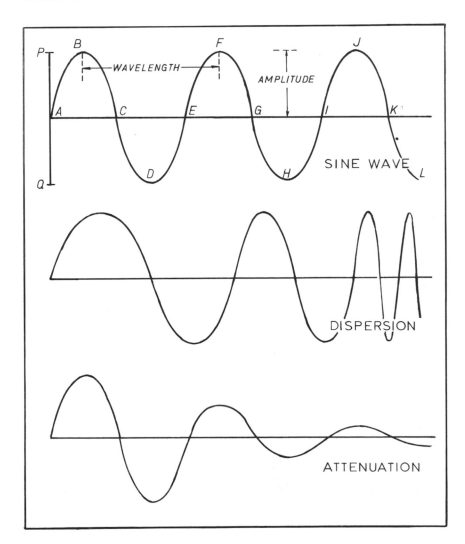

*Fig. 35: Wave motion. The distance between the successive crests or troughs of a wave is called the* wavelength, *and the maximum excursion from the zero position in either direction the* amplitude. *The sine wave shown at the top has a constant wavelength and a constant amplitude. If the wavelength changes with time, as in the middle example, the wave is said to be* dispersed, *and if the amplitude decreases as in the lower example it is said to be* attenuated.

If we look at the tail end, or *coda* of a seismogram, where the L-waves are recorded, we will see that the waves of longest period apparently arrive first and that shorter and shorter ones come progressively later. This process is known as *dispersion,* and it results from the fact that although an earthquake produces surface-waves of many different periods all mixed up, they travel at different speeds, depending on their period, and gradually sort themselves out as they travel. If we know when and where an earthquake took place, we can work out the speed of travel for waves of each particular period, and plot the result in the form of a graph called a dispersion curve. The shape of the curve we get will depend upon the thickness and composition of the outermost layers of the Earth along the whole path between the epicentre and the recording station.

Surface-wave measurements are evaluated by a rather tedious trial-and-error process. First you must guess the likely thickness and speed of travel in each layer of the crust, and then use your model to calculate a dispersion curve. Finally, you compare the result with the curve you obtained from your earthquake record. If they don't fit, you change some of your figures, and try again. Fortunately, the electronic computer has relieved us of a great deal of this drudgery, and it is usually possible to find a model that fits the observations quite closely, even when there are complicated changes in crustal thickness along the path. Figure 36 shows how Love waves and Rayleigh waves behave when they travel over paths that are mainly continent or mainly ocean.

There are, of course, other ways of getting information about the crust. The geologist has obtained useful data by analysing the kind of lava that comes out of volcanoes in different parts of the world. Precise measurements of the pull of gravity tell us whether the rocks beneath us are heavier or lighter than normal. Measurements of electric currents in the ground, and of the Earth's magnetic field can also provide information about the deeper parts of the crust. All of these studies help to complete the picture we get from seismic refraction measurements and surface waves.

Below the crust, we are no longer concerned with rocks of a familiar kind. At a depth of 30 km, the temperature is about 1200° C. and we might expect them to melt, but they do not become liquid. The great weight of material on top prevents it. Nevertheless, they gradually lose their individual identities, and become fused into one great mixture. Some small localized variations in composition remain, but the diversity that is typical of the crustal rocks has gone.

Perhaps the best way to think of the physical condition of the rocks at this depth is to liken them to solid pitch. Even if it is so solid that it can be shattered by a hammer blow, it will still flow and spread if you leave a lump on the bench overnight. If we treat it gently, it behaves as a liquid; but if we apply sudden forces to it, it behaves like a brittle solid. As far as waves are concerned, the upper part of the mantle is elastic, but for the slower processes of geological deformation, it is plastic, and within it slow movements are taking place.

Among the most important of these movements are those due to convection, and we shall consider their effects in a later chapter. Convection is the transfer of heat from one place to another by bodily movement of the hot substance. A body of rock that is heated by contact with hot material in the deep interior of the Earth will expand, becoming less dense than its surroundings, and consequently tending to rise. On nearing the surface, it is able to lose its heat and, contract, thus becoming denser and sinking again. This process sets

*Fig. 36: Dispersion of Love and Rayleigh waves. When the speed of the components of a complex wave depends upon their period, the resultant wave is dispersed. The way in which a surface wave is dispersed depends upon the structure of the crust along the path it travels. The graphs show the differences in behaviour of waves that have travelled over typical continental and oceanic paths.*

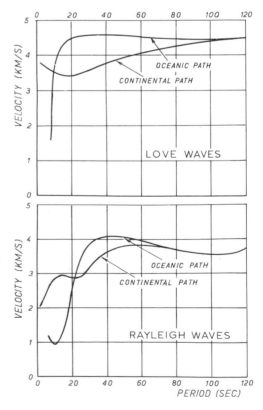

up great circulating convection currents, ascending and descending as they convey heat from the interior of the Earth.

Because the descending currents are denser than the rising ones, there are regional differences in the composition of the mantle, but here we shall consider only how its properties change with depth. Very broadly speaking, seismic waves travel faster and faster the more deeply they penetrate into the mantle. Just below the Mohorovičić discontinuity the velocity of *P*-waves is about 8·1 km/sec, and this increases to 13·6 km/sec at the boundary of the core. The corresponding figures for *S*-waves are 4·4 and 7·3 km/sec. There is no obvious change at a depth of 700 km, the greatest depth at which earthquakes occur, but deep earthquakes are confined to certain limited parts of the Earth, and we can expect any associated changes in the physical properties of the mantle to be similarly localized.

The speed of a seismic wave depends upon the density and the rigidity of the material through which it is travelling. An increase in density will slow it down, and higher rigidity will make it go faster. At greater depths the material should be more and more compressed by the increasing weight on top, but the fact that the speed of the waves increases shows that the increase in density must be less rapid than the corresponding increase in rigidity. However, there are some exceptions to the general rule which were first noticed in connection with the behaviour of sound-waves from explosions in the deep ocean.

In the oceans, it gets colder quite quickly down to a depth of about fifteen hundred metres, where the temperature is close to freezing point. At greater depths the decrease takes place much more slowly. Since the speed of sound in water depends on both the temperature and the pressure, the result of the two acting together is to make it travel more slowly at this depth than either above or below it. If we fire a small explosive charge at this depth, not all the waves will be able to reach the surface. Unless they leave the source at a great angle to the horizontal they will be bent backwards and forwards and trapped within a narrow channel. Most of them are transmitted to very great distances in this way before they are ultimately absorbed. The explosion of small bombs containing only a few kilograms of explosive can be recorded quite easily at distances of several thousand kilometres. This sound channel in the ocean is called the SOFAR layer, and it has been suggested that ships, rafts, and aeroplanes in distress could use it to signal their whereabouts to specially equipped listening stations by firing a small charge.

In the uppermost part of the mantle, between the base of the crust and a depth of about a hundred kilometres, something similar goes on. This region is known as the *asthenosphere* (from the Greek *a*, without, and *sthenos,* strength). The rocks in it have been weakened by the increase in temperature to a greater extent than they have been consolidated by the weight of material on top. The result is that the speed of seismic waves in this region drops below that at the base of the crust. At still greater depths the effect of the increasing pressure is to make it rise again, and so form a low-velocity channel like the one in the ocean. This channel interferes with the travel-times of *P*- and *S*-waves recorded at distances between about 15° and 20°. Professor Caloi of Rome University first realized that the fall in velocity in the asthenosphere was responsible, and that waves were being channelled through it like sound waves around a whispering gallery.

The rocky material that lies above the asthenosphere is called the *lithosphere,* from the Greek *lithos,* a stone. Older writers used the term lithosphere to mean the crust. We now apply it to a much thicker region — how thick is hard to say, for there is no sharp boundary like the Mohorovičić discontinuity to define it.

The asthenosphere channel is not the only low-velocity channel in the Earth. Professor Gutenberg has suggested that in many parts of the world there could be one within the crust. Under the influence of heat and pressure, quartz changes its physical state, and this change should occur at a depth of about ten kilometres, producing the drop in velocity needed to create the channel (Figure 37). In continental regions waves have been detected that appear to have been directed through the channel. Its presence affects our estimates of the thickness of continental crusts by a few kilometres, but oceanic ones are less than ten kilometres thick and do not contain a channel.

This interpretation would dispose of two long-standing difficulties. When we measure the speed of the waves produced by an explosion at the surface of the Earth, we get a slightly higher value than we obtain when we measure earthquake waves. Since they are known to be the same kind of waves, and to travel through the same rock, this is ridiculous. If there were any difference, we would expect the earthquake waves to take the deeper path and to have the higher velocity. By assuming that the earthquake foci lie in the low-velocity channel, Professor Gutenberg was able to explain the observed results quite satisfactorily. At the same time, it was possible to avoid the odd result that *P-* and *S-*waves from some earthquakes did not appear to leave the focus at the same insant.

In 1957 and 1958 the world's geophysicists organized a special programme of cooperative research projects known as the International Geophysical Year. This resulted in a great many additional crustal studies, and in the establishment of new seismograph stations in Antarctica and other parts of the globe that had previously been inadequately covered. The success of the operation was so apparent that in 1960 Professor V. V. Beloussov of the Institute of Physics of the Earth in Moscow suggested that there should be a further programme directed towards the study of the upper mantle. Most geophysicists agreed with him that the answers to many puzzling questions were likely to be bound in the region immediately beneath the crust.

One of the most spectacular schemes intended to contribute to the Upper Mantle Project was an American proposal to drill a hole right through the crust and to obtain a sample of the mantle for direct

*Fig. 37: The crustal low-velocity channel. If the velocity of waves at any particular depth in the Earth is less than at depths above and below it, waves that leave the focus of an earthquake at that depth in certain directions are trapped within a 'low-velocity channel'. In this sketch the velocity has been assumed to increase from 6 km/sec. at the surface to 7 km/sec. at a depth of 10 km. It then falls again to 6 km/sec. at 15 km., and increases once more to about 7·5 km/sec. just above the Mohorovičić Discontinuity. Waves directed steeply upwards from the focus, as at A, can reach the surface directly as a normal Pg phase. Those directed steeply downwards, as at D, are reflected from the discontinuity. If a little less steeply inclined they are refracted by it, as shown at C, travelling beneath the discontinuity and returning to the surface as Pn. Over the range of inclinations intermediate between these groups, the waves are trapped within the channel, as at B.*

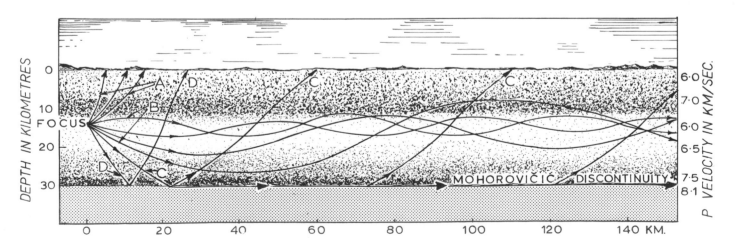

study and analysis in the laboratory. Under most land areas the Mohorovičić discontinuity lies beneath at least twenty or thirty kilometres of rock, so it was decided to drill the Mohole (as it had been irreverently christened) through the comparatively thinner oceanic crust, working from a floating barge. Enormous technical difficulties were expected, but it turned out that the political ones were even greater. In 1966 the U.S. Congress decreed that Project Mohole should be abandoned, we are still without a sample of the mantle.

Fortunately the less ambitious parts of the Upper Mantle Project went ahead more smoothly, including some deep drilling in several parts of the U.S.S.R., more crustal thickness measurements and some fresh work on seismic travel-times. We shall return later to consider the processes going on in the upper mantle, many of which have only been understood within the last decade.

When the Mohorovičić discontinuity is ultimately pierced, what can we expect to find beneath it? Chemically, the mantle is composed for the most part of silicates of magnesium, with lesser amounts of iron and aluminium oxides and traces of sodium and calcium. If we had to name an actual rock the most likely one seems to be a dense ultrabasic one called dunite, which is mainly olivine, but this is at best an informed guess.

The change from mantle to core is abrupt, occurring within a few kilometres at most. Two changes are involved – a change of material, and a change of state.

At the core boundary, the *S*-waves meet an impenetrable barrier, but *P*-waves can continue, although their speed is once again reduced to 8·1 km/sec (Figure 38). On the surface of the Earth, inability to transmit *S*-waves is regarded as a most important sign that a material is a liquid. Although the core is liquid by this test, it is misleading to think of it as behaving like water. A reliable analogy is difficult to find, and we must be content to think of the material of the core as quite unlike anything we have ever met at the surface of the Earth. The core is much denser than the mantle. The density of the whole Earth is about 5½, whilst the average of the surface rocks is only about 2½ times as heavy as a corresponding bulk of water. In the mantle, the density averages less than 5, so that there is a good deal of weight to be made up in the core, which has a density of 10 to 12 for most of its bulk, and may rise as high as 16 or 17 at the centre. Some geophysicists think that this great density is due to a concentration of heavy metals, like iron and nickel, whilst others think it can be accounted for merely by supposing that the atoms of the materials forming the rest of the Earth have been changed under the pressure so that they can be more tightly packed together in the core. This is a question which is not likely to receive a final answer for a long time.

The existence of a sharp boundary between the mantle and the core gives us a further clue to the Earth's internal temperature. At this depth, it must be hot enough to melt the metal of the core, but not so hot that it can melt the silicate material of the mantle in contact with it. This sets quite narrow limits, and the probable temperature works out at about 3600° C. Since the core is metallic it is a good conductor of heat, and there cannot be much further rise of temperature within it.

I have already hinted that the core is not a simple structure with the same properties all the way through. In 1936, Miss Inge Lehmann, the Danish seismologist, examined records of a number of large earthquakes, including the New Zealand shocks at Murchison and

*Fig. 38: Density and seismic wave velocity inside the Earth. The velocities of P- and S- at different depths within the Earth are known within fairly close limits. The densities deduced from them are less certain, particularly in the outer and inner core, as indicated by the shading in the lower graph.*

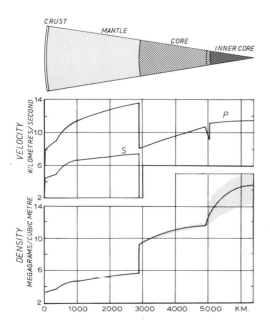

Hawke's Bay in 1928 and 1931. It was clear from these records that a *P*-type wave was arriving at stations which should have been within the shadow zone. This can be explained if there is an inner core, about 1250 km in radius, and of rather greater density than the outer portion. When naming a phase which has travelled through the inner part of the core, we use the letter *I* if it is a *P*-type wave, and *J* if it is an *S*-type wave. The phase *PKIKP* has now been definitely observed, but the existence of *PKJKP* is still very doubtful. If it exists, there are reasons to believe that it will not be very strong, so that we can expect it only in big earthquakes. It is probable for other reasons that the inner core is solid, but a record of *PKJKP* would provide a welcome proof. Figure 38 shows the way in which the density and the velocity of seismic waves change with depth below the Earth's surface. We are now in a position to draw a complete picture of the interior of the Earth, and this has been done in Figure 39.

*Fig. 39: The Earth's interior.*

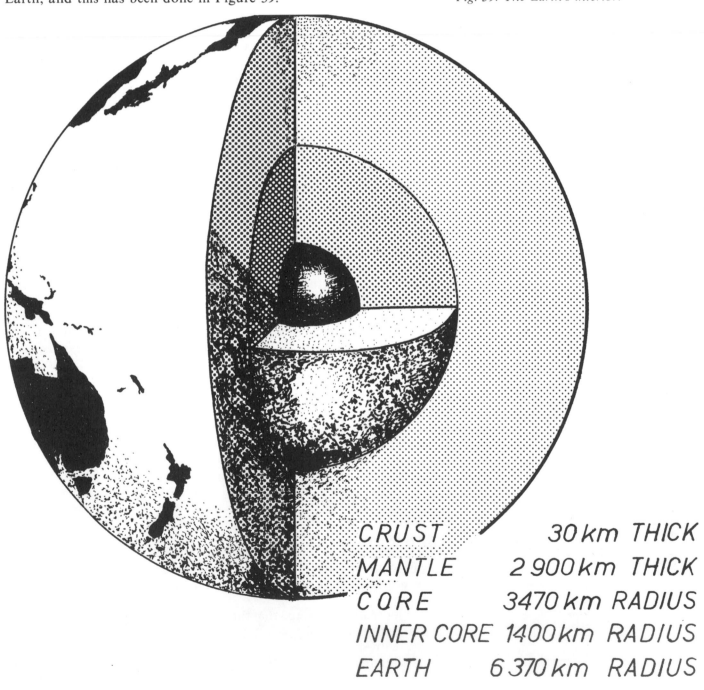

CRUST          30 km THICK
MANTLE       2 900 km THICK
CORE          3470 km RADIUS
INNER CORE  1400 km RADIUS
EARTH         6 370 km RADIUS

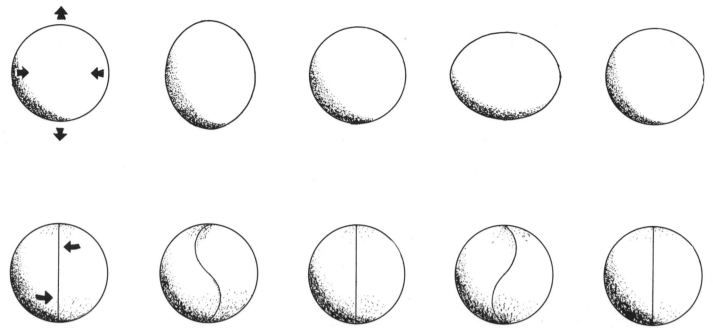

*Fig. 40: Free oscillations of the Earth. Very large earthquakes can set the whole Earth vibrating. There can be radial movements that distort its shape, as in the upper set of diagrams, or transverse movements that leave it the same shape but distort the surface, as in the lower set.*

Although we are reasonably sure that the inner core is solid, its density is very uncertain. It is unlikely to be less than 15, and on some reasonable assumptions it could be as high as 18 or 20. The study of surface-waves of very long period offers a possible way of finding out.

The longer the period of a surface-wave, the deeper are the parts of the Earth involved in transmitting it, so the introduction of ultra-long-period seismographs means that the usefulness of surface-waves is no longer limited to the study of the crust. First the properties of the mantle, and more recently those of the Earth as a whole have been investigated with their help.

Very large earthquakes like those in Chile in 1960 and Alaska in 1964 have set the whole bulk of the Earth in vibration like a great jelly. Two basic kinds of wobble are possible, known as the *torsional* and *spheroidal* modes (Figure 40). In torsional oscillation the surface of the Earth is displaced sideways, the simplest case being when the two opposite hemispheres move in opposite directions. During spheroidal vibration the particles move in and out radially, so that the Earth alternately bulges at an equator and stretches at the poles, in the manner of a rugby football. This kind of vibration is like that of the outside of a great bell, or it can sometimes be seen in a suspended water-drop.

These oscillations are of course very slow, the deep fundamental note having a period of nearly an hour, and there is a complicated series of overtones. The exact period of this note, the relationship of the overtones to it, and the way the whole series of vibrations dies away are all related to the distribution of density and elasticity throughout the whole bulk of the Earth. Once vibrations of this kind have been started, they take a very long time to die out, and suitably designed pendulums can still detect them several days after the earthquake.

# 8 Continents and oceans

Some force whole regions, in despite
O' geography, to change their site:
      Samuel Butler, *Hudibras*

The fact that there are continents and oceans needs an explanation. If the Earth began as a molten mass surrounded by vapours, it might very well have ended up as a smooth ball covered to an even depth by sea. Studies of the crust have shown that the continents and oceans are different in structure, thickness, and chemical compositon. It is simpler to see why these differences, once they have arisen, should persist.

Compared with the radius of the Earth the thickness of the crust is small. The difference in average level between the continents and the ocean floors is smaller still, a mere five kilometres. To be sure, it is nearly twenty kilometres from the bottom of the deepest ocean trench to the summit of Everest, but these large departures from the average are unusual, and the processes of geology are active to reduce them. The basic difference in level between continent and ocean, however, is in a different category.

If we were to float a number of pieces of wood of different shapes and sizes in a trough of water (Figure 41) we would find, provided that they were all made of the same kind of wood, that a big block sticking a long way out of the water also went well down underneath, while a thin plank that was almost awash didn't go far under the water at all. The comparatively light material that makes up the continents rests upon the denser material of the mantle in a way that is not very different from floating. If each bit of the continent could find its own level independently, we could expect the bottom of the crust to lie very much deeper under the mountain ranges than it does beneath the plains, and the base of the thin oceanic crust to be nearer the surface than the base of a continent. This kind of balance is known as *isostasy*, from the Greek *iso*, equal, and *stasis*, standing.

There are several indications that isostasy is operating in the Earth. Waves from near earthquakes that have to pass under mountain ranges are delayed by their roots, for example, but the usual method of investigation is to make measurements of gravity.

Imagine that we have hung up a plumb-bob somewhere in the middle of a great continental plain (Figure 42). Below us the light rocks of the crust and the material of the mantle underneath them lie in even layers stretching away in all directions. Under these conditions the pull of gravity will make the bob hang straight down, pointing to the centre of the Earth. Suppose now that without altering anything else we pile a mountain range on top of the crust, to one side of the bob. There is now more mass on that side than the other, and the gravitational attraction of this mass will try to pull the bob a little in its direction.

When we make measurements near real mountains, we find that their pull has very little effect. The reason is that underneath, the mountain has a root sticking down into the mantle. This root is composed of the same kind of rock as the crust, and drives out

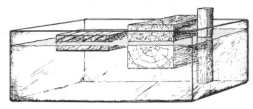

*Fig. 41: The principle of isostasy. The distance to which a floating block extends beneath the surface can be judged from the amount that appears above it.*

*Fig. 42: Deflection of the plumb-line. When there are no local irregularities, a plumb-line hangs vertically, pointing in the direction of the centre of the Earth, as in A. The gravitational attraction of a large mass like the range of mountains in B should pull it to one side, but if the mass of the mountain is compensated by a root of light crustal material driving out part of the heavier mantle, the total mass on all sides of the bob remains the same, and it continues to hang vertically, as in C.*

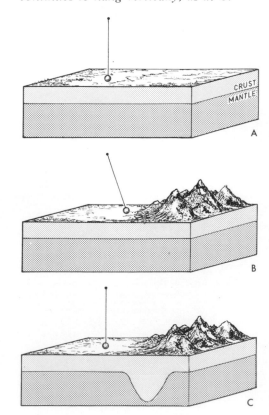

enough of the heavy material to leave the same total mass on all sides of our pendulum.

Regions in which the balance is perfect are said to be isostatically *compensated*, and large parts of the Earth seem to be very close to the condition of balance. In others the balance is upset, and we say that there is a *gravity anomaly*. Measuring the displacement of a suspended plumb-bob is difficult, but portable instruments called gravimeters (Plate 20) have been devised to simplify the mapping of the Earth's gravitational field. Basically they are no more than a delicate spring with a weight hanging from the end. When the pull of gravity on the weight increases, the spring gets longer, and when the pull is removed it contracts again. In practice, the changes in pull are very small, so the springs have to be very delicate, and protected against changes in temperature and mechanical damage. Even then, there are problems in interpreting the readings, for complicated allowances have to be made for the configuration of the country, for the height above sea-level, and for departures from normal density in the near-by rocks due to localized geological peculiarities.

The gravity anomalies in uncompensated regions may be either positive or negative. Regions where the pull is greater than normal will have a tendency to sink, and those where it is less will tend to rise. There are many reasons why anomalies should exist. When mountain ranges are eroded away, and their rocks transported to the sea by rivers and dropped on the bottom, the trim of the continental rafts is

*Plate 20: Gravity measurements. Differences in the pull of gravity at different places on the Earth's surface can be measured with portable gravity-meters like this one being used in the Antarctic. The part of the meter that responds to the varying pull is enclosed in a vacuum, and is rather like a vertical seismometer. For transportation it is placed in a sprung and padded compartment in the aluminium cylinder seen standing behind it.*

upset, but the material beneath the crust yields only slowly, and it takes time for them to reach their new stable positions. Under these conditions, the mountain ranges have a continual tendency to rise, and the crust beneath the shallow seas where the material is deposited becomes warped downwards. These differential processes cause strains in the region between.

Isostatic forces alone are insufficient to account for all the folding, fracturing, and uplift that is evident in the rocks around us. The crust is also stressed by the slow but powerful movements of the mantle beneath, generated ultimately by the Earth's internal heat.

Each of the continents contains a nucleus of very old crystalline rocks. Most of its former relief has been weathered away, but it has been untouched by the processes of deformation and tilting that are so much in evidence at the active continental margins. To all appearances these stable nuclei, which are known as *shields*, have been unmoved, if not since the beginning of time then at least since the pre-Cambrian, which for most human purposes approximates to the same thing. Appearances deceive. The continents are floating rafts, and rafts can move without disturbances to the cargo.

As long ago as 1620 Francis Bacon was struck by the similar shapes of the coastlines on opposite shores of the Atlantic, but it was not until 1910 that Alfred Wegener, a German meteorologist, seriously suggested that they had once been united, along with Australia and Antarctica, to form a single super-continent that he called *Pangaea* (Greek for 'all the land', Figure 43). Pangaea was supposed to have remained in one piece until about the beginning of the Mesozoic, when it rifted into pieces that gradually moved apart to become the present continents. This hypothesis is known as *Continental Drift*.

Geologists quickly found that the similarities between formerly united pieces of Pangaea went far beyond a similarity in general shape. Whole sequences of rocks in widely separated continents were found to match in extraordinary detail. Botanists and zoologists, who had previously insisted that there must once have been now

*Fig. 43: Continental drift. The present continents are probably fragments of a single primitive continent called Pangaea, which broke up in the Mesozoic era about 150 million years ago. The pieces have since drifted apart and their shapes have been modified. In the reconstruction above Africa and the Americas are easily recognized. Australia and India nestle against eastern Antarctica. The Indian fragment later collided with Eurasia and became part of it.*

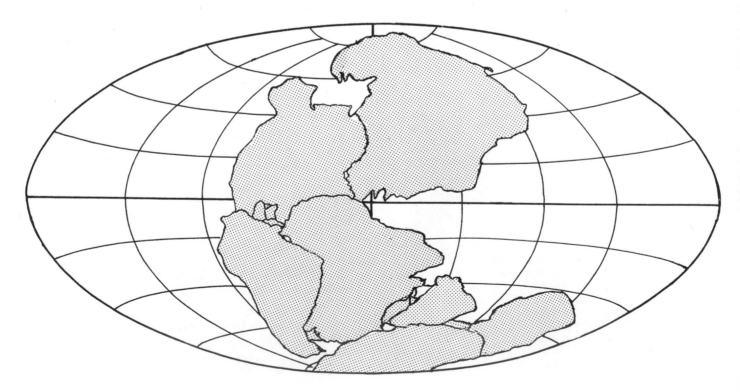

sunken land-bridges across the oceans to account for similarities in plants and animals, gave the hypothesis a warm welcome.

Geophysicists were less enthusiastic. They were prepared to grant that for the purposes of isostasy the continents acted like great rafts of granite floating on the denser material beneath; but although that material was plastic, they knew that it was also extremely viscous, and they knew of no forces great enough to move the rafts apart. Wegener had written of *Polflucht*, a flight from the poles. This idea they were inclined to dismiss as German mysticism. Yet geophysicists were gathering data that could only be explained by supposing that something of the kind had in fact occurred. The clues lay in the magnetism of the Earth.

The Earth is a magnet, but not because of the permanent magnetism of the iron and nickel in the core. At that depth the temperature is far too high for permanent magnetism to be possible. The fact that a suspended lodestone or compass needle would point towards the pole has been known since very ancient times. At the end of the sixteenth century it was realized that it did so only approximately, and that the direction in which it actually pointed slowly changed. This happens because the Earth's magnetic field varies in a rather complicated way.

To begin with, it has two parts, one originating within the Earth itself, and the other resulting from an interaction between the ionosphere (the electrically charged layer of the upper atmosphere that reflects radio waves) and streams of electric particles emitted by the Sun. An eruption of sunspots or solar flares can upset the balance of this interaction, causing magnetic storms during which radio communications are disrupted and auroral displays may be seen; but these storms are short-lived and less relevant to seismological problems than the slower changes that affect the internal field.

The core of the Earth is fluid, and it is a good conductor of electricity. The fluid is in motion, and there are electric currents circulating within it. Taken together these movements constitute a kind of self-exciting dynamo, which generates the internal magnetic field. This dynamo has a most important property. It is unstable. While the Earth's rotation ensures that the magnetic poles remain somewhere close to the geographical ones, a very small disturbance in the internal currents could make the entire external magnetic field reverse its direction, so that the end of a compass-needle that had previously pointed north would now point south.

This kind of upset has not occurred in historic times, but we do not have to go far back into the geological past to find that the rocks contain a record of many such reversals. The study of this magnetic record is called *palaeomagnetism*, and provides the most persuasive evidence for the reality of continental drift and the existence of convection currents within the mantle.

A rock can become useful for palaeomagnetic study in a number of ways. When substances are heated beyond about six hundred degrees Celsius they lose their magnetism, but if they are allowed to cool again in the presence of a magnetic field they become re-magnetized in the direction of the field. The natural magnetism of igneous and metamorphic rocks is therefore a record of the direction of the Earth's magnetic field at the time they cooled. Sedimentary rocks can also preserve a record. While magnetic particles are floating, they behave like tiny compass-needles, so that under calm conditions they are deposited on the bottom all pointing the one way, aligned in the direction of the field. In a very thick stratum it may be possible to follow the changes in direction from the time the oldest material was deposited at the bottom until the most recent was formed at the top. Even artificial materials like the clay bricks in the ancient hearths and ovens uncovered by archaeologists have proved useful to the palaeomagnetician.

The practical difficulties of palaeomagnetic work are very great, for there are many ways in which the original magnetism of the rock could have been disturbed, but by taking many samples a reasonably consistent story can be pieced together. After proper allowance has been made for reversal of the field, the orientation of a continent at the times its rocks were formed can be worked out, and its wanderings traced. The details of the story differ a little from the one originally told by Wegener, but it is now generally accepted that large bodily movement of the continents has taken place.

Magnetic measurements at sea are a less tedious business than the collection of carefully-oriented rock specimens and the delicate laboratory measurements called for on land. All that is needed is to tow a continuously recording magnetometer behind a ship, and because the geological history of the ocean floors has usually been less disturbed than that of the continents, the elaborate mapping needed before proper allowance can be made for the tilting and folding of the rocks since they acquired their magnetism is also unnecessary. This is fortunate, for the difficulties facing a marine geologist are daunting.

The sea covers seventy percent of the Earth's surface. Most of our geological knowledge has been gathered from the other thirty percent, and no matter what allowances we make, geology alone is bound to give us a distorted picture. Oceanographers realized that corrective measures were needed, and in the 1950s, particularly at the time of the International Geophysical Year, a great many important oceanographic cruises were made. The Americans were active in both the Atlantic and the Pacific, the Russians tackled the Pacific and the icy problems of the Arctic, and the French, the Japanese, and the Danes also mounted major expeditions. Their enormous contributions to biology and their work on ocean currents, sea-temperatures, and salinities do not concern the seismologist. What does is the detailed mapping of the topography of the ocean floor, the sampling of the sediments on the bottom, and the measurement of their thickness by seismic methods.

It was already known that the Atlantic was divided into eastern and western halves by a great range of submarine mountains that poked above the surface in Iceland, and in a chain of smaller islands like the Azores, St Helena, and Tristan da Cunha. It was also known that similar ridges crossed the floors of the other oceans. What was new was the realization that these mid-oceanic ridges are connected to form a single great system that branches and snakes its way over most of the globe.

There were other puzzling discoveries. One was that none of the sea-floor sediments was very thick, and that all of them were very young. The oldest bottom-samples then found were Cretaceous, about 135 million years old. To explain this two American oceanographers, R. S. Dietz and H. S. Hess, revived an earlier suggestion that the sea floor was in motion. In 1963 F. J. Vine and D. H. Matthews of Cambridge University realized that the magnetized rocks on the sea bottom contained proof of it.

It had been observed in the North Atlantic, the Antarctic, and the Indian Oceans that bands of magnetic anomalies lay parallel to the

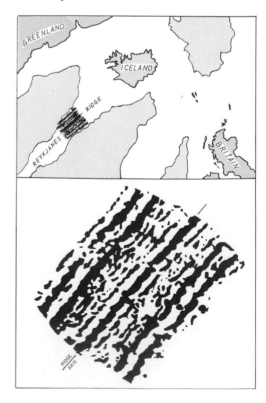

*Fig. 44: Magnetic striping of the sea floor. This diagram shows the symmetrical pattern of oppositely magnetized rocks on the sea floor on opposite sides of the Reykjanes Ridge, south of Iceland.*

crest of the oceanic ridges, and that the patterns on opposite sides of the ridge were almost mirror images of one another. This was not easy to explain. What Vine and Matthews suggested was that the basalt lavas that make up most of the sea floor originated in the volcanoes that are found along the ridges, and were then carried outwards by convection currents in the material underneath. When the lavas cooled, they became magnetized by the Earth's field, and the reason why the striped pattern was the same on both sides was that every time the Earth's magnetic field changed polarity, the new lavas were magnetized the opposite way round (Figure 44).

In this new way of looking at things the ocean floors have become huge conveyor-belts carrying material outwards from the submarine ridges, and the pattern of magnetic striping provides a measure of the rate at which they are moving. In most places it is only a couple of centimetres a year, but in the course of geological time it can move continents, and provide the horizontal forces needed to build mountains, and to fold and fracture the crust.

What happens to the material reaching the ocean margins? There are two possible answers. It can pile up and form mountains, or it can be drawn into the mantle by the now descending convection current. In either case, we can expect to find a region of vigorous geological activity, and we shall return later to consider what happens in more detail. One thing that happens is the occurrence of earthquakes, and we must first see how seismic activity fits into the overall pattern of crustal movement.

# 9 How earthquakes happen

The emperor Justinian prohibited, under penalty of death, certain kinds of sexual offences, together with blasphemy and the practice of swearing by the hair of one's head, on the grounds that such practices notoriously provoked thunderbolts and earthquakes. This seems to me a sound reason. One cannot tolerate conduct which causes earthquakes any more than one can tolerate conduct which leads to riot and disorder.

A. H. Campbell, *Justice and Toleration*

We are now ready to leave the broad association of earthquakes with the development of the Earth's geological and geophysical features and consider how the slowly accumulating tectonic forces are transformed into a sudden burst of seismic waves.

The crust of the Earth is fractured in many places. When the rocks on either side of a fracture have been displaced so that the strata no longer match, the geologist calls the crack a *fault* (Plate 21). The forces that produced it may have been forces of compression, or tensions, or shearing. Each will result in a different kind of displacement, and this is the basis of the usual method of classifying faults. Figure 45 shows the basic kinds of movement possible, their names, and the names given to the different parts of a fault. Plates 22 to 28 show the actual appearance of faults of different kinds in a variety of settings.

*Normal* faults are usually considered to be the result of tension, and *reverse* faults the result of thrusting. Because the movement is along the direction of the *strike*, the name given to the bearing of the fault trace, *transcurrent* faults are also known as *strike-slip* faults. When the opposite side of the fault moves towards the observer's right the movement is said to be *dextral*, or *right lateral* and *sinistral* or *left lateral* when it moves to his left. Transcurrent movement may of course be accompanied by a greater or lesser amount of normal or reverse movement, but it is usual for one or the other to predominate. The word normal should not be taken to imply that this kind of fault is more usual than the other kinds.

The total displacement of a fault has usually taken place in several steps. In any particular region, the forces responsible tend to go on acting for long periods of time; but this is not always the case. They may be transferred elsewhere, be interrupted and renewed, or may even reverse their direction.

Geologists have noted that the appearance of fresh fault-breaks on the Earth's surface, or renewed movement on existing faults has sometimes accompanied a large shallow earthquake. The first clear instance to be reported was in 1819 when an earthquake near the present border of India and Pakistan resulted in some 1500 deaths, and a fault-scarp some three metres high rose across the coastal salt flats of the Rann of Kutch. This became known as the Allah Bund, or God's Dyke, from its similarity to the levées thrown up by the local ruler for irrigation purposes.

After the San Francisco earthquake of 1906, H. F. Reid examined the impressive transcurrent movement that had affected three or four hundred kilometres of the great fracture known as the San Andreas

*Plate 21: Geological faulting. Where the Nukumaru Fault reaches the coast it appears as a break passing through cliffs about 6 metres high. Because of surface erosion, the right side is higher than the left, but an attempt to match the corresponding rock layers will show that it is the left side of the fault that has moved upwards.*

Fault, and the deformation of the country for some distance on either side of the fault trace. As a result of his observations he put forward the hypothesis known as the *elastic rebound* theory.

*Plate 22: Vertical faulting. This famous picture was taken in 1891, and shows the faulting at Midori in the Neo Valley that accompanied the Mino-Owari earthquake. The almost vertical scarp is six metres high, but inspection of the road on the right will show that there has also been a sinistral movement of about four metres.*

*Fig. 45: Geological faulting. The upper pictures show the three main types of faulting. In most real faults tension or compression is combined with shear, and any one of the three may predominate. The strike of a fault is what seamen would call its bearing — the angle its trace makes with a north-south line, measured from north towards the east.*

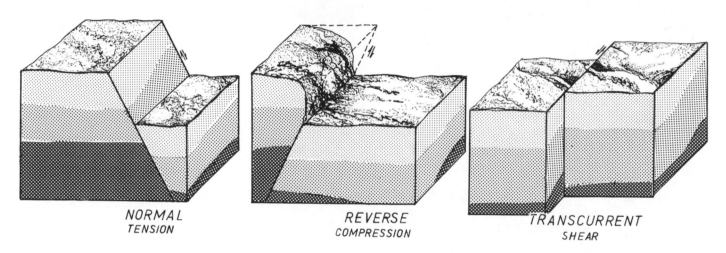

NORMAL
TENSION

REVERSE
COMPRESSION

TRANSCURRENT
SHEAR

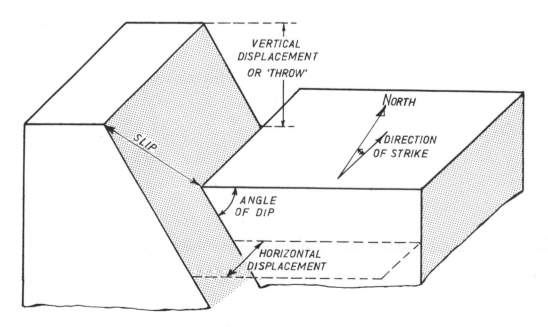

VERTICAL
DISPLACEMENT
OR 'THROW'

NORTH

DIRECTION
OF STRIKE

SLIP

ANGLE
OF DIP

HORIZONTAL
DISPLACEMENT

*Plate 23: Vertical faulting. This fault scarp at Quiches, in the Peruvian Andes, is three metres high and appeared in the Ancash earthquake in 1946.*

*Plate 24: Transcurrent faulting. Faulting during the Imperial Valley earthquake in 1940 displaced the rows of trees in this Californian orange-grove.*

*Plate 25: Transcurrent faulting. A sinistral movement of about four and a half metres that occurred in the Dasht-e-Bayaz earthquake in Iran in 1968. When there is little vertical movement, as in this case, the surface trace is often quickly destroyed by erosion and human activity.*

*Plate 26: Mole tracks. The appearance of a fault trace often depends as much upon the nature of the surface as upon the movement of the underlying rocks. In soft ground a common effect is the appearance of what the Japanese call 'mole tracks'. This example comes from Sampazari, in western Anatolia, and made its appearance in the Mudurunu Valley earthquake in 1967.*

*Plate 27: Faulting and topography. Faulting can often be distinguished from superficial slumping by its relative independence of the topography. The downhill side of this fault in the Nimbluk Valley, near Boskabad in Iran, moved upwards about thirty centimetres in the Dasht-e-Bayaz earthquake in 1968.*

*Plate 28: The stronger wins. When this fault break in the Turkish earthquake at Gediz in 1970 encountered a grove of trees, it found it easier to divert through the soft ground than to break the roots of the trees.*

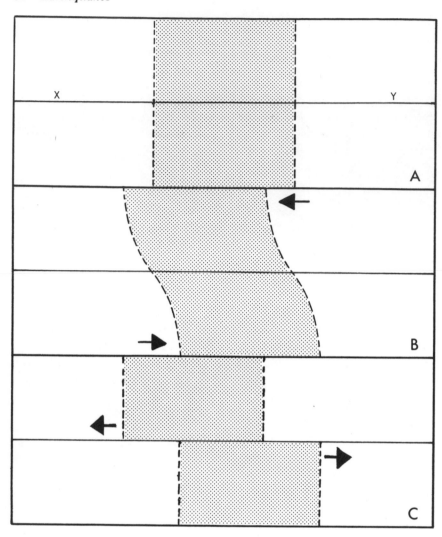

*Fig. 46: Elastic rebound. The top figure shows a tract of country whose weakest rocks lie along the line XY. Regional forces slowly distort it until it assumes the shape shown in B, at the same time storing elastic energy in the rocks. When the accumulated strain. becomes too great for the strength of the rocks they break along the line XY, releasing their stored energy in the form of earthquake waves and creating a geological fault, as shown at C.*

Suppose that Figure 46A represents a tract of country perhaps 50 or 100 kilometres across, and the weakest rocks in it lie along the line XY (which could for example be an old fault). Imagine that the broken lines are very long straight fences built at right angles to the line of weakness, and that the country is being slowly deformed by regional forces in the crust. In time the fences will assume the shapes shown in Figure 46B. All the time this has been going on — and the process may go on for a century or more — elastic energy is being stored in the rocks, just as it is when we wind a spring. Eventually the strain may become so great that the weaker rocks can no longer resist it, and they suddenly break along the line of weakness. This releases the stored energy, as if the coiled spring were suddenly let go. On either side of the break the rocks rebound to their unstrained positions. The movement is greater near the break and becomes less and less as we go away to either side. It is the waves set up by this sudden rebound movement that we call an earthquake.

The block diagram (Figure 47) shows the same process in a slightly different way. The movement can be horizontal as shown here, or vertical, or a combination of the two, according to the manner in which the rocks had been strained. If Reid is correct earthquakes are not a sudden abnormal happening, but a return to normal after a prolonged period of strain.

The elastic rebound theory has not been without its critics. In 1927 two Japanese observers reported that the fault trace of the Tango earthquake did not appear until *after* the destruction of their houses. Similar observations had been made in 1891, and this has led some Japanese seismologists to maintain that faulting is the result of earthquakes and not the cause. It should be remembered, however, that a mechanical failure of this kind must develop from some definite point of greatest weakness. This point is the focus of the earthquake, and it is generally buried at some considerable depth. The rate at which the fracture can spread from the focus is less than the speed of seismic waves, and the maximum shaking will in all probability precede the appearance of the dislocation at the surface. If the main energy release did not take place in a limited area, and in a comparatively brief instant of time, a seismogram would present a very complicated appearance, instead of the comparatively orderly sequence of pulses we can observe.

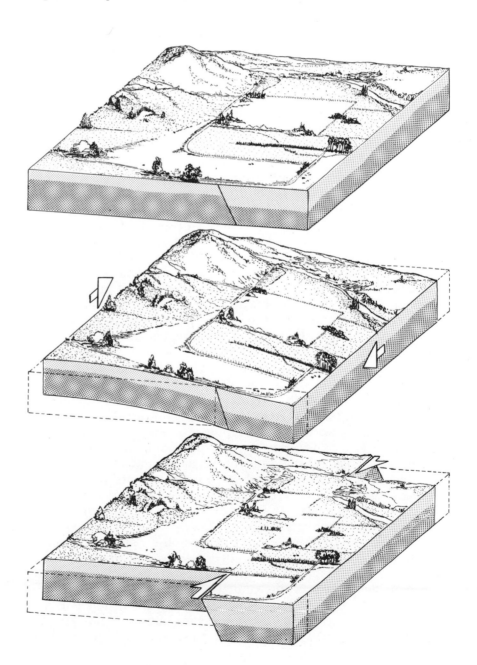

Fig. 47: *Elastic rebound. This block diagram of a landscape traversed by a fault shows its gradual distortion by regional stresses until the strain is released by an elastic rebound along the fault.*

The rebound theory certainly gives a satisfactory account of the deformations that can be observed at the surface of the Earth, but examination of surface faulting can tell us little about conditions at the focus, several kilometres underground even in the shallowest shocks. It could be that most of the energy comes from something other than elastic strain, and that surface faulting is only a form of earthquake damage. In the early 1960s this was the view of most New Zealand seismologists, and some of their Japanese colleagues agreed. For several decades the seismologists of Europe and America had been busy with problems to which the actual mechanism of the earthquake was irrelevant, or in which it was at most a minor consideration, and serious physical objections to the theory seemed to have been overlooked.

We have seen that earthquakes occur, at least in some parts of the Earth, down to depths of about 700 km. Because of difficulties in measurement, we cannot be so sure whether there is a shallow limit, but the shallowest shocks of any great size have focal depths of a few kilometres at least. As we penetrate deeper and deeper into the Earth, the pressure and the temperature both increase. The increase in pressure means that the frictional forces acting to prevent a fault from moving also become greater and greater. At the same time, the increasing temperature makes it easier for the rocks to deform and flow. Unless the rocks are fairly rigid, it is not possible for them to accumulate enough elastic strain energy to overcome the friction, and faulting by simple brittle fracture would probably become impossible at any depth greater than that of the very shallowest earthquakes. Dr. E. Orowan has estimated that at a depth of 600–700 km, the friction would be at least a thousand times the strength of the rock. For reasons of this kind, many seismologists who found elastic rebound a satisfactory explanation of shallow earthquakes had reservations about deep ones. If there were really two quite different sorts of earthquake, why did they produce such similar records, and why did they tend to happen in the same parts of the world?

Doubts were to be strengthened by a discovery in California where the rebound theory had originated, and where belief in it was very strong. In 1948 a wine-grower near Hollister had built himself a new reinforced-concrete winery. A few years later, the walls on opposite sides of the building had cracked. As time went on, the cracks became wider, and the concrete slabs that made up the floor were displaced. The building had been so sited that part of it lay on one side of the San Andreas fault, and the rest on the other. Although there had been no earthquake strong enough to damage the building, and certainly no earthquake strong enough to cause a visible fault-break, the opposite sides of the fault were slowly creeping along at an average rate of about one or two centimetres a year. No building could be expected to stand up to that sort of treatment. Seismographs and instruments for measuring the amount and the rate of the creep have been installed, and although it is found that local earthquakes speed up the movement temporarily, the steady movement appears to be unrelated to earthquake activity.

This is not the first time creep has been observed. As far back as 1932, it had been found that oil-wells drilled through the Buena Vista fault in Kern County, farther to the north, were being sheared off by continuous movement of this kind. The number of faults transfixed by oil-wells or straddled by wineries is not great, and it is still uncertain how general fault creep will turn out to be. Several New Zealand faults are now being watched to see if creep is taking place, but so far none has been detected. If strain can be continuously relieved in this way, it is clear that there will be no stored energy to produce the waves radiated from a large earthquake.

A final objection was based on the very small number of earthquakes that were known to have produced fresh fault movements. In 1954 Professor C. F. Richter considered that there were only thirty-six 'clear and well authenticated cases', and among these there are some that could be questioned. Since then closer observation has added significantly to the list, but even when due allowance is made for shocks under the sea and in other inaccessible places the total number of examples is surprisingly small in comparison with the yearly total of recorded earthquakes.

In spite of these apparently strong objections, few seismologists would now question the broad correctness of the elastic rebound theory. Three lines of research have silenced the objectors. The first was the result of a shift in attention from the Earth's surface to a renewed concentration on events at the actual focus. The theory of the method used to study them was first worked out by H. Nakano in about 1922, and it had been extensively applied by Kawasumi and other Japanese seismologists over the next two decades, but instrumental limitations and the small number of good recording stations had limited their success, and it had found little application outside Japan.

Let us imagine the origin of an earthquake to be surrounded by a sphere, just big enough to enclose whatever is going on, with the focus of the shock at the centre of the sphere. If we join the focus to each recording station by a line along the path the *P*-wave takes, each line will pass through the sphere at some different point. Now, if the first movement that reaches the station is a compression, the corresponding point on the focal sphere must have moved outwards, and if it is a rarefaction, the point must have moved inwards. If we can collect records from enough stations right round the Earth, it should be possible to build up a picture of what happened at the focus.

In practice, these studies are very difficult. Not every earthquake begins with a clear movement, and many stations turn out to have only emergent phases, almost lost in the background of microseisms. It is also difficult to get a set of observations well spaced around the focal sphere, not only because seismograph stations are unevenly scattered around the globe, but because the layered structure of the

*Fig. 48: First-motion studies. The first movement recorded at a particular seismograph station may be either towards it (a compression, C) or away from it (a dilatation, D). The stations that record compressions and dilatations are usually distributed in alternate quadrants about the epicentre. This can be used to work out the direction of the fault-plane and the direction of movement, but the results are ambiguous. A dextral movement of the fault shown in A produces the same pattern of compressions and dilatations as a sinistral movement on one at right angles to it, as shown in B.*

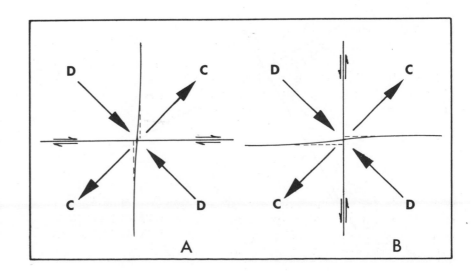

Earth bends the rays in such a way that for shallow shocks all the waves from the top half of the focal sphere reach the surface within a hundred kilometres or so of the epicentre. In theory we would need half our stations within this distance to get proper coverage. Fortunately the position is a little better for deep-focus earthquakes.

There is a still more serious problem. The results are ambiguous. Figure 48A shows a fault with its plane perpendicular to the paper. The direction of regional strain is such that rocks on the upper side of the fault will move to the right. When this strain is suddenly released by elastic rebound, all the seismographs in the quadrants marked C should record compressions, and those in the alternate quadrants marked D should record dilatations. Figure 48B shows a second fault, at right angles to the first, but with a sinistral instead of a dextral movement. The pattern of compressions and dilatations is the same in both cases.

If the earthquake mechanism were not some kind of shearing movement, some very different patterns of first motion could be expected. Explosions, for example, should produce nothing but compressions, and collapses should produce only dilatations, provided that there was no change of shape. If there were a change of shape at the same time as the change of volume a quadrantal pattern, or even something more complicated, could be superimposed upon the simple pattern of compressions or rarefactions.

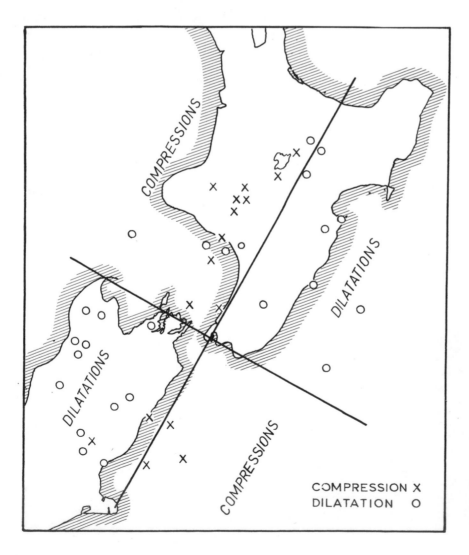

COMPRESSION X
DILATATION   O

*Fig. 49: First motions at Wellington. If all the faults in a region have much the same orientation, as is often the case, the earthquakes that produce compressional first motions at a particular station and those that produce dilatations are distributed in alternate quadrants.*

In spite of the difficulties first-motion studies became a very popular field of research during the 1960s, particularly careful work being done by the teams of workers under Dr. J. H. Hodgson in Canada, Professor Keilis-Borok in the Soviet Union, and Professor Honda in Japan. Although the confidence that could be placed upon the observations of a single earthquake was small, regional patterns were found and these lent support to the developing ideas of sea-floor spreading and plate tectonics.

When there are dense networks of recording stations, it becomes possible to apply first-motion techniques to local earthquakes. In many parts of the world large concentrations of portable instruments have been used to record very small shocks in limited regions for short periods. The large numbers of clear first motions recorded during these projects are of great value in understanding the patterns of regional strain, and how they vary with depth.

When the faults of a region share the same general orientation, a single station is sufficient to show the sense of movement. In central New Zealand, for example, most active faults run in a roughly north-east or south-west direction. Figure 49 shows the direction of the initial movements observed in Wellington for a number of shallow earthquakes. Granting the assumptions involved, the map suggests that there is a dextral displacement, that is, that the north-western side of the faults moves north-eastwards with respect to the south-eastern side. This is in accord with the geologists' observations of the faults at the surface.

The second line of research was mathematical. Professor Leon Knopoff in California and Dr. M. J. Randall in New Zealand worked out in detail the kinds of wave that would be radiated by different possible source mechanisms. Their results showed not only whether the first wave would be a compression or a rarefaction, but what amplitude it would have, and what proportion of *P*-type and *S*-type waves were to be expected. Dr. Ari Ben-Menahem worked back from records of surface-waves to conditions at the focus, and other American seismologists concerned themselves with details of fault-rupture and the waves it generated. All of these studies showed the importance of some form of shear, as the elastic rebound theory indicated. What had been little more than a qualitative hypothesis was becoming a proper mathematical theory.

The final and most recent line of study has removed the objection that at quite shallow depths friction would effectively prevent a fault from moving. Laboratory work on the behaviour of rocks at high pressures showed that the presence of liquid in the pores of the rock could result in the lubrication of a crack that would otherwise have been locked. This idea was supported by the observation that an increase in the number of earthquakes had followed the impounding of water in a number of large dams. In these cases, however, increases in pressure on the lake bottom were also involved, and it is not possible to be sure of how great a part the water is playing. More startling evidence of the importance of water was obtained near Denver, Colorado, in 1962. The United States Army, wishing to get rid of a surplus of toxic gases, dissolved them in water and pumped them down a well over three and a half kilometres deep. By the end of 1965 more than 700 earthquakes had been recorded in an area which had experienced none since 1882, and the frequency with which they occurred was linked with the amount of pumping. We shall return to this question of fault lubrication in a later chapter.

# 10 Where earthquakes happen

... the smoke and stir of this dim spot
Which men call Earth.
John Milton, *Comus*

One Thursday in February 1750, an earthquake was felt in London. Most New Zealanders have felt earthquakes, and so have most Japanese, but most Englishmen have not and there was much alarm. The alarm increased when a second shock followed four weeks later. Now, as John Wesley once observed, 'there is no divine visitation which is likely to have so general an influence upon sinners as an earthquake', and it is no surprise to learn that the churches were full the following Sunday, and that the recent 'divine warnings' provided most of the preachers with their text. Their number included the Rev. Dr William Stukeley, M.D., F.R.S.

Stukeley believed that earthquakes were due to electricity, and later expounded his views to the Royal Society in three papers that have earned him a corner in the history of seismology; but whatever natural agency was involved, Stukeley had no doubt that the hand of God was ultimately responsible. 'The chastening rod' he told the congregation of St George's Church, Bloomsbury, 'is directed to towns and cities, where there are inhabitants, the objects of its monition; not to bare cliffs and uninhabited beaches'. It was a reasonable guess, but it could not have been supported by observation.

During the nineteenth century a number of attempts were made to compile systematic catalogues of earthquakes, so that by the time the seismograph was invented the broad pattern of the world's seismic belts was known, and Montessus de Ballore had made the important observation that they approximated closely to the belts of young fold mountains.

*Plates 29 and 30: Weak buildings. In many parts of the world the high casualty rates in moderate earthquakes are a direct result of the traditional building practices. The inherent weaknesses of piled stones or sun-dried brick can be only slightly improved by wooden framing, and even this may be beyond the resources of the people. These examples are from Turkey, but similar ones could be found in South and Central America, and in other parts of the Middle East. Intensities as low as MM VIII could destroy structures of this kind. Below, Plate 29 (rubble); opposite, Plate 30 (adobe).*

There are still many uses for lists of damaging earthquakes, but they have serious limitations as a basis for the study of seismicity. Where there are no people there are no observations, and a large part of the Earth's surface is unwatched. At the other extreme, the large numbers of casualties that are often reported from some parts of South America, North Africa, and the Middle East indicate the folly of housing dense populations in buildings of piled rubble and mud brick, rather than the number and severity of the earthquakes in those places (Plates 29, 30). For an undistorted picture instrumental records are essential.

Figures 50 and 51, which are taken from Gutenberg and Richter's classic *The Seismicity of the Earth,* show the epicentres of all the large earthquakes in roughly half a century. Although the maps were drawn in 1954, and the accuracy of some of the early epicentres is low, they are still the best maps available for showing the relative vigor of the activity in the main seismic regions. Unfortunately there are some quite active regions in which all the shocks were too small to be included. The most serious omission is the activity that follows the mid-oceanic ridges. The ordinary shallow shocks and the deep-focus ones have been shown on separate maps so that they can be distinguished more clearly.

The mid-oceanic ridges are seen very clearly in Figure 52, but in these maps no attention is paid to magnitude. As a result the western United States, where there are many recording stations and very small shocks can be detected, appears far too active.

The active belts in which most earthquakes occur lie at the edges of stable regions which are not entirely without earthquakes, but in which the shocks are infrequent and usually small. The most vigorous of these active belts follows the greater part of the Pacific margin, and is characterised by both deep and shallow activity, which are not exactly superimposed. A second and only slightly less active belt joins it in the southern Philippines, and passes through Indonesia, Burma, and the Himalayas to the Mediteranean. It closely parallels the great mountain ranges and is often called the Alpide Belt.

When these belts are examined in detail, it will be found that they are not strictly continuous. The maximum depth of the activity, the relative positions of the deep and shallow shocks, and the patterns of association between the earthquakes and other geological and geophysical features vary strikingly from place to place. On small scale maps the individual segments merge to give an illusion of continuity which is nevertheless the result of a real tectonic pattern we shall discuss further.

Compared with the activity of the Circum-Pacific and Alpide belts, the seismicity of the mid-oceanic ridges is minor, the earthquakes being neither so numerous nor so large.

There are two kinds of region that are characteristically stable – the great ocean basins, and the continental shields – but they may contain active fractures such as the African Rift Valley – which has volcanoes as well as earthquakes – and the line of activity crossing South Australia from Spencer's Gulf to Lake Eyre. Perhaps the only part of the Earth that can validly claim to be earthquake-free is Antarctica. This is something of a seismological puzzle, as Antarctica has both young mountain ranges and active volcanoes, which seem to be associated with earthquakes in most other places. A proper understanding of this would probably teach us something important about the mechanism of earthquakes.

Professor F. F. Evison has pointed out that it is useful to classify

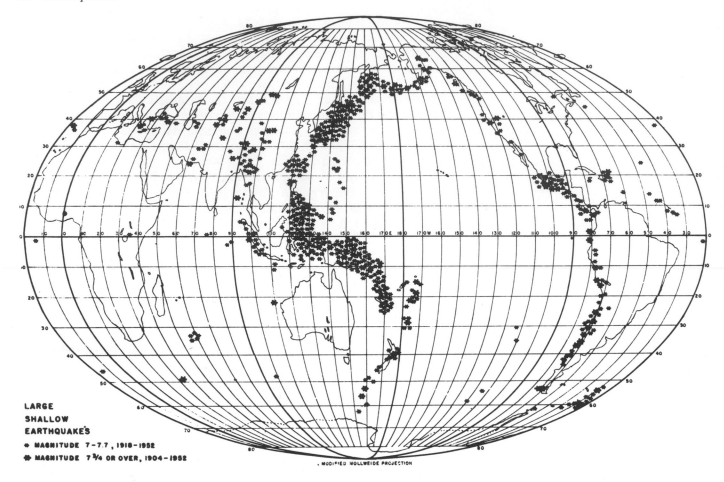

LARGE
SHALLOW
EARTHQUAKES

✦ MAGNITUDE 7-7.7 , 1918-1952
✤ MAGNITUDE 7¾ OR OVER, 1904-1952

. MODIFIED MOLLWEIDE PROJECTION

*Fig. 50: Seismicity of the Earth. Epicentres of large shallow earthquakes, 1904 — 1952. (From Gutenberg and Richter.)*

seismic regions as symmetrical or asymmetrical, according to their relationship with other geophysical features like volcanoes, gravity anomalies, and submarine trenches. The symmetrical systems, which include the mid-oceanic ridges and the rifts, are not so active and all the earthquakes are shallow. In the asymmetrical systems, the deeper shocks are increasingly displaced to one side of the shallow activity.

The ideas of continental drift and spreading of the sea floor provide a possible explanation of the world pattern and of the differing arrangements of geophysical features. The hypothesis that has been developed is known as *plate tectonics*.

According to this idea, the outer layers of the Earth behave like rigid plates that fit the main body of the Earth like loose caps, which are free to move about. Their thickness is a matter of some controversy. They must be substantially thicker than the crust, or they would not be able to withstand horizontal pressures without breaking. On the other hand they cannot extend below the weak layer in the asthenosphere, which probably provides the surface on which they slide. About 100 kilometres is therefore a likely figure. There are seven main plates, shown in Figure 53, and a few minor platelets needed to complete the pattern. The plate boundaries lie along the mid-oceanic ridges and active continental margins, following the belts of seismic activity.

Assuming that the plates are not immovably jammed together, there are three things that could be happening at a boundary between two plates – they could be moving apart, they could be driven together, or they could be slipping sideways with respect to one other.

At the mid-oceanic ridges they are being forced apart, and the force responsible is thermal convection in the Earth's mantle. Rising currents are injecting lavas that are continually being added to the edges of the plates (Figure 54) creating new sea-floor and forcing it outwards, leaving a record of the process in the pattern of magnetic stripes already described in Chapter Eight.

Convection depends essentially upon circulation. Rising currents of hot material must be balanced by descending currents of the material that has cooled. These descending currents are to be found near the active continental margins, and in the neighbourhood of the deep submarine trenches. This is confirmed by measurements of heat-flow taken with probes forced into the sea bed, and in drill-holes on land. There is little difference in the figures on land and at sea, but near the ridges the values rise to several times the average.

Where two rather similar plates collide, the result may be a chain of fold mountains. Contact of this kind between the Indian and Eurasian plates is the basic explanation of the Himalayas. Where the plates are dissimilar and there is a descending convection current, the situation becomes more complicated. The ocean floor is pulled downwards producing a submarine trench, but the continental material consisting of lighter rocks is unable to sink, and rides over the top. The result is a *subduction zone* in which the material of the ocean floor is once more carried downwards until the rising temperature melts it and absorbs it again into the mantle.

The presence of the descending material reveals itself in several ways. Being cooler and denser than the surrounding mantle it creates a gravity anomaly, it alters the appearance of the seismograms of earthquake waves that have had to pass through it (Figure 55), and it

*Fig. 51: Seismicity of the Earth. Epicentres of large deep and intermediate earthquakes, 1904 — 1952. (From Gutenberg and Richter.)*

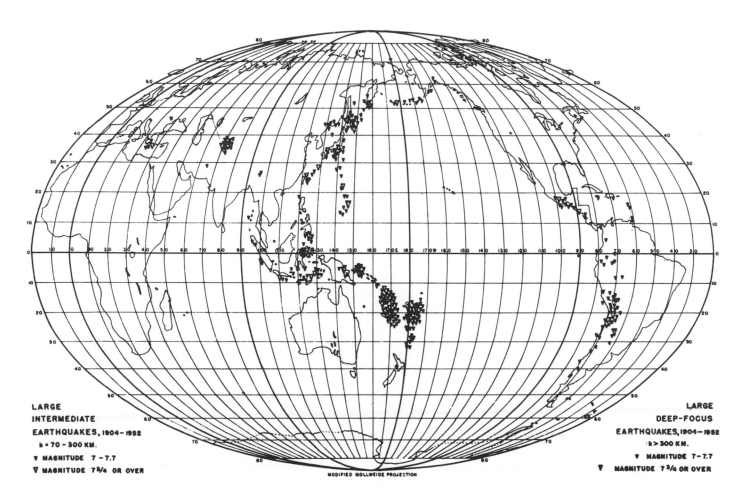

LARGE
INTERMEDIATE
EARTHQUAKES, 1904-1952
h = 70 - 300 KM.
▽ MAGNITUDE 7 - 7.7
▼ MAGNITUDE 7¾ OR OVER

LARGE
DEEP-FOCUS
EARTHQUAKES, 1904-1952
h > 300 KM.
▽ MAGNITUDE 7 - 7.7
▼ MAGNITUDE 7¾ OR OVER

MODIFIED MOLLWEIDE PROJECTION

traps the energy of the deep-focus earthquakes that occur within it, giving them very characteristic isoseismal patterns.

Deep-focus earthquakes are found only where there is descending material of this kind. Some writers call the volume within which the foci of deep shocks occur the 'down-going lithospheric slab', and others call it the *Benioff zone,* though Dr Hugo Benioff's view of these regions was not very like the one held now.

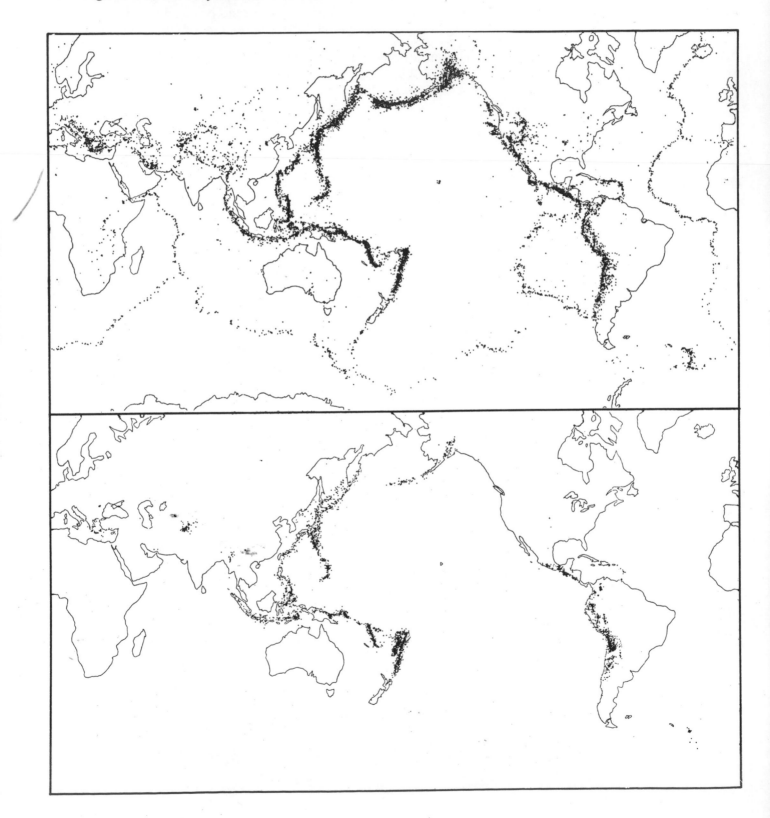

In both symmetrical and asymmetrical regions the different geophysical features – earthquakes, volcanoes, gravity anomalies and so on – occur in a definite pattern. That of the mid-oceanic ridges is the simpler of the two. Shallow earthquakes occur close to the axis of the ridge, along which there is usually a central rift or chasm. There are active volcanoes, emitting fluid basaltic lavas that cool to produce the pattern of magnetic striping on the ocean floor. The age of the volcanoes increases with their distance from the axis of the ridge.

The essentially asymmetrical features of a subduction zone are most clearly seen at active continental margins and in the formations known to the structural geologist as *island arcs* (Figure 56). These great arcuate systems occur along many segments of the Pacific margin, the most spectacular example being the Aleutians. On the outer, convex side of the arc there is a deep oceanic trench, with a narrow but active belt of shallow earthquakes just inside it. Here the values of gravity are lower than normal, and there may be a few small islands where the ocean bottom again rises in a ridge, as in the Mentawai Islands off the south coast of Sumatra. Within this ridge, the gravity again becomes normal, but continues to increase. The earthquakes become rather deeper, with foci at perhaps 50 or 100 kilometres. Then come the main islands of the arc, usually formed in the Cretaceous or Tertiary period, and often having active volcanoes. These are sometimes violently eruptive, and emit stiff andesitic lavas. Further inland, there is an older or secondary arc with extinct or nearly extinct volcanoes, and earthquakes at depths of about 200 kilometres. Continuing still further there may be a shallow sea before the continent proper is reached. The seismicity does not always continue, but if it does, its depth goes on increasing up to the maximum of about 700 kilometres.

Not all the features enumerated are present in every asymmetrical system; indeed, it would be difficult to find an example in which they had all been adequately observed, but when they do occur they

*Fig. 52: Seismic geography. The upper map shows the epicentres of shallow earthquakes, and the lower one those of earthquakes with focal depths of 100 km or more from 1962 to 1967. They show the positions of the mid-oceanic ridges and the deep earthquake zones very clearly, but since the magnitude of the shocks shown is not the same everywhere, they give a distorted picture of the relative seismicity of the different zones. (After Barazangi and Dorman.)*

*Fig. 53: Plate tectonics. The Earth's lithosphere is divided into a number of rigid plates at the boundaries of which most of the world's earthquakes occur. The names of the main plates are shown, and minor platelets are identified by numbers: 1 Philippines Plate, 2 Cocos Plate, 3 Caribbean Plate, 4 Nasca Plate, 5 Arabian Plate.*

*Shading indicates the main zones of deep earthquakes, and the arrows indicate the directions in which the plates are believed to be moving.*

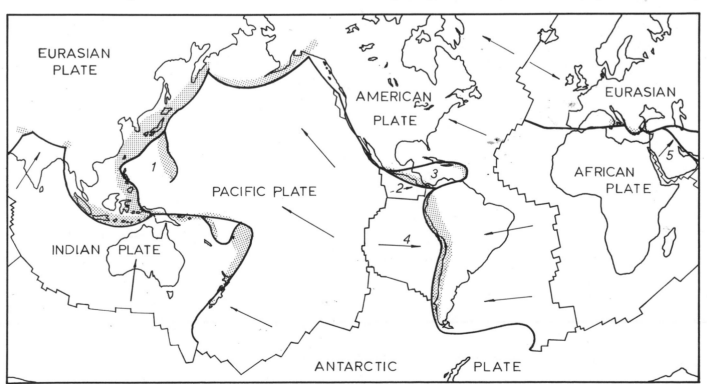

EURASIAN PLATE

AMERICAN PLATE

EURASIAN

AFRICAN PLATE

PACIFIC PLATE

INDIAN PLATE

ANTARCTIC PLATE

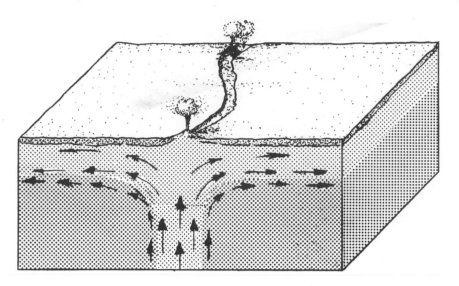

*Fig. 54: A spreading ridge. Rising convection currents produce vulcanism along the mid-oceanic ridges, adding material to the edges of the lithospheric plates that make up the sea floor, and driving them apart.*

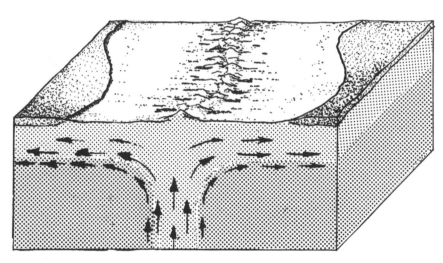

occupy the relative positions that have been described. The minor differences betweeen island arcs and active margins are adequately explained as the result of differences in the more superficial parts of the structure.

If we consider the number of earthquakes that occur at different depths we find that about two thirds of them are shallow, and that

*Fig. 55: Attenuation in a subduction zone. Two seismograms of a small deep earthquake on January 6, 1977 (Magnitude 4·5 and depth 189 km). The wave paths to Tuai, where the upper record was made, lie within the lithospheric slab and high frequency vibrations are recorded; but the paths to Karapiro (lower record) lie mainly in the asthenosphere, and the more rapid movements are missing.*

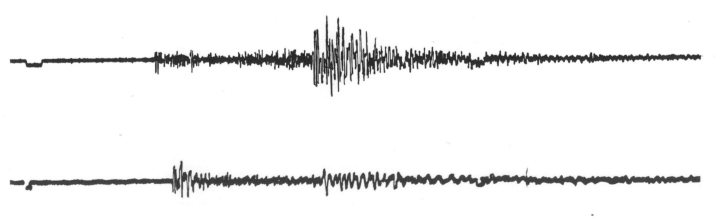

*Fig. 56: Subduction beneath an island arc. Shallow earthquakes occur over the whole breadth of the arc, but deeper shocks are confined to the descending lithospheric slab.*

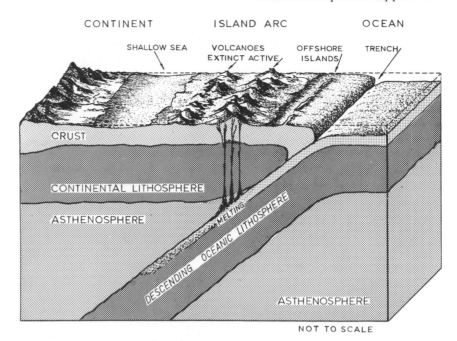

less than five percent have depths greater than 450 kilometres. At this depth there is a minimum, but an average based on world figures is unlikely to mean very much, as the detailed pattern varies greatly from place to place, and there are often complete gaps in the range. In New Zealand there are no shocks at all between 380 and 550 km, and similar gaps exist in Kamchatka and in South America.

Most really deep shocks occur around the Pacific or close to it, the deepest known shocks being at about 720 kilometres beneath the Flores Sea. The striking exception to this rule is a shock near the Straits of Gibraltar in 1954, which had a depth of 640 km. Otherwise it is rare to find depths of more than 100 km outside the Pacific. The main exceptions are in the eastern Mediterranean, particularly in the Vrancea district of Romania; and in the Hindu Kush where a vigorous grouping of shocks at about 220 km marks the western end of the Himalayas.

# 11 Sizes and numbers

It is shaped, sir, like itself, and it is as broad as it hath breadth; it is just so high as it is, and moves with its own organs . . .

Shakespeare, *Antony and Cleopatra*

So far we have talked rather loosely of large and small earthquakes. It is of course possible to compare one with another by giving the number of people killed, or the value of the buildings destroyed, but these things are not really measures of the earthquake itself. They depend upon outside factors like the density of the population and the level of social development in the shaken region.

Maximum felt intensities depend a little more directly upon the earthquake, but even they can be upset by secondary factors. A small variation in depth produces a big change in the size of the felt area and the way the intensities are distributed, and if the epicentre lies off the coast or in rugged and inaccessible country it may be impossible to get a direct estimate of the maximum intensity. A really satisfactory measure has to sum up the total effect of the earthquake and must be easily worked out from the records of existing seismograph stations.

The way to get such a measure was found by Professor Charles Richter of the California Institute of Technology, who devised the scale of earthquake magnitudes. The *magnitude* is a measure of the total energy in the seismic waves. The number used indicates the maximum amplitude of the trace that would be recorded on a standard kind of seismograph put at a standard distance from the earthquake. The instrument chosen was a Wood-Anderson torsion seismometer with a period of 0·8 seconds, critical damping, and a magnification of 2 800, but the magnitude can be found from other instruments at other distances by fairly simple calculations.

On this scale, any earthquake with a magnitude of eight or more is a very big one indeed. The largest shocks of which we have instrumental records were the Colombia-Equador earthquake on Jan. 31, 1906, and the Sanriku earthquake in Japan in 1933, both of which reached magnitude 8·9. Judging from its felt effects the largest shock ever was the Lisbon earthquake in 1755, which might have reached 9, but there is now no way of telling for certain. The San Francisco earthquake in 1906 and the one in Alaska in 1964 reached 8·3 and 8·4 respectively, but the only New Zealand earthquake to approach magnitude 8 was the South-west Wairarapa shock in 1855. The biggest since there have been seismographs was the Hawke's Bay earthquake in 1931, with a magnitude of 7·9.

Any earthquake much above magnitude 7 can be a major disaster if it happens near a populated area, particularly if it is in a part of the world where the buildings are poor. A magnitude 5 shock can damage chimneys and plaster, and break goods stacked up in window displays. Most of the small felt shocks in New Zealand have a magnitude of at least $3\frac{1}{2}$, but in California where the shocks are shallower, earthquakes of magnitude $2\frac{1}{2}$ are often reported. It is unusual for shocks smaller than magnitude 2 to be felt anywhere.

The size of the smallest shock possible is not easy to determine, but a value not far below magnitude 0 seems likely. Magnitude 0 is just a number on a scale; it doesn't mean that there is no energy in a shock that size, any more than a thermometer reading of $0°C$ implies that there is no heat left in the bulb. For very tiny earthquakes we use minus magnitudes, just as we use temperatures below zero when it gets sufficiently cold. No matter how big or how small an earthquake is, it can be assigned a magnitude. Journalists who write of the Richter scale 'of 12 degrees' are probably confusing magnitude with intensity, and those who write of the 'open-ended Richter scale' are stating the obvious. They never seem to find it necessary to point out that our scales of mass, length, time, temperature, and electric power are also 'open-ended'.

It is important to stress the difference between the total energies given on the magnitude scale, and the felt intensities of the modified Mercalli, MSK, and Rossi-Forel scales. A shock has different intensities in different places – as many intensities as there are observers – but it has only one magnitude, even if the estimates of it made by different observatories disagree. Newspaper, radio, and television reporters the world over seem desparately anxious to keep the public confused about this, their usual method being to substitute the word 'force' for magnitude and intensity alike, apparently considering the proper terms too technical for their readers. A more subtle gambit is to insert the words 'on the Richter scale' after any unqualified number in the original report. It is a great pity that so many reporters think that their duty is done when they have obtained a number from the nearest observatory. The earlier generation of newsmen who printed homely descriptions of the happenings in their neighborhood have left stories of permanent scientific value.

Having berated journalists for confusing the public about the magnitude scale, the seismologist must also admit to a degree of guilt. The original magnitude scale, as we have seen, depended upon the records of a Wood-Anderson seismograph. In California and New Zealand, where there were networks of these instruments, it came into general use almost at once, but in other parts of the world different instruments were in use, and the Wood-Anderson ceases to be useful for shocks at distances beyond about 1 000 kilometres. It was natural that attempts should be made to apply the scale to the teleseisms recorded on long-period instruments.

The first result was a magnitude scale that depended upon surface-waves. It was intended to give the same numbers as the original scale, but closer study showed that there were small differences. To distinguish the two scales, seismologists now call the original local magnitudes $M_L$ and the surface-wave magnitudes $M_S$. The differences are not serious for large shocks, but below magnitude 5 the values obtained from distant records may be as much as half a magnitude too low.

There are two difficulties facing a magnitude scale based on surface-waves. The first is that deep-focus shocks do not generate them, and the second is that their amplitudes are seriously reduced when the path to the recording station follows a route with complicated changes in crustal structure. In order to get round these troubles Professor Gutenberg suggested using a quantity he called the 'unified magnitude', which depended upon the amplitude of body-waves like *P, S,* and *PP.* This turned out to involve even bigger differences from the original scale. There is reasonable agreement for shocks of magnitude 6·6, but above this the unified magnitude (usually written $m$ or $m_B$) falls increasingly below the Richter magnitude, so that a shock with a unified magnitude of 8·0 would have a Richter magnitude of about 8·7. Below magnitude 5, $m$ is slightly greater than $M_L$.

Unfortunately not all seismograph stations make it clear which magnitude they are reporting, and although the differences are not very important in the middle range, they can be serious in the case of large shocks that attract a great deal of public interest. The U.S. National Earthquake Information Center often quotes $m$, and this becomes transposed in the course of transmission by teletype. The term 'Richter magnitude' should be reserved for the original M, which will be used for all magnitudes quoted in this book, the distinction between $M_S$ and $M_L$ being made in the few cases where it is important.

Although the magnitude of an earthquake is related to its total energy, the relationship is not quite straightforward, for the scale is a 'logarithmic' one. Instead of its steps being equal they increase in a regular way, so that the amount of additional energy in any particular step is about 27 times that in the previous one. Thus, a magnitude six shock releases 27 times as much energy as a magnitude five, and 27 times 27, or 729 times as much as a magnitude four.

There are many more small earthquakes than big ones. Over the range of magnitudes from about 2 to 8 the number of shocks increases about eightfold for each decrease of one magnitude step. Over the whole Earth there are about twenty shocks each year that exceed magnitude 7, nearly a thousand over magnitude 5, and over 100 000 that are strong enough to be felt. Of course this trend cannot go on indefinitely. If it did we should have to put up with a continuous tremble from a succession of minute shocks, but the total number of shocks picked up by our seismographs cannot be far short of a couple of million a year.

We can be thankful that the eightfold relationship breaks down at the top end too, so that there is a limit to the size of earthquakes. The strength of the rocks sets a limit to the amount of elastic energy that can be stored. To reassure the timid that this is not mere theorizing, we can point out that if the relationship still held for very big shocks we would have a magnitude ten earthquake about every ninety years. Such a devastating event would shake the whole Earth, and we can be quite sure that nothing so catastrophic has happened in all recorded history.

If we know the magnitude and the focal depth of an earthquake we can deduce a great deal about its effects in a given place, but the uncertainties that remain can be of serious practical consequence to engineers. The same amount of energy can be released in different ways. It may have been stored in a small but highly-strained region, or it may have come from a much larger region strained to a smaller extent. This will affect the spectrum of the radiated waves, that is to say, what proportion of the energy will go into waves of any particular frequency. A highly-strained source region produces a large drop in stress and radiates a much greater proportion of waves of short period than would come from a larger source region and a smaller drop in stress. Which kind of shock we can expect will depend upon the strength of the rocks involved, and the degree to which they have been previously fractured.

Long-period records can be used to work out a quantity that supplies much of the missing information. It is called the *moment* (from the Latin *momentum,* importance), and is related to the drop in stress and the amount of movement of the fault. A comparison of the magnitude and the moment of a shock reveals whether a high or a low stress-drop was involved. The volume of the source, the displacement of the fault, the magnitude, the moment and the drop in stress are all connected, so that if we can find any three of them, we can calculate the other two. The moment is not so easy to work out as the magnitude, but Dr S. J. Gibowicz has found a method that can be used for routine work, and the moments as well as the magnitudes of many shocks are now available.

Earthquakes do not happen at regular intervals, but they are not completely random events. If an earthquake has just occurred, the probability that there will be another in the same area is increased. To put things less formally, most big earthquakes are followed by aftershocks.

The simple elastic rebound theory does not make it at all clear why these aftershocks should occur. If the main shock releases the energy stored in the strained country, why doesn't the fault go on moving until all the strain is gone? The accumulation of enough energy to unlock the fault again after it has once stopped moving should take considerable time; yet the early aftershocks are sometimes almost as big as the main shock itself. It had often been suggested that the main shock might re-distribute the remaining stresses in the area, so as to make energy available which could not be released by the first shock itself, and that the fault, once it had been unlocked, would probably move more easily if it hadn't had time to cement up again. A few years ago, Dr Hugo Benioff, who designed the seismograph already described, made a study of the magnitude of these small shocks and their relation in time to the main shock, and has been able to put forward a much more convincing explanation. In order to understand it, we must first make a study of what happens to materials when we compress them.

Suppose we have a sample of rock in our laboratory, which can be squashed in a special hydraulic press, and some means of measuring just how much we squash it. If we apply the pressure, and leave it for a long time, measuring the change in bulk from time to time, we will get results which can be plotted on a graph like Figure 57. When the pressure is first applied, at A, the rock will immediately contract to a smaller bulk, B. If we continue to exert the same pressure, it will continue to contract for a long time afterwards, but at an ever decreasing rate. When the point C is reached, we release the pressure again. The rock recovers at once, but it does not come right back to its original size. It comes back quickly to D, so that CD represents the same amount of change as AB, and then takes its time about the rest of the recovery. This recovery process is known as 'elastic afterworking' or 'creep-strain recovery', and Benioff considers that it is responsible for aftershocks.

Elastic rebound can release only the stored energy corresponding to CD; this causes the main earthquake. But stress across the fault is immediately set up again as the elastic afterworking takes place. This energy is released in small aftershocks, for the fault can move more easily and extend further now that it has been freed by the movement causing the main shock. By adding up the energy stored in a sequence of aftershocks, and plotting it on a graph, Dr Benioff has been able to show that the creep strain recovers in exactly the way that would be expected from laboratory studies of the effect of pressure upon rocks. One very curious thing happens. In most cases, the strain is a mixture

*Fig. 57: Elastic creep. When pressure is applied to a sample of rock, part of the compression occurs at once, but very slow contraction continues to take place for a long time afterwards. When the pressure is released the first part of the contraction is immediately recovered, but the rest is only very slowly released during a period of 'elastic afterworking'.*

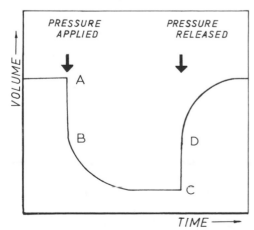

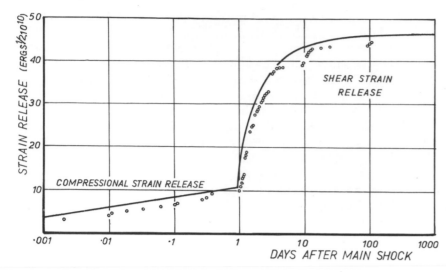

*Fig. 58: An aftershock sequence. This graph shows the strain released in the series of aftershocks that followed the Cheviot earthquake on January 10th, 1951.*

of compression and shear. When both types are present, no shear energy is released until all the compression has gone. Because of this, the graph is broken into two portions of different shape; and the shapes are those laboratory experiment has led us to expect. Figure 58 shows the graph for the sequence of aftershocks which followed the Cheviot earthquake of 10th January, 1951.

After a shallow earthquake in an average tectonic setting the biggest aftershock is very often a little more than a magnitude smaller than the main shock, a statement sometimes called 'Båth's Law' after the Swedish seismologist who first noticed it. The number of shocks occurring becomes less as time goes by until the aftershocks merge with the normal activity of the region, but in any group of shocks the proportion of large to small ones stays much the same. This means that the biggest aftershock may come long after the main earthquake, and it is quite possible for large shocks to happen near the end of a sequence.

The shallower an earthquake is, the more likely it is to have after-shocks. At depths greater than 100 km extended sequences are rare, but it is quite common for deep shocks to occur in pairs or groups of three of nearly equal magnitude, at intervals that range from three or four minutes or less up to several days or perhaps weeks.

Groups of shallow earthquakes can sometimes take on the character of an earthquake swarm. Swarm earthquakes are usually small but very numerous, and of much the same magnitude, so that it is not possible to pick a principal member of the group. Small swarms are fairly common in both New Zealand and Japan, but they are also known in Europe, in Tasmania, and in other places where the normal level of seismic activity is low.

# 12  Earth waves and sea waves

They take the rustic murmur of their bourg
For the great wave that echoes round the world.
            Tennyson, *Idylls of the King*

There is a limit to the useful magnification of a seismograph. The Earth is never completely still. If our instrument is sensitive enough, we will record small continuous movements even when there is no earthquake. They are called *microseisms*. If the magnification is great enough to show the microseisms, there is no advantage in increasing it any further, as the only effect will be to confuse the record. Microseisms are very regular in period, generally in the range from four to six seconds, although there are others of shorter period which can be quite troublesome to some seismographs. Their amplitude is not constant, but changes from day to day. Occasionally violent 'microseism storms' occur (Figure 59) when they become so large as to make the records unreadable.

Some microseisms, especially the short period ones, are probably due to human activity. If the recording station is near a town, the short period vibrations will largely disappear at night when heavy machinery in the factories is stopped, and the amount of traffic falls. We can get away from these disturbances to some extent by putting the recorders in suitable places, but there are still natural microseisms to be dealt with. It has long been known that they are less troublesome inland than near a coast, but the exact way in which the earth waves and the water waves are connected has only recently come to be understood.

When there are long straight coasts or lines of cliffs, it has been suggested, the constant breaking of the surf could generate waves in the ground, and be recorded as microseisms. There is no doubt that some microseisms do originate in this way, but when an attempt was made to track down the source of others, it was found to lie far out to sea.

During the Second World War special networks of seismographs, known as tripartite stations, were set up on the islands of the Caribbean Sea in the hope that the microseisms they recorded would turn out to have a close connection with major weather disturbances. It was found that they had their origin at the centre of intense meteorological systems such as tropical cyclones, and that the specially designed seismographs could be used to follow the movement of the storms. After further study it was found that ocean waves set up by the storm exert a kind of pumping action on the sea bottom, and communicate their energy to the Earth. Once started, these trains of waves will travel many thousands of kilometres, but suitable equipment will usually enable the various separate sources to be distinguished.

Although the method showed promise, seismographs for recording microseisms have not become a regular part of the weather forecaster's equipment. Some further research into North Atlantic storms was carried out in Denmark, and the Royal Observatory in Hong Kong has found the microseisms recorded on its standard instruments of some value in following typhoons, but radar and satellite techniques seem destined to drive the seismologist from the field of storm warning.

In addition to these storm microseisms, which have periods in the range from four to six seconds, and the artificial machinery and traffic vibrations of a second period or less, there are other short-period movements which result from quite local meteorological conditions. Chief among these are rain microseisms and frost microseisms, whose names are sufficiently self-explanatory.

Microseisms are for the most part a mixture of the different types of surface wave, and although their main origin appears to be linked with storms over the ocean and a few great lakes, there is only a small decrease in their amplitude as we travel inland. They can still be recorded in such places as the centre of the North American continent, and at the Soviet stations in Central Asia. It is quite possible that the presence of the low-velocity channel in the crust may play some part in the fact that they can be efficiently transmitted over such vast distances.

Now that meteorologists have spurned the microseism, the seismologist is likely to resume his traditional view that microseisms are nothing but a nuisance. They certainly make it very difficult to find good recording sites on small islands. New Zealand seismologists with a responsibility for much of the South-West

*Fig. 59: A microseism storm. A section of a record made at Christchurch on a Galitzin seismograph. Each line covers a period of about 7 minutes, and successive traces are half an hour apart. The increase in microseism level was associated with the passage of a meteorological front.*

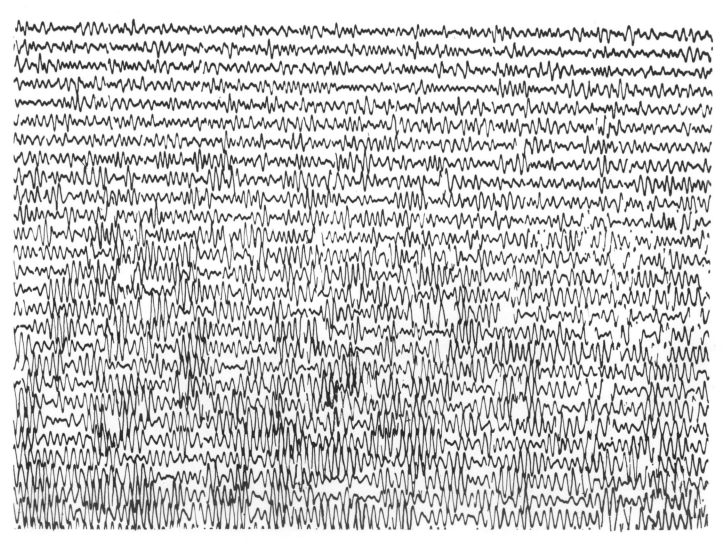

*Plate 31: Tsunami damage. The great Alaskan earthquake in 1964 created a wave 12 metres high, devastating buildings, docks, and railway yards along the shores of Prince William Sound.*

Pacific and a country that contains no place more than sixty or seventy kilometres from the sea look with some envy at the quiet stations at Charters Towers in Queensland and Chieng Mai in northern Thailand, whose instruments run at several hundred times the sensitivity of their own. At Scott Base, beset by Antarctic storms for part of the year, the magnification can be raised when the ocean freezes over for the long polar night.

The best known link between earthquake waves and the waves of the sea is the *tsunami* or seismic sea-wave that can follow a large earthquake under the sea. Tsunamis are popularly known as 'tidal waves', but they have nothing to do with tides, and as there *is* such a thing as a tidal wave it is better not to run the risk of increasing the confusion. The Japanese word tsunami, which is now in fairly wide use, really means 'harbour wave'. Since the effects of seismic sea-waves are frequently most severe in narrow estuaries and bays the term is both appropriate and convenient.

The way in which a tsunami is started is not completely understood. It is clear that water must be displaced when there is faulting, slumping, or uplift of the sea-bed, but Professor Gutenberg has established a number of cases in which the epicentre of the shock was clearly on land, and it seems that the passage of surface-waves across a shallow continental shelf or perhaps along a submarine canyon can sometimes start a sea-wave.

Earthquakes can also set up wave movements in ponds and lakes. The water in a lake or an enclosed arm of the sea has a natural tendency to 'slop' at some particular frequency that depends on its size and depth. If this frequency coincides with that of the earthquake waves the water will resonate, and the waves will be magnified as if by a seismograph. These oscillations are called *seiches*, and they may be set up by the wind and other causes besides earthquakes. The passage of a tsunami or a large storm wave past the entrance to an enclosed harbour has sometimes set the water inside it into seiche oscillation.

The very largest earthquakes seem to be particularly effective in generating seiches, possibly because the very long-period waves still have an appreciable amplitude at distances far beyond that to which the shock can be felt. After the great Lisbon earthquake in 1755 seiches were reported from France, Italy, Holland, Switzerland, England, and even from Norway and Sweden, some 2 800 kilometres from the epicentre. After the Assam earthquake in 1950 there were oscillations recorded on the depth gauges of several English reservoirs, and also observations in Scandinavia. It is also on record that a seiche caused by an earthquake in the Aleutians put a sudden and undignified end to a formal gathering beside a swimming pool in Texas.

Tsunamis can be extremely destructive, and some of the stories told about them are so alarming that it is not easy to separate fact from fiction, but their destructive power is not apparent until they reach a coast. In deep water the waves are extremely wide from crest to crest, so that they cannot be detected by shipping even when they are several metres high. Their speed depends upon the depth of the water, and when shallow water is reached the wave is abruptly slowed down, so that the front piles up and breaks with tremendous force, particularly if it is confined within an estuary or a narrow bay. Even a wave only one or two metres high can damage small vessels moored in shallow water by bumping them on the bottom, and can be powerful enough to destroy boatsheds and coastal roads and embankments (Plates 31, 32, 33).

Once a tsunami has been started it can travel for many thousands of kilometres with little diminution in size. Tsunamis from South

*Plate 32: Tsunami damage. All that remained of Hawaiian beach houses and coconut palms after they had been struck by a tsunami 7 metres high in 1975.*

*Plate 33: A tsunami wave. The tsunami that followed the Niigata earthquake carried these boats against the bridge at Iwafune, and is still flowing up the river.*

American earthquakes have proved troublesome in New Zealand, Japan, and Hawaii, which has also been affected by tsunamis from Japan and from the Aleutians.

Very large tsunamis are fortunately rare, but around the Pacific Ocean they are frequent enough to pose a serious problem, and a regular warning system has been organized. This has its headquarters in Hawaii and depends upon the cooperation of major seismograph and tide-gauge stations in many countries. Stations that record an earthquake that could possibly have generated a tsunami radio sufficient data for Hawaii to determine the epicentre, and if it proves to be a submarine earthquake to ask the nearest tide-gauge stations to watch for abnormal movements of sea level. Although the speed of a tsunami can reach more than 600 kilometres an hour in the open ocean, there is still time for many places to get an estimate of the arrival time and probable size of the wave, so that shipping and people in coastal areas can be warned and if necessary evacuated.

The tsunamis that affect Hawaii most often come from the Aleutians, and warning is given by the tide-gauges on the Alaskan and Canadian coasts, but in the Aleutians themselves and in Japan the earthquakes responsible are often too close to allow much time. However, the Japanese have arranged for urgent telegraph messages to be passed from any place that is affected to the places the wave has not yet reached. The Soviet authorities operate a similar system in Sakhalin and Kamchatka.

The greatest seismic sea-wave on record is perhaps not strictly a tsunami. It occurred at Lituya Bay in Alaska in 1958. Here a magnitude eight earthquake set off a great landslide that fell into the bay and shot one wave over an opposite spur, removing the forest to a height of over 500 metres, and sent another down the bay to break at a height of 290 metres on the far shore. Two fishing vessels were sunk with the loss of two lives, and some ten square kilometres of forest were destroyed. There have been some other large waves started by landslides, but no earthquake has been involved. It appears that the record for a normal tsunami is still held by the wave that struck Cape Lopatka, at the southern tip of Kamchatka, in 1737, breaking at a height of 70 metres.

Not all countries with earthquakes off their coasts have a tsunami problem. Something in the contour of the sea-bottom or the mechanism of the shocks prevents the generation of a wave. This is true of New Zealand. The magnitude eight South-West Wairarapa earthquake in 1855 raised a long stretch of coast and disrupted tidal patterns in Cook Strait, but does not seem to have caused a large wave. The only clear instance of a locally generated tsunami was in 1947 when the wave that followed a moderately large shock off East Cape washed away the bridges over small streams along the coast to the south, and damaged a small seaside hotel.

Waves of distant origin are more often observed. Early in 1976 a shock near Raoul Island in the Kermadecs generated a wave that gave the many pleasure-craft in the bays of the Northland peninsula some anxious moments. Fortunately the earthquakes of the Kermadec region, like those nearer to New Zealand, do not often cause tsunamis, even though large shocks are fairly frequent. The most troublesome waves have come from Chile. In 1868 waves from a Chilean earthquake reached New Zealand with sufficient force to attract general attention in the ports on both coasts, and there was a drowning in the Chatham Islands.

Similar surges followed another Chilean shock in 1960, and disrupted shipping movements in the port of Lyttelton for some hours. Upsetting as this was, it was much less serious than the effects of the same tsunami in more distant parts of the Pacific, such as Japan, where it attained destructive force. The difference can be explained by the presence of the Campbell Plateau, a large area of comparatively shallow water to the south-east of the South Island. When the wave reaches the outer edge of this, it is forced to slow down and a large part of its energy is dissipated before it reaches the New Zealand coast.

Sometimes the sea gives warning of the approach of a tsunami by withdrawing before the wave arrives. When this happens, it is wise to make for high ground at once, but curiosity frequently gets the better of people and leads them to explore the area of sea-bed that has been uncovered. This withdrawal does not always take place, and is certainly not a reliable enough effect to be used as the basis of a warning system.

One or more secondary waves may follow, at intervals of an hour or more, and the disturbance can upset normal tidal patterns for some days.

Japanese observers have sometimes recorded flashes of light at sea before the arrival of a tsunami. There is no reason to doubt the reports, and it has been suggested that they might be caused by disturbance of the small marine organisms that make the wake of a ship so luminous in tropical waters. Whatever the truth of this, it still affords no basis for any kind of practical warning.

The frequency with which tsunamis occur is hard to determine. The only lists that have been published are obviously very incomplete, and can often offer only a guess at the position of the epicentre responsible. Sizes are seldom given, and do not mean very much unless they are measured on an open coast or in deep water. Even small islands may sometimes cause a large 'shadow' and protect the places on the far side quite effectively. It would seem that the Pacific has one or two a year, but that the majority of them are quite small.

# 13 Earthquakes and volcanoes

BANQUO: The earth hath bubbles, as the water has,
      And these are of them.
                      Shakespeare, *Macbeth*

Many people associate earthquakes and volcanoes. In New Zealand we have plenty of both; but the earthquakes do not happen just because there are volcanoes in the Tongariro National Park and hot springs at Whakarewarewa. Volcanoes and earthquakes are different outcomes of the same underlying geological processes, and there is therefore a broad similarity between the world pattern of earthquake belts and the pattern of active volcanoes.

When we discussed the interior of the Earth we saw that it was hot, but that there was no world-wide layer of molten lava just below the surface, waiting to pour from any convenient hole. The enormous pressure of the overlying rocks effectively prevents melting. Nevertheless, there are localized exceptions. The circulating convection currents in the mantle can create 'hot-spots' beneath the oceanic ridges, or the surface material being carried downwards at an ocean trench or a continental margin may become molten during the process of re-absorption. The molten material formed in this way is called *magma*, and is able to force its passage through cracks and along lines of weakness in the solid material.

Usually it does this by a comparatively unspectacular process known as *intrusion*. The magma, having forced itself a certain distance through the crack, or along the interface between strata, solidifies to form a *dyke* or a *sill* of igneous rock. If the conditions are suitable, and the magma behaves in a less controlled manner, a volcano may result.

Eight or nine hundred of the world's volcanoes can be considered active, but there are often long periods of quiescence, and the school geography book's distinction between active, dormant, and extinct volcanoes is often hard to make. At any one time, only a few of them are in eruption, no more than twenty or thirty in a typical year.

A volcano starts as a vent through which escaping gases and ash can reach the surface. Scoria, pumice, ash, and so on piles up around the vent, and usually builds up the typical cone-shaped mountain. The rate of growth of the cone is often extremely rapid. At Parícutin in Mexico the local farmers knew of a hole in a paddock that kept reappearing whenever they filled it in, so they gave up and left it to form a small pit. One afternoon in February 1943, the pit cracked across and began to send up a small column of greyish ash. Twenty-four hours later, lava and scoria were coming out and piling into a cone fifty metres high. By June it had reached the village three kilometres away, by September it had destroyed it, and the lava covered some twenty-five square kilometres. After two years, the cone was five hundred metres high, but the eruption had begun to slacken, and nine years after it started, it stopped. This is one of the few cases in which a volcano has been studied right from birth.

It is usual to distinguish between the molten magma still within the Earth and the lavas that issue at the surface, losing dissolved gas and steam before they cool and solidify. The streams of molten lava and the explosions of burning gas are often spectacular, particularly at night, but the temperature of the molten material is seldom more than about 1 200°C. This is only just sufficient to keep it molten, an indication that we are dealing with a comparatively superficial process.

Lavas differ greatly in chemical composition, the two extremes being represented by the very liquid basaltic lavas that erupt along the mid-oceanic ridges to form the sea floor, and by the acid andesitic lavas that come from the volcanoes of the island arcs and continental margins. Most people regard the graceful cones of Fujiyama, Egmont, or Mayon as the typical shape of a volcano (Plate 34), but this is true only of those emitting fairly stiff andesitic lavas. Basaltic volcanoes, like Mauna Loa in Hawaii, or Kilimanjaro in northern Tanzania are gently dome-shaped, like an inverted saucer. In some cases, basaltic lavas may be so liquid that they do little more than fill the hollows in the ground, but repeated eruptions of this kind from many neighbouring fissures can build up great plateaus, like the Deccan Plateau in India, consisting in all of some seven hundred thousand cubic kilometres of erupted material.

*Plate 34: An andesitic cone. Merapi volcano in central Java, during the eruption in 1961. Lava is spilling from the left-hand side of the crater.*

*Plate 35: A vulcanian eruption. Mt Ngauruhoe, in the central North Island, during the eruption in 1975. This explosion on February 19 was accompanied by a small earthquake of magnitude 3·4. The large blocks that are being hurled within the cauliflower cloud are about twenty metres across.*

*Plate 36: A nuée ardente. During the eruption of Merapi in 1961 a nuée cut this broad path through the jungle on its lower slopes for a distance of several kilometres, and left it covered in thick white ash.*

*Plate 37: A nuée ardente. One of several villages at the foot of Merapi destroyed by the nuée in 1961. This one stood at the side of the path and did not experience its full force.*

The potential destructiveness of a volcano depends to a great degree upon the kind of lava it habitually emits, and it is possible to classify volcanoes by their usual manner of eruption, but most of them change their habits in the course of time. The quietest type is the Hawaiian eruption, which is seldom violent. Instead, the volcano prefers to pour out quantities of very liquid basalt, building up a mound of scoria close to its vent.

In the next type, like Stromboli, the lava is still basaltic in composition, but much less liquid, and is often thrown up in gas fountains and small explosions. The Vulcanian type, named after the original Vulcano, also in the Lipari Islands off the coast of Italy, has an even stiffer type of lava, composed of more acid rock which tends to harden inside the crater. Volcanoes of this type often send up great clouds of fine ash in a 'cauliflower' cloud, and the wind disperses the material over very wide areas (Plate 35). In New Zealand there are thick deposits of ash from ancient eruptions of this type all over the Tongariro-Taupo region in the centre of the North Island. The last type of volcano, the Peléean, is named after Mont Pelée in Martinique, the scene of a disastrous eruption which destroyed the town of St. Pierre in 1902. These volcanoes send out what are called *nuées ardentes* — dense clouds of gases and incandescent material which tumble over the edge of the crater and roll swiftly down the slope (Plates 36, 37). The lava in these volcanoes is so stiff that it can form an apparently solid plug in the mouth of the vent. Sometimes the pressure underneath forces the plug high into the air to form a 'spine'. The material is soft, and soon erodes away when exposed to wind and weather. The spine of Mont Pelée was originally a most impressive affair several hundred metres in height.

Between eruptions many craters fill with the water that drains from the surrounding slopes, and a crater lake is formed. The crater wall is often little more than a pile of ash in which a breach can easily be formed, either by further volcanic action, or because the wall can no longer support the growing weight of water behind it. When this happens a turbulent mass of ash, bolders, mud, and snow may be carried down the mountain side at great speed. This is called a *lahar*, or volcanic mudflow (Plate 38). New Zealand's worst railway disaster occurred when a lahar from the Ruapehu crater lake carried away a bridge over the Whangaehu River in the Tongariro National Park. All through the park there are rocky mounds composed of material deposited by past lahars. A crater lake is not essential to the creation of lahars. In Indonesia there have been instances where heavy rainfall has been sufficient to start serious mudflows.

The explosions that accompany a violent eruption can send waves through the Earth that can be recorded on seismographs and may even be felt as earthquakes. Most of these explosions take place either in the crater or in the vent of the volcano, but sometimes there are underground explosions or movements of magma that can truly be called volcanic earthquakes. Compared with the tectonic earthquakes to which most of this book is devoted volcanic shocks are usually very minor affairs. This is because most of the energy of the explosion goes into the air as a sound wave rather than into the ground, and because the comparatively weak rocks fracture before very large pressures or strains can build up.

When the air-wave from a great eruption strikes a building, the shaking can be mistaken for an earthquake. Waves of this kind can travel very great distances. Sounds from the great eruption of Krakatoa in 1883 were heard from Sri Lanka and northern Thailand to Alice Springs in central Australia. Big noises are not always heard at shorter distances, as the sound is carried more effectively in the high atmosphere, and there is a zone of silence around the volcano itself. Explosions of Ngauruhoe and Ruapehu that were not heard in the National Park area have been reported from Taranaki and from Wellington suburbs over two hundred kilometres away.

In most countries where there are dangerous volcanoes close to centres of population, the authorities have organized some kind of a watch for impending eruptions. Unfortunately volcanoes are so individual in their habits that it is often difficult to know what to watch for. It is usual to install a seismograph, but many eruptions are well advanced before the first earthquakes are recorded. Other indications, like increasing ground tilts, or changes in the temperature of hot springs and crater lakes are often better pointers to a coming eruption.

Volcanic earthquakes and crater explosions are most frequent when the volcano is visibly active. When the activity is on the increase nearby seismographs show a kind of movement known as *volcanic*

*Plate 38: A lahar. Ash from beside the crater lake of Mt Ruapehu swept down the mountainside, cutting a path through the snowfield.*

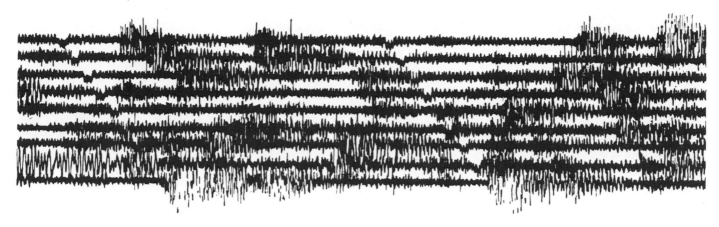

*Fig. 60: Volcanic tremor. Explosions and shallow earthquakes against a background of volcanic tremor, recorded on Raoul Island during the 1964 eruption.*

*tremor.* This takes the form of very rapid vibrations, generally less than half a second in period. When tremor first appears, it lasts only for an hour or two at a time, but as the activity of the mountain increases, it becomes more violent, and increases in amplitude. When the eruption is at its height, it is much less regular in appearance, not so much because the period changes, but because the vibration keeps changing phase; that is to say, it breaks off in the middle of a movement, and begins all over again. Hawaiian volcanologists have suggested that the tremor may be caused by molten lava rushing past the edges of projecting underground strata, making them vibrate like the reeds of a mouth-organ. Shimozuru has found that the tremor is a mixture of body-waves and surface-waves, and that the more deep-seated its origin is, the longer its period becomes. He suggests that as the magma releases its gas to become lava, rhythmical oscillations of the lava can be set up in the underground conduits and in the vent of the volcano, and these generate the tremor.

The seismogram shown in Figure 60 was obtained by the New Zealand expedition to Raoul Island in the Kermadec group during an eruption at the end of 1964. Explosions in the crater and shallow earthquakes centred beneath Denham Bay appear against a background of volcanic tremor many times the amplitude of the normal microseisms, and of much shorter period.

Regions in which there are active or recently extinct volcanoes, like parts of Japan and the North Island of New Zealand, often experience earthquake swarms. These are outbreaks of numerous small to moderate earthquakes, no one of which can be clearly identified as the main member of the group. From May to December 1922 the small township of Taupo experienced an outbreak that has been quoted in several textbooks as a typical swarm. There were many hundred shocks, the largest of which caused minor damage, surface faulting was observed a few kilometres to the west, and a stretch of the lake shore subsided about two metres.

In 1922 this area was sparsely populated, and there were no seismographs capable of recording local shocks. It now seems probable that a moderate earthquake was responsible for the faulting, and that what followed was a normal but unusually vigorous sequence of aftershocks. At the end of 1964, however, the same district experienced a more typical swarm. There is now a permanent seismograph station at the Wairakei geothermal electric power station, a few kilometres to the north, and it was possible to move portable recorders to the district. In normal periods the Wairakei seismograph records about five close shocks a month. At the peak of the swarm it recorded over nine hundred in one day. The foci turned out to lie under the western part of the Lake, not far from the bays where the fault traces appeared in 1922, but there was no sign of renewed fault movement.

Public opinion tended to blame the occurrence upon the exploitation of geothermal steam, but no changes in the quantity or the quality of the steam were noticed by the power-station staff, and none of the field investigators who regularly measure spring and bore-hole temperatures reported anything abnormal. Few true swarms have been reported from non-volcanic regions, but their link with volcanic activity is at best indirect, and it cannot be claimed that the mechanism that produces them is properly understood.

We saw when discussing island arcs that the earthquakes directly beneath active volcanoes were often at a depth of about 150 kilometres. The French volcanologist Claude Blot has suggested that deeper earthquakes over a wider area may also be involved in the eruptive process, pointing to a number of sequences that begin with a deep earthquake, continue with shocks that get shallower and closer to a volcano, and end with a volcanic eruption. Although his statistics are superior to those commonly employed in political argument, they have not been good enough to convince most geophysicists and his hypothesis at present remains an interesting suggestion.

Dr Trevor Hatherton of the New Zealand Geophysics Division and his Californian colleague Dr W.R. Dickinson have discovered an interesting relationship between the depths of the earthquakes under andesitic volcanoes and the amount of potash present in their lavas, which increases as the earthquakes become deeper. This kind of analysis should give us additional information about the physical as well as the chemical properties of the material at the depths at which melting occurs.

The subject of volcanism is wide enough for a book in its own right, and only an outline can find a place in a book about earthquakes, so we shall say nothing of hot springs, boiling mud-pools, or geysers. Readers who want to know more will find them discussed in books on geology, some of which are listed in the Appendix.

# 14 Earthquake prediction

CASSANDRA . . . Destroyed again, and this time utterly!
CHORUS: She seems about to predict her own misfortunes . . .
Of your prophetic fame we have heard before,
But in this matter, prophets are not required.
Aeschylus, *The Agamemnon*

Astronomers can predict eclipses and other spectacular conjunctions of the heavenly bodies with an accuracy that is in no small degree responsible for the respect with which their more dubious speculations are treated. The meteorologist's predictions, if less reliable, are accurate enough to exact a measure of confidence. The seismologist, who issues no warnings, is frequently chided for neglect, and if he protests that prediction is none of his business, he is left in no doubt that most people think that it should be.

At first sight, it would seem that an earthquake prediction would need the astronomer's kind of accuracy before it was of any use at all. A prediction that there will be a disastrous earthquake in California on 5th November, or that Manila will have a big earthquake within the next few years, even if correct, affords little basis for practical action. It is not possible to evacuate all California, or even to bring business to a standstill.

After New Zealand's disastrous Hawke's Bay earthquake in 1931, when more than 250 of the inhabitants of Napier and Hastings were killed, a local seer claimed that he had 'correctly'predicted it. In fact, he had placed the centre south of Hawke's Bay, in the Wairarapa, but a distance of a hundred and fifty kilometres is little hindrance to a determined prophet. Had the authorities believed his warning, it is not improbable that the inhabitants of Masterton, the chief township of the Wairarapa, would have been evacuated to Napier or Hastings to become additional casualties. As it was, they escaped with a severe shaking.

Prediction of individual earthquakes will need to specify the time, place, and size of the shock with high accuracy, or at the very least provide a good indication of the degree of uncertainty involved, or they will do more harm than good.

It is not only the soothsayer whose predictions can pose problems for the civil authorities. Quite recently an English academic (not a seismologist) considered that he had found a method of predicting earthquakes, and decided to tell the press. He added that he was expecting a large one in New Zealand. The British press passed the news on by cable. Fortunately their New Zealand colleagues decided to get expert comment before printing the story, and only very timid souls were upset. New Zealand's official displeasure was conveyed to the prophet, who is understood to have muttered darkly about interference with academic freedom.

Even it if were precise, the prediction of an individual earthquake could bring only problems to a community whose buildings had not been designed to withstand it. Something might be done to minimize casualties, but knowledge of the impending losses would result in social and economic confusion. This would be even worse if false predictions could be issued maliciously. Fortunately one useful kind

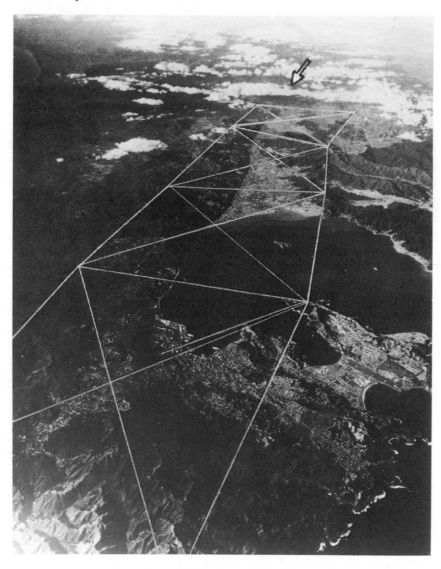

*Plate 39: Regional strain. Repeated surveys of this network of triangles across the Wellington Fault are being undertaken in order to keep track of the accumulation of regional strain which could lead to an earthquake. Similar work is being undertaken near many active faults. The fault follows the western (left hand) side of the harbour and the Hutt Valley beyond it to the north.*

of prediction is possible. The statement that 'During the next 100 years, this bridge will have to withstand ten shocks of intensity seven or more' is quite useful to the design engineer. Seismologists have concentrated upon making reliable statements of this kind, to be embodied in building codes and zoning provisions, but this does not mean that they have given up hope of making more precise forecasts.

Early seismologists spent much time looking for regular periodicities in the times at which earthquakes occurred, but without success. As the elastic rebound theory gained acceptance it became clear that the build-up of the forces responsible for the shock was a slow process, and that what should be looked for was some form of 'trigger' that determined the exact instant at which the stored energy would be released. If no trigger were involved, exact prediction would be very difficult indeed. We should need to know the exact dimensions of the fault, the strength of the rocks that surrounded it, the roughness of the surface, how much force was pressing the faces together, and many other uncertain quantities before we could have any hope of estimating the amount of strain needed to start it slipping.

It is a simpler matter to detect the accumulation of strain. Accurate surveys repeated at intervals should reveal whether a tract of country is being deformed or not. These have become much simpler and cheaper since radar instruments for the precise measurement of distance supplanted the older methods of triangulation with a theodolite. Surveys for this purpose are now being made regularly in California, Japan, and New Zealand (Plates 39, 40). As the Japanese seismologist Suyehiro pointed out to a meeting of American engineers many years ago, it is no use worrying about the trigger being pulled until you know whether the gun is loaded, particularly as the earthquake-gun will go off without the trigger being pulled when the charge in it has grown large enough.

Changes in pressure have always been considered among the more likely triggers. Tidal loading and a variety of meterological factors come under this heading. Some investigators have looked at planetary attractions, but these are so much smaller than other variable forces at work that they are unlikely to have the deciding effect. Nevertheless, if an earthquake is just on the point of happening, a very small effect indeed could determine its precise instant.

Signs of triggering are possibly present during aftershock sequences and swarms, when the conditions for another earthquake can be considered more than usually favourable. For example, R. C. Hayes found that the aftershocks of a Cook Strait earthquake in early 1950 tended to be more frequent when the tide was falling and the barometer lower than normal. Similar observations have been made in Japan. In the Himalayas and in the Mississippi Basin it has been reported that the frequency of small tremors is linked to flood conditions, a high rate of change in the intensity of the flood being likely to trigger off minor swarms.

Dr T. H. Heaton of the California Institute of Technology points out that what probably matters is the relative rates of change of the triggering and the tectonic stresses. The gravitational pulls of the Moon and Sun affect not only the water in the oceans but the solid body of the Earth, raising a tide that can change its radius by as much as forty centimetres. This creates elastic strains that change much more rapidly than the slowly accumulating tectonic strain released in

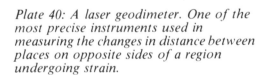

*Plate 40: A laser geodimeter. One of the most precise instruments used in measuring the changes in distance between places on opposite sides of a region undergoing strain.*

an earthquake. Whether the tidal change is big enough to act as a trigger should depend upon the orientation of the fault. He examined 107 shocks in which this was known and found that large shocks within the crust appeared to be triggered if the fault displacement was vertical or oblique, but not if it was transcurrent. This was what his mathematical analysis had suggested. Deep shocks did not appear to be triggered. He does not think that shocks smaller than magnitude 4 should be triggered, as the rate of change of the other forces involved would, on our present theories, be greater than that of the trigger. So far he has not been able to check whether this suggestion is true.

Most countries have some popular tradition of 'earthquake weather'. In his *French Revolution* Carlyle remarks that 'Hope ushers in a revolution as earthquakes are preceded by bright weather', but most Englishmen, Shakespeare among their number, have pictured earthquakes as the fitting climax to a storm:

> LENNOX: The night has been unruly: where we lay
>           Our chimneys were blown down . . .
>           . . . some say the earth was fev'rous, and did shake.
> MACBETH: 'Twas a rough night.
> LENNOX: My young remembrance cannot parallel a fellow to it.

The Japanese consider that earthquake weather is hot and humid. Omori examined the weather conditions during eighteen major Japanese shocks spread over 530 years, and found that twelve of them happened on fine days, two on cloudy days, and four on rainy days. This tells us more about the Japanese climate than it does about the earthquakes.

The rescue operations that followed New Zealand's Hawke's Bay earthquake in 1931 were aided by an abnormally long period of fine weather, but the Murchison earthquake two years previously occurred in an equally abnormal period of storm and rain. Local folk-lore has it that earthquake weather is hot and still.

Instances are known when the sharp change in barometric pressure that accompanies the passage of a meteorological front has coincided with a local earthquake, and Richter observes that in California, minor shocks tend to increase at the beginning of the rainy season, when large air masses are shifting and the load on the Earth's surface is consequently changing. If pressure changes play any great part in triggering earthquakes we might expect shocks under the sea to depend greatly upon the tides, as the daily changes in pressure on the sea bottom as they ebb and flow are ten times greater than the changes in air pressure. Nothing of the kind has been observed.

It is widely believed that a sharp increase in the number of small earthquakes heralds the approach of a large one, but this is the exception rather than the rule. Except in the case of the shocks that precede a volcanic eruption there are seldom more than one or two foreshocks, and there is no way in which a foreshock can be distinguished from the normal minor activity until after the main event.

Japanese seismologists have observed that some large earthquakes have been preceded by abnormal tilting of the ground, and special tiltmeters were installed to study the matter more closely. Although further instances were recorded, they had no success in finding any kind of regular pattern. Tiltmeters are not easy to keep in good adjustment, and there have been few attempts to duplicate or follow up the Japanese work.

The most promising work so far began in Soviet Central Asia. For many years Soviet seismologists have made a particularly close study of the earthquakes in the Garm district of Tadzhikstan. In 1962 Kondratenko and Nersesov announced that they had found a regular pattern of changes in the speed of seismic waves that had crossed a part of the region about to have an earthquake.

Under normal circumstances the speeds of *P*- and *S*-waves through most kinds of rock have almost exactly the same ratio to one another; the *P*-wave is about 1·77 times as fast as the *S*. If, however, the rocks are under very great strain the ratio falls, until when they are just at the point of breaking it is a little above 1·5.

The Russians kept a watch on the waves from the small earthquakes that are always occurring in the district and found that when they had passed through an area about to have a larger earthquake their velocities were abnormal. Low velocity-ratios developed and persisted for quite long periods, and just before an earthquake they suddenly returned to normal. The size of the earthquake depended upon the time for which the abnormal conditions had persisted (Figure 61).

The first problem in using this effect for prediction is that the region in which abnormal velocities are found is quite small – only a few tens of kilometres even in the case of a large shock. Several methods of detection have been tried. The one used by the Russians was originally devised by the Japanese seismologist Wadati, and depends on having about a dozen or more stations at close range. If the *S-P* interval at each station is plotted against the time of arrival of *P*, the points lie on a straight line whose slope represents the ratio of the velocities. An alternative method, which has been tried in New

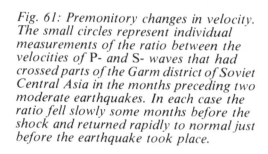

*Fig. 61: Premonitory changes in velocity. The small circles represent individual measurements of the ratio between the velocities of P- and S- waves that had crossed parts of the Garm district of Soviet Central Asia in the months preceding two moderate earthquakes. In each case the ratio fell slowly some months before the shock and returned rapidly to normal just before the earthquake took place.*

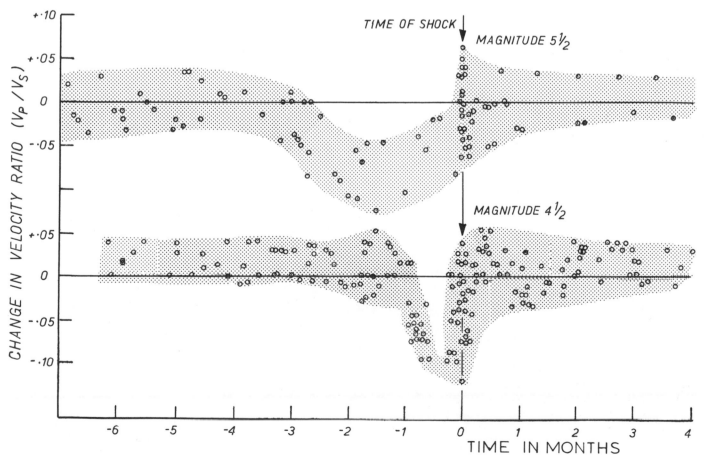

Zealand and in the U.S.A., depends upon recording the arrival of *P*-waves from distant shocks at a station actually within the region of abnormal velocity. If the region is strained, the waves arrive later than the travel-time tables suggest they should.

So far, most predictions have been made long after the event. Seismologists have looked through their records to find an earthquake close to a seismograph station, and then found that the anomaly was there beforehand. In New Zealand it was present before the Gisborne earthquake in 1966, and in California the speed of *P*-waves fell three and a half years before the San Fernando shock in 1971. Both Russian and American seismologists have been making cautious predictions in private with some success, though the shocks predicted have been small. The best publicised prediction so far was of a magnitude 7·3 earthquake in the Liaoning province of China in early 1975 (Plate 41). Reports indicate that the Chinese authorities felt sufficient confidence in the prediction to ask people to leave their homes, offering the inducement of outdoor movies! Most people complied, and although many houses were destroyed there were few casualties.

It was some time before the pioneer work of the Soviet seismologists attracted attention elsewhere. When it did, the first problem was to find out whether similar velocity changes occurred in

*Plate 41: Earthquake prediction. Chinese seismologists successfully predicted the Liaoning earthquake in 1975, but although casualties could be minimized, there was no way of preventing the economic loss represented by the damage to this factory and the office building opposite.*

other parts of the world, or whether they were due to some local geological peculiarity of the Garm district. Once it became clear that they were not a purely local effect, it was natural to ask why they happened. It was easy enough to understand why the velocity-ratio fell, but what caused the return to normal that seemed to be most significant in deciding the instant of the shock?

The answer that is most generally accepted was given in 1972 by Amos Nur of Stanford University. He suggested that the explanation was *dilatancy*. Dilatancy is a curious phenomenon with a curious history. It was discovered as long ago as 1886 by Osborne Reynolds, an English physicist who was looking for the properties of ether, the mysterious all-pervading medium that was then thought to be responsible for transmitting light and radio waves. He found instead that he had come upon a general property of almost every granular substance, like sand or piles of grain.

In 1972, few seismologists had heard of dilatancy, although it was familiar to engineers working in the field of soil mechanics, and in 1965 Dr F. C. Frank had published a review paper in an American journal drawing attention to its possible involvement in the mechanism of earthquakes. What is dilatancy? Suppose the grains in a heap of rock particles are packed as closely as possible, and we try to compress it further. We can compress it in the direction of our push, but it will move out in other directions to compensate. As it was already packed as tightly as possible, the only way in which it can change its shape is by dilating and occupying a bigger total volume. The odd thing is that in the process it becomes stronger, probably as a result of the increased pressure between the grains at the points of contact, and it is consequently in a condition to store still more elastic strain before it eventually collapses.

A complication arises when the pores of the dilatant material are filled with fluid. This is the case with the rocks inside the Earth. At shallow depths, ground-water is present, and farther below there will be magmatic material that can move through the pores of the more solid rock. When external pressure causes the rocks to dilate, they do so by increasing the volume of pore space, more probably by the formation of minute cracks than by rearrangement of the grains. Since the spaces that contain it are now bigger, the pressure of the pore fluid must fall, but beyond the dilatant region it will remain normal, and there will be a flow of liquid into the region until the pressure is once again equalized. As this happens the dilatant rock loses its increased strength. When the pressure of the pore fluid falls, the velocity of *P*-waves through the region also falls, returning to normal when the pressure deficiency has been made good by the influx of fluid from beyond the strained region.

We can now describe the elastic rebound process in more convincing detail. As regional strain builds up towards breaking point tiny cracks begin to form in the rocks, and they become dilatant. In the dilatant condition they become stronger and can store further strain, but while this is going on fluid from beyond the dilatant region is flowing in and weakening them once again. They are already strained beyond their normal capacity, and the rate at which they fall in strength determines the instant of failure (Figure 62).

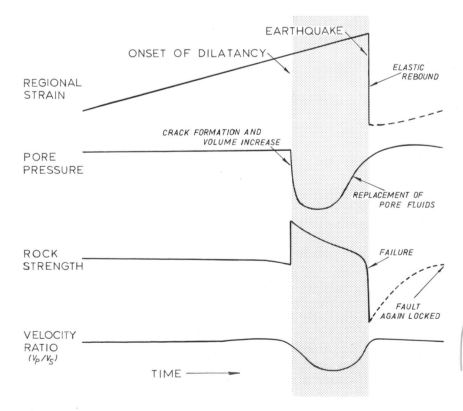

*Fig. 62: Dilatancy and earthquake mechanism. When regional strain increases sufficiently the rocks become dilatant. The pressure of the fluid in the pores falls, increasing their strength and making it possible to store more strain. As the fluid is replaced the strength of the rocks falls again, triggering an elastic rebound and producing an earthquake.*

If this dilatancy theory of earthquake mechanism is correct, keeping a watch on *P*-waves or changed velocity ratios may not be the only way to detect dangerous conditions. It may now be possible to find some pattern in the apparently erratic uplifts and tilts that Japanese seismologists have reported, and geophysical measurements of the movement of ground-water may be simpler to make than purely seismological measurements.

One method that the Russians have found promising is to measure the electrical resistance between buried electrodes several kilometres apart. As the ability of rocks to carry an electric current depends to a large extent upon the amount of pore fluid they contain, the resistance can be expected to rise when they become dilatant. By changing the spacing between the electrodes and the strength of the current it is possible to test rocks at different depths. A less obvious method that was tried in the Garm region depends upon the fact that many crustal rocks are to a greater or lesser extent radioactive. When cracks open in the rock, the area in contact with the ground-water increases, and the result is to increase the amount of radon it absorbs. This can be watched by sampling the water in deep wells, and testing it with a geiger counter in a laboratory. Before long, a number of reliable methods of detecting dilatant regions should be available.

If these methods live up to present hopes, the warnings will come in two stages. The first alert can be given when a region has been dilatant for long enough to produce a significant earthquake. The longer it is delayed, the bigger the expected shock will be, but how big a shock a given delay implies depends upon the strength of the rocks and the rate at which strain accumulates. It will therefore have to be found for each particular region, but it seems likely that there will be at least a year's warning of a shock of magnitude 7. The danger period and final alert would begin when the anomalies started their return to normal. The speed at which they do this will depend upon the porosity of the rocks and the availability of fluid. It will certainly be different in different regions, and in some places may well vary seasonally. The final warning could come only days before the shock, but indications are that the alert will be soon enough to be useful.

Professor F. F. Evison has noted a pattern of events that has preceded several earthquakes in New Zealand and California. First, there is a closely-grouped set of earthquakes of about the same magnitude that he calls the 'premonitory swarm'. This is followed by a period called the 'premonitory gap', during which there are no earthquakes in the region nearby. Eventually there is a 'main earthquake' whose size depends upon the size of the 'swarm' earthquakes and the duration of the gap. The 'swarm' is believed to attend the opening of the cracks that signal the onset of dilatancy, and the gap to last thoughout the dilatant period. The possibility of basing predictions upon this pattern is obvious, but there are difficulties in distinguishing 'premonitory swarms' from other similar groupings of earthquakes, and there have not so far been any indisputable successes. Russian and Japanese seismologists have also reported a decrease in the number of small earthquakes in the period preceding a major shock.

The discovery of changes preceding a shock by some days gives some support to the popular belief that birds and animals can sense that an earthquake is imminent. There is no difficulty in explaining periods of warning of half a minute or so. Many creatures are more sensitive to sound and vibration than humans are, and at least some instances of apparent prescience are due to the animal's response to the weak *P*-wave of a shock in which humans could feel only the *S*.

It is much harder to verify and explain the persistent reports of animals being disturbed for a day or more before the shock, and most long-period predictions by animals remain open to question. It now seems possible that the reports of abnormal behaviour of sheep and cattle some 15 minutes before the Inangahua earthquake in 1968 and other similar reports are accounts of animal response to some preliminary ground deformations that were not perceptible to humans. There were no instrumentally recorded foreshocks.

Similar stories are told of the sensitivity of fish, which can be seriously affected by the passage of strong *P*-waves through the water. Numbers of dead fish apparently killed by submarine concussion have been observed after many large earthquakes from the South-West Wairarapa shock in 1855 to the Alaskan earthquake in 1964.

Professor Tsuneji Rikitake, Director of the Earthquake Research Institute of the University of Tokyo, has drawn attention to a curious consistency in the length of warning that we can expect different kinds of precursory signs to give. It depends upon the magnitude of the coming shock, and applies to changes in wave-velocity, earth currents, radon content of ground-water, changes in the rate of fault creep, and a number of other possible indicators. For a shock of magnitude 3 we can expect only about one day's warning, but for one of magnitude 4 the time is about 10 days. For a magnitude 8 shock we would have 25 or 30 years in which to prepare. The fact that a number of different indicators all give similar results raises hopes that a practical method of prediction is at last in sight.

The problem of what to do with a prediction remains. Few seismologists would feel that their duty had been done when they had telegraphed their warning to the Prime Minister, and many of them are trying to interest sociologists in finding out what the public response to a prediction is likely to be. The ordinary citizen is unlikely to welcome the news that his house is likely to fall down in an hour or two, but that the City Council is turning on free movies in the town square.

There can be little doubt that the social and economic consequences of issuing a prediction will be serious, but exactly what is likely to happen depends a great deal upon the nature of the prediction. At present, it looks as if the seismologist will first issue a long-term warning, perhaps some years in advance, and then gradually make the time and place of the shock and its probable magnitude more and more definite as the time of the shock gets nearer. Once such a prediction is published, insurance and property values are likely to be seriously upset, there may be a movement of population, new constructional projects are likely to be postponed, and there may be unemployment among people engaged in painting and repairing buildings. On the other hand, camping gear, fire extinguishers, and emergency rations could be in demand, with shortages and high prices following.

An important distinction should be made between a prediction the source of which may or may not be worthy of belief, and a warning, which should be an official instruction or advice to take some definite action. Even those governments and local bodies that have been active in the field of civil defence, and have excellent plans for dealing with unexpected disaster, have so far thought little about the consequences of prediction.

Even more serious from the legal and administrative point of view would be the adoption of a suggestion by some American geophysicists that the earthquakes of California could be controlled. What they suggest should be done is to drill holes along the San Andreas fault, several kilometres deep, and about half a kilometre apart. They would then pump fluid from a pair of holes, and force it into a third hole between them. This should trigger off an earthquake, but its magnitude would be limited by the fact that the fault was locked at the two outer holes. By moving systematically along the fault they could remove the regional strains before they became dangerous, and California need experience only minor shocks. The cost of the project would be no more than a few thousand million dollars.

Whatever the prospects for prediction or control, it is certain that earthquake casualties and economic loss can be greatly reduced if we turn our ingenuity and our labours to framing sound building codes, and devising better methods of construction.

# 15 Safe as houses

They dreamt not of a perishable home
Who thus could build.
    William Wordsworth, *Ecclesiastical Sonnets*

In the confusion that follows an earthquake there are more urgent tasks than the compilation of statistics, and it is no easy matter to estimate the total of the damage and loss of life they have caused. Even official figures can be misleading. Some countries habitually minimize disasters, while others exaggerate the casualty figures in the hope of increasing the flow of aid. When the horrifying results of the Tang Shan earthquake in 1976 have finally been assessed, however, the figure of a million deaths in the last half century is unlikely to prove an under-estimate.

By and large, earthquake disasters can be prevented. It is not earthquakes that kill people, but the things we build. Purely natural phenomena, like landslides and tsunamis, certainly play a part, and lack of foresight and the limitations in our engineering skills take their toll, but whenever there are big casualty figures it is usual to find the combination of a poor country, dense population, and primitive building methods. It is not necessary to have a large earthquake.

*Plate 42: Inadequate cross-bracing. Proper diagonal bracing of the lower floor might have prevented this damage to a top-heavy warehouse at Port Ahuriri in the Napier earthquake of 1931.*

5·8 caused ten to fifteen
Quizvan in Iran in 1962,
h toll was over twelve
n Peru, with a magnitude
ide and flood, killed sixty
t we find that Chinese
00 people in the Shansi
total ever claimed, but it
nother shock in the same
alled in Tokyo in 1923 and

le in the San Francisco
ter. The 256 deaths in New
wke's Bay earthquake of
of deaths on the road, but
ght to be concerned. The
t only our homes, offices,
bridges and public utilities
are reasonably likely to

ity scale, like the modified
see that serious damage to
in quite large earthquakes,
been taken to make them
resistant, but we cannot assume that all
buildings are well-built, or that there has been no deterioration with
age.

In New Zealand, where most people live in what Englishmen
would call wooden bungalows, and Americans term single storey

frame houses, the average man is probably safer than in countries where it is usual to live in a brick apartment block. The typical house is firmly bolted to a reinforced concrete foundation with broad footings. The framing is adequately cross-braced, and the covering of overlapping weatherboards nailed to every upright gives it further help in resisting deformation, though not always enough to prevent cracking of the plaster on the interior partitions. The older houses have a tin roof of galvanized corrugated-iron sheet fixed to wooden rafters with lead-headed nails. This fashion gave place to tiles, and later to flat roofs covered with fabric, tarred, and sanded. Still more recently, steep gables have again become the vogue, and there has been a return to galvanized iron and aluminium, which can now be produced in sufficient length to span the building in a single piece. A variety of sheet plastic materials, and squares of metal with ceramic coatings that imitate tiles or shingles are also in use. In some instances, a veneer of bricks replaces the weatherboarding, but stucco is now uncommon.

From the point of view of safety in an earthquake, the tiled roof was a step back from the tin one. Tiled roofs are heavy – many times the weight of the structure which has to support them – and some varieties absorb more than their own weight of water. This results in a top-heavy building, and the situation can only be partly relieved by additional cross-bracing of the framework. The warehouse at Port Ahuriri seen in Plate 42 is an interesting example of the behaviour of a top-heavy building with inadequate cross bracing. This was taken after the Hawkes Bay earthquake in 1931. Tiles are easily dislodged in a shake, and even if they do not cascade to the ground and strike the passers-by or the occupants of the building as they rush outside, they will probably be so badly cracked that they are no longer watertight.

It is sound advice not to run outside in an earthquake, whatever the building you may be in at the time.

The maximum violence in a destructive shock is generally reached within ten seconds of the first tremor, and all that can be done is to follow the advice of Dr. Bailey Willis: 'Stand still and count to forty. At the end of that time, it makes no difference what you do.'

The best thing to do, Dr Willis's advice notwithstanding, is to get under some part of the structure which is reinforced, such as a doorway, or under a strong desk or table that will support the weight of anything that collapses on top. Falling material is responsible for

*Plate 44: Bricks and tiles. The cracks in the walls of this house at Inangahua show that bricks are not always stronger than the mortar that holds them together. Falling tiles have caused many deaths. The combination of an inadequately braced chimney and a tiled roof is to be avoided.*

*Plate 45: Differences in natural period. The difference in period between the tower of the Hastings Post Office and the rest of the building resulted in its collapse. Although a passer-by was killed, the occupants escaped uninjured.*

most earthquake casualties, and as a rule more rubble falls into the streets than inside the buildings. In the Hastings Post Office the tower collapsed, killing a passer-by, but there were no casualties amongst the people inside.

Fortunately, there is seldom serious structural damage to the wooden house. The frame has considerable resilience, and can put up with a great deal of distortion before anything snaps. This flexibility does, however, contribute to the most common type of damage – a cracked pan in the water-closet. Since the cistern is fastened to the wall and the pan to the floor, a comparatively mild shake in the right direction will break it. Isolated instances are reported in shocks of strength between MM IV and MM V, but this is exceptional. Perhaps there is a case for flexible plumbing.

Damage to the water-closet is inconvenient, but hardly dangerous. This is not the case with the next most common form of damage – cracked and fallen chimneys. These begin to fall about MM V. Builders assure me that there is no reason why a properly erected chimney should ever fall, but they undoubtedly do. Some 20 000 chimneys in Wellington and the Hutt Valley were in need of attention after the Masterton earthquakes of 1942. The most common types of failure are a separation of the bricks, often along a diagonal or in a kind of X-pattern, or a snapping off at roof level (Plate 43). Individual bricks, or even the whole top section of the chimney can crash through a roof. Sentimental attachment to the open fire is responsible for the largest single earthquake hazard in the country.

The failure of brick buildings is often attributed to the use of poor mortar, but a careful examination of Plate 44 will show that in a number of cases the strength of the bricks themselves has been exceeded. It is most important that the corners of brick buildings, and those portions which may try to vibrate independently of the rest of the structure, should be well tied together. The failure of towers, like the one on the Hastings Post Office (Plate 45) is probably quite as much due to a difference in natural period from the rest of the building as to any inherent structural weaknesses.

It may be thought that the danger is limited to that of being hit by a falling brick. This is unfortunately not the case. Failure due to separation of the bricks is the greater hazard, but its operation is indirect. This occurrence of secondary damage is a commonplace to the insurance man. A small earthquake may, for example, break a pipe, and the escaping water may damage large quantities of stored goods. In any large earthquake, community services such as water, gas, and electricity are put out of action. Under these circumstances many a housewife is tempted to prepare a meal, or at least to boil tea on the open fireplace. If the chimney has a crack concealed behind the

*Plate 46: Inertia. This water-tank has a well-braced metal stand that could probably have withstood the shaking, but the tank was not fixed to it, and the scratches on its underside record the story of its wanderings.*

*Plate 47: Chimneys. Not everything that breaks falls down at once. Happenings like this increase the risks in aftershocks. The twisting of this tall factory stack probably indicates an intensity of MM VIII — but note that the tiled roof seems to be intact.*

*Plate 48: Inverted pendulum. A tall support for a large mass needs to be strong. Brickwork is too brittle for a job like this.*

woodwork, the risk of fire is very great. Once a fire starts, the normal fire-fighting services are not available to put it out. This is not just a far-fetched possibility. Records of the great San Francisco shock, and several more recent Japanese ones, show that the damage by fires lit after the earthquake was many times more costly than that caused by the shock itself.

There are two main factors in earthquake damage: resonance with the incoming waves, and inertia. The hazard from inertia seems to be less obvious to members of the public and the ordinary small builder. When the ground beneath an object moves, it will have a much greater tendency to resist the movement if it is heavy, like the water-tank shown in Plate 46. Hot-water cylinders that are constrained only by their supply and outlet pipes have been responsible for a great deal of expensive secondary damage that could have been prevented with a simple ring of nails around the base. Heavy wardrobes and bookcases are all too seldom screwed to the wall behind, and stoves, refrigerators and pianos are almost never secured in any way. All of these can move about (or more correctly, tend to 'stay put') in quite moderate earthquakes.

Securing the contents of our buildings may be in large measure a matter of common sense, but it is no use bothering if the buildings themselves are going to fall down. How can we design buildings that are adequate to resist the earthquakes they are likely to experience?

Even in the epicentral regions of magnitude eight and a half earthquakes, some buildings have been left standing. A crude approach would be to copy them, and to forbid other types of construction, but most communities would consider this too harsh a restriction upon their development. We must find out why buildings collapse, and apply the principles to new planning and design. From the beginning it was clear that this approach would involve both the study of earthquakes and the study of structures. It was rather longer before it was realized that the properties of soils and foundations, which form the connection between the earthquake and the building, are equally important.

Even if the earthquake engineers can solve these problems, some element of risk is likely to remain. When the question is posed in the abstract, most people will say that this is not acceptable; yet in other fields – in transport, in public health, and in damage from tempest, fire, and flood – they undoubtedly face far greater risks than they do from earthquake. It is possible to analyze these events and arrive at some kind of a measure of public acceptability. Most engineers and framers of anti-seismic laws would say that their aim was to bring the risks well within this limit at the least possible cost. A world without risks of any kind is an unattainable ideal.

During an earthquake, a building behaves like a crude kind of seismograph, responding to the incoming waves in accordance with its natural period and damping. The design of a seismograph is purposely kept simple, so that its behaviour can easily be calculated, but most buildings are rather complicated structures. The different parts may have different resonances, and different degrees of internal damping and friction, and these may vary with the amplitude of the imposed vibration. Analyzing the different components of the response is not an easy matter, and finding the characteristics of the incoming waves in a strong earthquake is no less troublesome a problem.

The records of observatory seismographs are of only limited help. They are too sensitive to produce clear records of near earthquakes unless they are very small, and they have the additional disadvantage that the speed of the recording paper is usually insufficient to open out the shape of the waves, so that the higher frequencies and the details of the wave-form cannot be adequately studied. Special strong-motion instruments have therefore to be used. They do not operate continuously, but have a trigger that starts the recording paper moving whenever there is a fairly strong earthquake. It can therefore move at high speed without using awkwardly large and expensive quantitites of paper. The first second or so of the record is lost while the paper gets up speed, but this is not usually the destructive part of the earthquake.

The small number of good strong-motion records available for study is still a matter for concern. We do not know where and when a large shock will happen, and it is difficult to lay a trap for one. In California and Japan the owners of large buildings are now compelled to install strong-motion seismographs, and in New Zealand, the Department of Scientific and Industrial Research has

*Plate 49: Framed masonry panels. The reinforced-concrete frame of this exhibition building at Skoplje saved it from collapse, but the brick infilled wall shows the typical X-pattern cracks resulting from shear.*

*Plate 50: Unreinforced brick. The first storey of this brick apartment building in Skoplje failed and collapsed, leaving the upper floors comparatively intact.*

Plate 51: *Complete collapse was common in the Andean townships affected by the Chimbote earthquake in Peru in 1970. Streets filled with rubble add to the difficulty of rescue operations.*

Plate 52: *Look both ways. This light tropical structure walled with mats has a relatively heavy roof. The end walls are probably stiff enough to resist a thrust at right angles to the page, but some kind of bracing was obviously needed on the mat-covered sides.*

spread a network of instruments across the country, and the Ministry of Works has built strain-gauges and other measuring devices into a number of its larger engineering structures. In spite of efforts like this in many parts of the world, no one has yet obtained a good record within the zone of maximum intensity for a magnitude eight shock.

The reinforced concrete or steel-framed building, which is typical of most of the larger constructions today, possesses both strength and flexibility; and although there may be superficial damage to partitions and curtain walls, they can be expected to remain substantially sound after even a large earthquake. In fairness to architects and builders, attention should be drawn to the fact that the great majority of well-designed modern buildings will survive all but the largest shocks, but much more attention needs to be paid to the problems of secondary damage and fire.

There is more to making a building earthquake resistant than constructing it of suitable materials and seeing that there are no loose bits to fall off, though small buildings and private houses can usually be made safe by applying simple rules-of-thumb embodied in local by-laws. The design of skyscrapers, factories, bridges, refineries, dams and the like calls for a more elaborate procedure.

*Plate 53: Traditional and modern. Two lessons from New Guinea. The foundations of the native building are without bracing, while the wall of the concrete block store had no reinforcing.*

*Plate 54: Lateral movement of the decking broke these bridge piers at Lianoning.*

*Plate 55: Poor bracing. The light unbraced foundations of this San Fernando building were inadequate to resist the sideways forces of the mass above.*

*Plate 56: Frame distortion. Poor bracing and a heavy roof caused the distortion of this San Fernando home.*

One of the earliest approaches was to lay down some definite horizontal acceleration that the building must be designed to withstand. This had the advantage that the engineer could use the design techniques he was accustomed to use when considering wind loadings, and could often combine the wind and the seismic factors and handle them together. The value of the acceleration adopted was usually about a tenth of the acceleration due to gravity. Experience has shown that normal buildings designed in this way perform quite well in most earthquakes, in spite of the fact that strong motion seismographs show the actual accelerations developed in even moderately damaging shocks to be much greater.

*Plate 57: Wooden houses. Wooden frame houses are good earthquake risks, provided they are built on an adequate foundation. Ground subsidence at Anchorage during the Alaskan earthquake in 1964 tilted this building without causing serious structural damage.*

*Plate 58: Fires follow earthquakes. After the 1931 earthquake, fire soon gained hold on the business centre of Napier. Very many large earthquakes have been followed by fire.*

*Plate 59: Rival neighbours. The differing periods of these two buildings at Niigata made them respond to the earthquake with different kinds of motion, so the stronger battered the weaker.*

*Plate 60: A building vibrator. The vibrator of the University of Auckland's School of Engineering attached to the parapet of a building. The two outer wheels revolve in the opposite direction from the centre one. A range of different weights can be bolted to them eccentrically.*

The reason for the discrepancy seems to be that the maximum accelerations developed are associated with periods that are shorter than those of most buildings, and are not characteristic of the whole duration of strong shaking. With the help of the information now being gathered the engineer can begin his calculations with a 'design spectrum' that specifies the strength of the building at certain definite frequencies.

Where the earthquake risk is believed to vary in different parts of a country, the code may contain zoning provisions varying the resistance required. In New Zealand the acceleration specified varies from 0·08 to 0·16 times that due to gravity.

In Japan, a more elaborate method is used. The country is divided into three regions, in which values of 0·2, 0·15, and 0·1$g$ respectively are taken as standard. These regional values are then multiplied by a factor varying from 0·5 to 1·5 which depends upon the building and upon the type of subsoil on which it is to stand. This type of code is gradually being replaced by a more elaborate consideration of the dynamic characteristics of the building, particularly in the case of tall or otherwise unusual structures.

Analysis of a design must establish not only that the building is strong enough to resist foreseeable earthquake forces, but that the movements during the shock are not excessive and alarming to the occupants. In the case of tall tower-like buildings the displacements can be very large before there is any chance of structural damage, but the truth of this statement will not necessarily be obvious to someone caught twenty storeys above the ground during an earthquake. Apart from this, the contents of the building may be thrown about, blocking stairs and exits.

The general availability of electronic computers has greatly changed the approach to practical design, and makes it possible to consider structures which would have been out of the question a few years ago, not because the principle on which their design depends was unknown, but because the necessary calculations would have been too laborious to be economic.

What if, in spite of all precautions, there is a shock large enough to cause severe structural damage? The designer has still a measure of control over the part of the structure that will fail first, and it is usually possible to arrange things so that the occupants of the building will be safe, even if the damage is so bad that it will have to pulled down and replaced.

If the movement of a building during an earthquake is to be limited, it must be well damped. Damping devices function by absorbing energy, and a common arrangement is to arrange that certain sections of wall will bear the brunt of the damage. New Zealand engineers have been experimenting with disposable components that can be built into bridges and similar structures. These can be metal links or sections that are intended to be strained and deformed far beyond their elastic limits, or piston devices that use the unwanted energy to force lead through a small aperture. After a severe shock these components can be readily removed and replaced.

It is important to see that the natural period of a building is not too close to the predominant period of earthquake waves. This period can be calculated from the stiffness of the materials and the way in which the weight is distributed, but these can be difficult to estimate, and the addition or removal of internal partitions or the storage of heavy goods can change it markedly. Fortunately it is possible to measure the period of a completed building by recording its vibration in high winds, or by shaking it artificially with a vibrator.

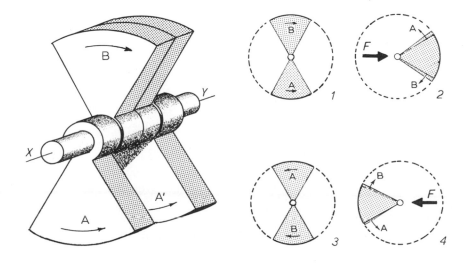

*Fig. 63: A building vibrator. Equal weights revolve in opposite directions. When they are in the vertical position as at 1 and 3 the centrifugal forces cancel out, but in the horizontal positions they act together to produce a horizontal force on the axle X Y, alternately directed to the right as at 2 and to the left as at 4. The gearing to produce the rotation of the weights, the variable speed motor and its controls, and the frame for clamping the vibrator to the building are not shown.*

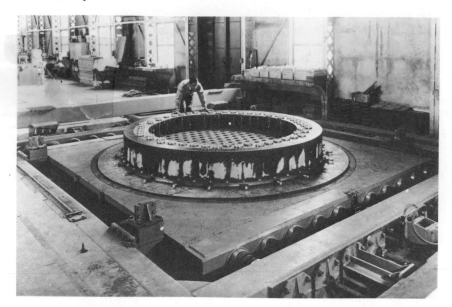

*Plate 61: The large shaking-table at the Building Research Laboratory of the Japanese Ministry of Construction can support a load of 17 tons and shake it with a vertical acceleration equal to that of gravity and a horizontal one twice as great. The period of vibration can be adjusted over the range from about 0.2 to 0.9 seconds. Here it is shown with the bottom section of an atomic reactor in position for testing.*

A building vibrator consists of a set of rotating weights driven by a variable-speed motor and geared to rotate in opposite directions (Figure 63, Plate 60). Each of the weights exerts a centrifugal force upon the axle XY. In positions 1 and 3 the forces pull in opposite directions and cancel out, but in position 2 they combine to pull the axle and the framework that carries it to the right. Half a revolution later, in position 4, the weights are again together, but the pull is now to the left. The machine therefore generates an alternating force $F$ with a frequency that depends upon the speed of the motor. So that the machine will not have a tendency to twist, the weight A is split into two halves, and B revolves in between them. This is much less trying for the gearing and the bearings. There are various ways of connecting the vibrator to the building. The actual size of the weights used depends on how safe it is to shake the building, and how sensitive a recorder is available to measure the vibrations. In America, certain old buildings due for demolition have been turned into vibration laboratories and literally shaken to pieces!

Not all vibration studies have to made on full-size buildings. Sometimes it is sufficient to use a model, or to test only part of the structure. The Japanese Ministry of Construction has a very large shaking-table (Plate 61) which was used to test the components of a nuclear power-station.

Another approach is to use an electrical analogue. An analogue is an electrical circuit in which the values of the components are arranged to give them a response to electrical vibrations that can be compared with the mechanical properties of the building. An ingenious photo-electric device converts the record of an earthquake into a varying electric current that can be passed through the analogue, which is then studied by the techniques of electrical engineering. The results can finally be reinterpreted in mechanical terms that will apply to the real building.

We have already mentioned the importance of the ground on which a building stands. An American study has shown that the intensity on good and bad foundations at the same distance from the epicentre can in exceptional cases amount to as much as four degrees of the modified Mercalli scale. These variations can be studied by examining damaged cities, but only strong-motion records on a variety of foundations will really give the engineer the information he needs. It is certainly a sound practice to build on a rock foundation, and to avoid building different parts of the structure on different kinds of subsoil, such as partly on rock and partly on filling. One of the most unsatisfactory foundations appears to be alluvium – the material brought down by rivers, to build up the floors of their valleys. Japanese results indicate that a foundation of alluvium has the effect of absorbing small earthquakes, but it amplifies the vibrations of the larger ones. Unfortunately, old river terraces make apparently desirable building sites, and many ports have grown up at the mouths of rivers.

The foundation characteristics of a building-site can be directly investigated by boring drill-holes, and in the case of large buildings, this is almost invariably done. It is desirable that the building regulations for a large city should be based on wider knowledge than can be gleaned from a limited number of arbitrarily spaced holes. In Japan, a method of investigating the subsoil by observing 'micro-tremor' has been used. It is found that the character of the continuous background of microseisms and artificial vibrations at a given site depends upon the nature and depth of the unconsolidated material

*Plate 62: Liquefaction of subsoil. The weight of this building at Niigata drove it so far into the loose sandy foundation that the ground storey was almost buried, and the canopy over the entrance door became a vantage point.*

*Plate 63: Sand craters. When shaking compacts loose subsoil, the ground-water is forced out, bringing quantities of fine sand and mud to the surface through craters like these. The upper picture was taken in Charleston, South Carolina, in 1886, and the lower one in Niigata in 1964.*

near the surface. A sample record can be made in a matter of minutes, and it has proved possible to identify three or four main types of subsoil in this way. Large cities like Tokyo, Yokohama and Osaka have been completely mapped.

No building can be much safer that the ground it stands on. When some kinds of clay are shaken they will flow like a liquid, with unfortunate effects upon any buildings on top (Plate 62), and one of the results of the settlement of unconsolidated gravel is to drive out the ground-water, along with quantities of fine sand and mud (Plate 63). Few people expect an earthquake to leave them standing up to the knees in swirling muddy water that seems to have appeared from nowhere (Plate 64). Railways and roads cannot always avoid areas of bad ground of this kind, and bridges and embankments are often the vulnerable points in any network of communications (Plates 65 to 69).

Perhaps the hardest problem that remains in the field of engineering seismology is posed by the existence of old buildings that are valued for their beauty or their associations. Even when expense is a secondary consideration, strengthening measures may destroy the character that makes the building worth preserving. New Zealand

*Plate 64: Ground water. Expulsion of ground water by the 1964 earthquake brought traffic in Niigata to a standstill and drove citizens to the roof-tops.*

*Plate 65: Broken communications. Both road and rail links with Inangahua were severed by the earthquake in 1968. A section of road crossing filled ground has slumped, and the railway tracks have been buckled by the movement of the ballast.*

does not face the problem of whether a York Minster or a Leaning Tower poses an unacceptable seismic hazard to its citizens, but the very absence of ancient buildings in a young country makes us most reluctant to destroy any building of character. Should an ornate Victorian building facing a main thoroughfare be allowed to remain? If the ornamentation is well secured to a sound structure, there is probably no reason why it should not. The problem is often to find out whether this is so without doing damage. The old plans and specifications may no longer exist, and if they do, they are still no guarantee that the workmanship was sound.

With the passage of time even our newest buildings will weaken and the history and sentiment that surrounds the older ones will increase. With the growth of public regard we can also expect a greater willingness to spend money on preservation. Further research should lead to better techniques of strengthening. In the meantime we should not lightly make the decision to destroy all 'potential risks', and before we grant the humanitarian proposition that no building is worth a human life, we should ponder upon the number of fatal accidents that now attend the construction of our dams, railroads, bridges, and major buildings, without giving rise to public outcry.

*Plate 66: Bridge piers. Movement of the piers of the newly-completed Showa Bridge at Niigata caused the decks to collapse. An old stone bridge with wide piers was unharmed.*

*Plate 67: Bridge approach. Even if the decking of the Showa Bridge had not fallen (see Plate 66) getting on to it would have been a problem. The approach has subsided and cracked because of inadequate compaction and failure of the side walls. Note also the sand craters in the foreground.*

*Plate 68: The weakest link. Design of this New Guinea bridge apparently stopped at the abutments. Subsidence of the approach has left a wall across the road.*

*Plate 69: Temporary diversion. Several bridge-spans have collapsed, putting this elaborate traffic fly-over near San Fernando out of action. The earthquake responsible, with a magnitude of 6·8, must be considered only moderately severe.*

*Plate 70: Poor foundations. The fate of these identical apartment buildings at Niigata depended wholly upon their foundations. All were strong enough to resist the shaking, but some have tilted, one is completely overturned, and others are quite unharmed. Note the sand craters in the foreground.*

*Plate 71: Soil creep. This soil cracking and building damage was caused by movement down a comparatively gentle slope during the Liaoning earthquake.*

# 16 Zoning and insurance

TAMBURLAINE: I will confute those blind geographers
That make a triple region in the world
Excluding regions that I mean to trace
And with this pen reduce them to a map.
Marlowe, *Tamburlaine*

Earthquakes are more common in some parts of the world than others, and it is possible to make generalizations about which regions are active and which regions stable. In stable regions, precautions against earthquake are unnecessary; in regions with a history of repeated destructive earthquakes it is equally obvious that something should be done. The enforcement of suitable building codes and insurance against economic loss are two possible counter-measures.

Where there have been earthquakes in the past, there will almost certainly be earthquakes again. Unfortunately, human memory is short, and the earthquakes of even a generation ago are often forgotten. The history of countries like Korea and Japan, which have kept earthquake records for centuries, reveals a further problem. Periods of activity alternate with periods in which there are few or no earthquakes. In countries like New Zealand that have only recently been inhabited, and in those whose inhabitants have only recently become civilized, it is difficult to learn much from history; but once it is known that there are earthquakes, any prudent administration must consider whether its building-laws should contain provisions for anti-seismic design, whether these provisions should be enforced over the whole country or only in part of it, and whether the provisions should vary in stringency from place to place. The division of a country into regions having different anti-seismic building codes is known as seismic zoning.

Seismic zoning is not the same thing as studying seismicity. It may, for example, be quite reasonable to insist upon a higher degree of earthquake resistance for a building that could collapse into a busy city street than for one that is surrounded by open country, even though earthquakes are equally likely in the two places. The degree of shaking experienced is markedly dependent upon the subsoil, and a building erected upon thick gravels needs to be stronger than one on hard bed-rock nearby. Less stringent regulations may be needed for a storage warehouse than for a theatre or cinema that could be crammed with hundreds of people, or for a dam that would flood a populated valley if it were to burst. All of these factors may legitimately influence zoning, but they have nothing to do with seismicity, and the seismologist is rightly indignant when considerations of this kind are represented to be his scientific findings about earthquake risk.

In countries with a long recorded history and a dense population, such as Japan, it is useful to draw maps showing the highest recorded intensity in each town or city. If the region, again like Japan, is a very seismic one, most places that are going to have earthquakes will already have had one, and the map will give a fair estimate of the likely intensity. Maps of this kind indicate the minimum precautions.

The longer the history on which they are based, the better they are likely to be; but it is unwise to trust them in matters of detail. The disastrous earthquake at Niigata in 1964 occurred in a region with a record of lower seismicity than other parts of Japan. It is therefore necessary to supplement the lessons of history with other investigations. Two lines of approach are used – geological mapping, and the instrumental study of the smaller earthquakes.

We have seen that there are many more small earthquakes than big ones, the number of shocks of any particular magnitude being about eight times the number of the magnitude above. By recording the number of small shocks in a limited period we can therefore get a rough idea of how often to expect a large one. Of course the exact relationship between the big shocks and the small ones varies from region to region, but it is wise to assume that where small shocks are frequent, larger ones are possible. How much further it is possible to go is a matter of controversy. In the Soviet Union special expeditions have been sent to several of the Central Asian republics to assess the seismicity. Dr M. V. Gzovsky and his colleagues consider that from their studies in the Tyan Shan, where they recorded earthquakes down to magnitude 2 or less for one or two years, they have been able to produce a reliable evaluation. While active regions can certainly be found in this way, it would be rash to conclude that because no shocks were recorded in so brief a time the region was inactive.

With the very sensitive portable seismographs developed over the last few years it is possible to record and locate even smaller earthquakes than was done in the Tyan Shan. A small network of stations can be installed in a district and left for a few days or a week until a reasonable number of shocks has been observed, and then moved on until a whole region has been covered. These so-called *micro-earthquake studies* have now been carried out in both North and South America and in New Zealand, and have thrown light on a number of tectonic problems. They can, for example, establish what parts of a fault zone are at present active and where the fault is locked, but there are obvious dangers in using these short-term studies to predict long-term trends.

Many kinds of geological observation are of value for seismic zoning purposes. If one part of a geological unit is seismically active, it is reasonable to assume that the rest of it shares the same risk. We have seen that a close relationship exists between large earthquakes and geological faulting, and precautions are obviously necessary in any region where conspicuously active faults have been mapped. Few earthquakes have been recorded along the central portion of New Zealand's Alpine Fault, and on parts of the San Andreas Fault in California, but no seismologist would suggest that we should relax precautions in those areas because they have been inactive in recent times.

Soviet scientists have been very active in the field of what they call *seismic regionalization*. This is rather more than simple zoning. It involves a most careful synthesis of all the lines of seismological and geological argument. Data are frequently collected by special large expeditions like the one already mentioned, and historical documents are searched for accounts of past earthquakes. Soviet geologists place much less emphasis upon faulting than most Americans or New Zealanders would do, concentrating instead upon the identification of zones with contrasting geological history, particularly where vertical movements are involved, and regarding the regions of transition from one zone to another with suspicion. In the parts of the world with which they are concerned, these are more often marked by 'flexures' than by great faults of the type that is familiar around the Pacific.

Faulting is not the only geological evidence of past earthquakes. Many shocks are accompanied by uplift, subsidence, or tilting of large tracts of land. This can be inferred from changes in shore-lines and beach terraces, by the position of wave-cut platforms in relation to the present water-level, and from geomorphological features, such as small streams in which the rate of down-cutting has suddenly increased. Extensive areas of landslide may be explicable only on the assumption that there has been a large earthquake, and so on.

Important as this evidence is, it is essential to stress that it is admissable only for the purpose of *extending* the zones arrived at by direct consideration of the positions of the known earthquakes and of the distance to which the effects of a large earthquake can extend. The absence of a fault, or of any other geological feature, does not establish that there have been no earthquakes; and the fact that only small shocks have been experienced in the past does not establish that this is the upper limit of their possible size.

No part of New Zealand is far from a known earthquake origin, and until recently a uniform code of anti-seismic building laws was recommended for the whole country. In spite of strong representations from seismologists, a new code has been introduced, which slightly increases the requirements in some areas, but reduces them in others that include two of our largest cities, one of which has since suffered minor damage from a shallow magnitude 5 shock almost directly beneath it.

National zoning schemes, at least in a free enterprise economy, usually concern themselves only with the question of public safety. It should be possible for the citizen to emerge alive (and preferably uninjured) from a damaged building. The man with a large capital investment in property may look at the matter rather differently. Even if his building is still structurally sound, it could cost him a great deal to repair and repaint cracked plaster and the like. He will probably look for insurance cover. It is in this context, rather than in that of zoning, that studies of earthquake frequency are important. The infrequent earthquake is as destructive as the frequent one, and failure to plan for it cannot be excused by telling injured men whose city lies in ruins, 'I didn't say that this wouldn't happen – only that it wouldn't happen often'. A degree of earthquake resistance sufficient to protect life is the minimum acceptable standard for any building in a seismic area. Whether it is cheaper to pay higher insurance or to strengthen the plaster may reasonably be left to the owner.

Geological fault-lines are not narrow zones of exceptional earthquake risk. A structure that actually crossed a fault would naturally be in danger if the two sides of the fault were to move but few buildings are in this position. Ground movement close to faults that have moved appear to be simple displacements rather than wave-motions, which become predominant only at some distance away. A building on solid rock near a fault is more likely to be safe than one on a poor foundation a kilometre or more from it. If there is a zone of crushed or broken rock at the fault, it would be unwise to build on it, but this is because of its fractured nature and not because of its nearness to the fault. So firmly does the public believe in the potency of faults that seismologists are more asked for a 'map of the faults' than for the information about earthquake risks that the inquirer really needs. The whole of a country like New Zealand is intensively faulted, but in many cases the age of the fault is very difficult to determine. The geologist knows that a fault must be younger than the youngest rock it cuts, and is consequently able to classify a number of them as 'Recent'. But Recent, to the geologist, may mean any time in the last twenty-five thousand years, and the fault may have no intention of moving again. The only certain proof that a fault is active is the knowledge that someone has seen it move. Earthquakes have sometimes resulted in a hurried re-classification of faults. The White Creek Fault, which moved in the Murchison earthquake in 1929 was previously though to be 'dead'. If an inquirer really does want to know about faults, he should be referred to a geologist. Geologists asked for information about earthquake risks should see that the questioner talks to a seismologist.

There is widespread belief that certain people live 'on the earthquake line', where shocks are more strongly felt than they are in neighbouring places. The announcement is often made with a kind of pride, and as far as I can gather, the 'line' is pictured as a kind of wriggly snake stretching its erratic and sinister length across the countryside. Many towns have localities which are reputed to lie on it. In Wellington, at least, the places I have heard so described are in the older parts of the city, where the buildings are undoubtedly more shaky. Certainly, not all parts of a city will feel an earthquake with equal intensity, but the reasons are related to the differences in foundation, and the 'earthquake line' is a pure fiction.

There may be room for argument about the appropriate degree of strengthening needed to make a building earthquake resistant, but if the existing level is adequate, there is as little excuse for raising it in some centres as there is for lowering it in others. Insistence that earthquakes are necessarily less frequent and less severe in areas that are without known active faulting can only be described as irresponsible. The unhappy coincidence of this view with lay misconceptions about faults diverts attention from the implications of the earthquakes that lie beyond the boundaries of the area of Recent transcurrent faulting, and from the fact that we are almost totally ignorant of the submarine geology off the shores of our long and narrow country.

In many parts of the world, zoning ensures that protection is given to people who would otherwise be without it. In New Zealand it must result either in the people within the supposed zones of lower risk being denied it, or in those in the high-risk zones being put to unnecessary expense.

Increasing attention is being given to the small-scale variations that result from the differing foundation conditions to be found within a single zone of earthquake risk. Measurements made in large earthquakes have established that the intensities reached on poorly consolidated ground may be several degrees higher than those on solid rock nearby. The assessment of these variations within the primary zoning scheme is known as *microzoning*.

Microzoning is usually based on the results of several different kinds of survey, because of the practical difficulties that face most techniques in a busy built-up area. Gravity surveys can be used to follow changes in the depth of the bedrock beneath alluvium and artificial fill. Direct geological surveys are possible to some extent, and samples of soil and rock from the exploratory drill-holes on building sites can be examined in the laboratory. In addition, portable seismographs can be used to record the frequency and amplitude of the microtremor. This is usually of artificial origin, but the response of the soil to artificial vibrations is an indication of its probable behaviour in natural earthquakes. The tremor shows sharp changes in character when the recording point is moved from one type of foundation to another. When all the available information has been pooled, a map can be drawn to show the troublesome areas. Microzoning studies have now been made in a number of Japanese and New Zealand cities, and in parts of California. The results of the different methods used are in good agreement.

Seismic zoning problems are linked to the problem of earthquake insurance, but the zones established for insurance and for building purposes should not necessarily be identical. Structural problems arise almost entirely from the larger earthquakes, but the total of the insurance claims that arise from damage to goods and to non-structural fittings in small shocks may be very great. The frequency of occurrence of the smaller shocks, and the relative numbers of shocks of different magnitude therefore become important. A further difficulty is that people in regions of low seismicity are unlikely to seek earthquake insurance, so that unless it is linked to some other risk such as fire the risks cannot be properly spread and premiums become high, perhaps unrealistically so.

The insurance scheme operated by the New Zealand Earthquake and War Damage Commission was started by the government after the Masterton earthquakes of 1942, and provides compensation to owners for damage resulting from earthquake, enemy attack, and certain other natural calamities. It is funded by a small compulsory surcharge added to the premiums for fire insurance, including the insurance of motor cars. When a property is mortgaged, half the surcharge can be recovered from the mortgagee.

By New Zealand standards, the sums involved are large. In a quiet year, the amount paid out for damage in minor shocks totals only a few thousand dollars, but a shock of magnitude 5 is sufficient to send the payments up by tenfold. Since the fund was established, the largest shock has been the magnitude 7 Inangahua earthquake in 1968. Although most of the townships affected were not large, and were some distance from the epicentre, payments rose to over two million New Zealand dollars.

The weaknesses of the scheme have been the difficulty of arranging re-insurance outside the country, the fact that public opinion and state intervention has forced relief payments to people carrying no insurance, or in some cases when the seismic origin of the damage was open to question. There is continued pressure from rural interests to have the fund cover damage from flooding, landslide, and similar misfortunes that have often been aggravated by their own commercial activities.

Insurance is not a method by which payment for damage can be avoided; it merely spreads the payments in time and place. The Earthquake and War Damage Commission therefore devotes some of its resources to encouraging improved standards of building, and generously aids the New Zealand National Society for Earthquake Engineering with grants for publication and research. It is interesting that payments from the fund have gone to all parts of the country from the extreme north to Stewart Island. This lends support to the seismologists' view that New Zealand should be treated as a single zone of substantially uniform earthquake risk.

# 17 Earthquakes and the bomb

... they contend not about matter of fact, nor can determine their controversies by any certaine witnesses, nor judges. But as long as they goe towards peace, that is Truth, it is no matter which way.

John Donne, *Biathanatos*

The use of explosions for seismic prospecting has been so successful that the observatory seismologist has sometimes been a little envious of his colleague in the field. The use of natural earthquake records for investigating the internal structure of the Earth is limited by uncertanties in the time and place and the depth of the shock. Controlled explosions need have none of these disadvantages, but a great deal of explosive is needed to generate elastic waves as well as an earthquake can. Until the last war, most big explosions were accidental, and although the place was known, the time was not, and no special recording arrangements could be made. As soon as the war was over, seismologists in many countries succeeded in persuading the military authorities to make surplus ammunition available for crustal-structure studies, or at least to explode it in such a way that the records would be of scientific value. For example, the seismologists of Europe cooperated in recording the great explosion at Haslach, in Germany, and on the island of Heligoland. In New Zealand, tons of naval depth-charges were exploded together in Wellington harbour, and recorded at mobile stations up to 150 kilometres away. All this was very gratifying, but the fortunes of war threw up a seismological tool of even greater potency – the atomic bomb. The pity is that soldiers and politicians consider (on grounds that are at least questionable) that they are better able than seismologists to decide how it should be used.

From the very beginning, seismograph records of atomic bomb explosions were made, but the first few were of limited value. At the first test in New Mexico, no proper record was made of the shot-instant, because of the 'somewhat confused and emotional circumstances'. Similar considerations no doubt obtained at Hiroshima and Nagasaki. The Bikini test was a different matter. Satisfactory records were obtained as far away as in California, and Gutenberg and Richter were able to estimate its magnitude.

About the time of the International Geophysical Year, Professor K. E. Bullen was leading an international agitation to have a number of bombs specially exploded for crustal structure and upper mantle studies. Those proposals proved politically unacceptable, but since then a number of nuclear tests have been studied in some detail, including the British test at Maralinga, in Australia, and most of the American ones. The Maralinga test was of particular value, as the region is without natural earthquakes, and it looked as if the crust of a major continent was likely to remain unexplored for a long time. Meanwhile, Professor Bullen was collecting routine recordings of nuclear explosions made at ordinary seismological observatories, and was able to use them both for the revision of the standard travel-time tables, and to convince the military authorities that there were certain facts they could not hope to keep secret. Since then, shot-

instants and other information necessary for seismological studies have been more readily made available.

Important as this work was, it was soon to become secondary to the problem of nuclear test detection. Agreement to ban nuclear explosions in the atmosphere had been reached, and it seemed likely that underground tests would be banned as well, if only it were possible to detect infringements. Explosions in the atmosphere are easy to detect – and so too, in fact, are underground ones. The difficulty is that the underground ones are almost, if not completely, indistinguishable from earthquakes (Figure 64). If agreement on a test-ban is to be reached, the problem will have to be solved. If it is, the only people to regret it will be the seismologists! Meanwhile, government money for earthquake research has become available to an unprecedented extent, and it is extraordinary how many fundamental seismological problems are now said to be closely bound up with the detection of underground nuclear explosions.

Although the detection of underground nuclear explosions was technically possible, the existing seismograph stations in many parts of the world were too thinly spaced, and had only obsolete equipment.

A committee of American seismologists pointed out that many more good stations would be needed if clandestine tests were to be adequately policed, and that if the characteristics distinguishing bombs from explosions lay in the finer details of the records, it would be desirable for all the recording stations to have identical equipment. If this ideal was to be reached, the instruments would have to come from the same factory, and stations in many different countries would have to be persuaded to install them. As most of the stations would not want to replace their existing equipment, the only possible method of persuasion would be to give them instruments for nothing. This the United States government generously decided to

*Fig. 64: Which is the bomb? The upper seismogram is of a nuclear explosion 180 km from the recording station at Tinemaha. The lower one is that of a natural earthquake 181 km away, in almost the same direction. The distance between the test site and the epicentre was 43 km. (After Press and Archambeau.)*

do, and there is now a World Network of about 120 Standard Seismograph Stations. Each has two sets of three-component instruments, Benioffs for the short periods, and Press-Ewing seismometers for the long. The equipment also includes an accurate electronic clock and a radio receiver for uniform timing, instruments for calibration, and for copying photographic records. Stations retain their own records if they wish, but the United States Geological Survey maintains a central archive from which copies of any record from any station can be obtained for a few cents. The only large parts of the Earth now without standard stations are Canada (except for one in the far north), China, and the Soviet Union, but part of a standard set is being operated in Moscow. New Zealand controls four standard stations.

We have seen in a previous chapter that the upper limit to the useful magnification of a seismograph is set by the background of microseisms. These are a little less troublesome below the surface, and several recently-developed seismometers are small enough to be lowered to the bottom of drill-holes a hundred metres deep.

There is another way in which we can counteract the effect of microseisms, by combining the outputs from seismometers a short distance apart. The records of a distant earthquake made at two places a kilometre or so apart are very much alike, except for a small difference in arrival time, depending upon the direction from which the earthquake waves are coming. The background of artificial disturbances at the two stations, however, is likely to be different, and in most cases, the microseisms will not be coming from the same direction as the earthquake. If we displace one of the records slightly to allow for the time-difference, we can superimpose the earthquake records, but not the unwanted background. By spacing out many seismometers in a regular pattern, known as an 'array', and combining the outputs electrically after introducing suitable time-delays, it is possible to construct an instrument that will detect very small earthquakes (or bombs) at great distances. The output of each seismometer in the array is usually recorded separately on magnetic tape, and can be played back through a variety of amplifiers and filters before or after combination with other records. Electronic computers automatically determine the appropriate time-delays to be introduced, and what combination will give the seismologist the information he wants about any particular event. Array seismographs are a powerful aid to research of many different kinds.

In 1962, the United Kingdom Atomic Energy Authority set up an array of twenty seismometers at Eskdalemuir, in Scotland. They are mounted on concrete foundations in shallow pits evenly spaced along two lines at right angles, each about eight kilometres long. The signals are fed to a central laboratory near the intersection of the two lines, and recorded upon magnetic tape. They can be converted into conventional paper records, or subjected to electrical filtering and intercomparison in many different ways. The whole array has been calibrated by exploding naval depth-charges in the North Sea and the Irish Sea.

A number of similar arrays, using different layout patterns, is being operated in the United States. A still more impressive installation at Billings, Montana, best described as an array of arrays, is spread over an area about a hundred and fifty kilometres square. The site of the Large Aperture Seismic Array, as it is officially called, was chosen because of its distance from sea coasts and from human activity, and for its geological uniformity. Altogether there are 525 seismometers grouped into twenty-one clusters known as 'sub-arrays'. Each sub-array consists of twenty-five instruments, disposed along six radii of a circle 7 kilometres across (Figure 65, Plate 72). In order to reduce background noise still further, the seismometers are placed at the bottom of drill-holes 120 millimetres in diameter, lined with metal pipe and set in concrete. Most of the holes are 65 metres deep, but the centre one in each array is slightly larger and goes down 170 metres (Figure 66).

The signals from the separate seismometers in each sub-array are fed to an underground vault where they are amplified and electrically transformed into a suitable form for transmission by micro-wave radio link to the data-centre at Billings, some 200km away. At Billings two electronic computers compare and record the signals from the seismometers and make periodical checks and calibrations of the seismometers and their associated electrical equipment (Plate 73).

*Fig. 65: A seismic array. At the top left is a plan of the great seismic array in Montana. Each of the dots represents a cluster of seismographs laid out in the pattern shown on a larger scale at the right. The cross-section at the bottom shows the central seismometer at a depth of 170 metres, and the four shallower instruments along the same radius of the pattern at a depth of 65 metres.*

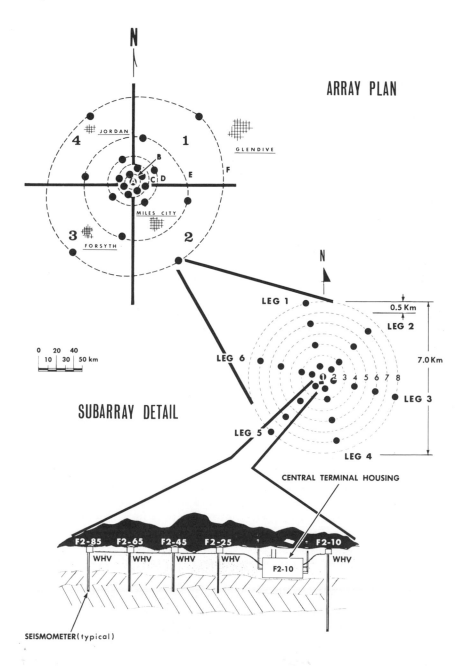

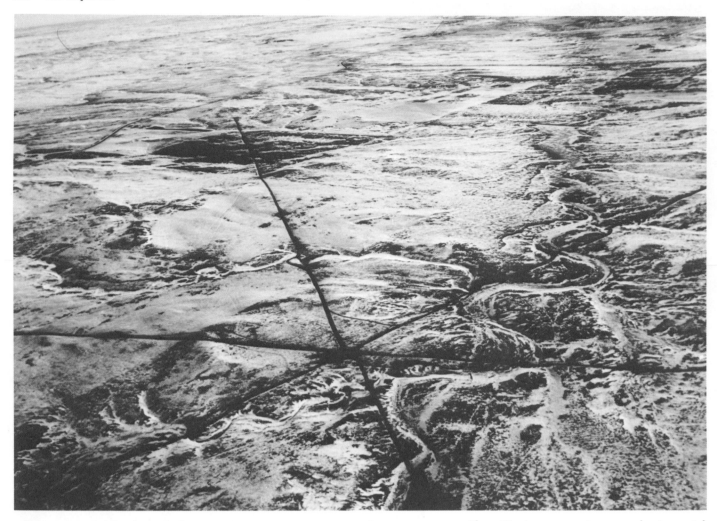

*Plate 72: An array seismograph. An aerial view of one of the twenty-one sub-arrays that make up the Large Aperture Seismic Array in south-eastern Montana, U.S.A.*

The cost of this gigantic instrument was over seven and a quarter million dollars, one million of which was spent on the computers and other equipment in the data-centre, over one and a quarter million on the drill-holes, half a million on seismometers and amplifiers, and the rest on buildings, radio links, land-lines, and fencing. The data-centre has a staff of seventeen, only one of whom is a seismologist. Another fifteen men are needed for routine maintenance of the array.

When we have recorded a suspicious event, whether by using an array, or at a conventional station, how are we to know whether it is a bomb or not? Figure 65 shows how similar earthquake and explosion records can be when the earthquake and the bomb are at almost the same distance from the recording station. The more obvious characteristics of the records seem to result from the ground structure, rather than from the mechanism responsible. It is possible that accurate depth measurements could help us. If the origin of the shock was more than a few kilometres deep, it must certainly have been an earthquake. But good depth measurements are not easy, and in order to make them we need records from places very close to the origin. In the event of a clandestine test, we are not likely to have them.

It was at first thought that observations of the direction of the initial movements on the seismograms would give a very simple method of distinguishing between bombs and earthquakes. We saw that an earthquake due to elastic rebound should give rise to a pattern of compressions and dilatations in alternate quadrants. In an explosion, it was argued, the pattern should be much simpler. All the ground particles near the source move outwards and nothing but compressions should result. It was also suggested that because the mechanism was all compressional there should be few S-waves or none at all.

*Fig. 66: A bore-hole seismometer. This is the arrangement used for each of the separate seismographs that make up the Montana array. The casing of each borehole ends in a 'well-head vault' consisting of a section cut from an ordinary 200-litre oil-drum, covered with a metal 'coolie hat' to keep out the rain. The vault contains an amplifier and the end of the land-line that feeds the signal to the centre of the sub-array. The stand at the bottom of the hole is a help in getting the seismometer into a vertical position.*

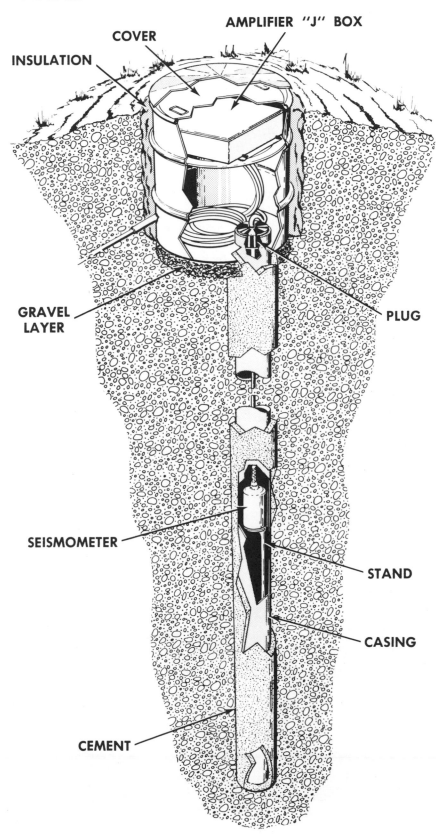

This is certainly not so. Even when conditions near the source are very uniform some shearing is inevitable, and shear strains already present in the surrounding rock can be released. Most records of atomic explosions therefore show significant S-phases, though small prospecting explosions sometimes do not. At present the most readily detectable difference between bombs and earthquakes seems to lie in the proportion of body waves to surface waves; that is, there is a difference in the magnitudes determined from the different phases. Taking all the methods now available together, it seems that the number of doubtful cases can be made small enough to make a ban on underground testing politically practicable, and at the time of writing new discussions on the subject have been announced.

Many members of the public are concerned that underground testing may increase the number of natural earthquakes taking place. Indeed, some of them accuse seismologists of concealing the 'fact' that such an increase followed the French tests in the atmosphere at Mururoa Atoll. For their part, seismologists have not attributed any significance to the fact that the period of the tests was one of less than normal seismic activity in the south-west Pacific.

The possibility that a large explosion could trigger an earthquake is not entirely without substance, but only in an area in which an earthquake would in any case occur. If the regional strain were already very close to causing elastic failure, the arrival of large elastic waves from an explosion might be enough to carry the rocks beyond their breaking strain and initiate rebound, but an event of this kind would only be possible when a natural shock was imminent. The bomb could determine *when* it occurred, but not *whether* it did.

We can be reasonably sure that if triggering of this kind is possible it does not extend to any great distance from the source. A 5 kiloton bomb radiates roughly the same energy as a magnitude 5 earthquake. If a bomb of this size could trigger earthquakes, we should expect the waves from the several hundred natural shocks of magnitude 5 that take place every year to set off further shocks, and the really large earthquakes to have spectacular repercussions in distant places. In brief, they don't. There are many highly creditable reasons for opposing atomic testing, but this is not one of them.

*Plate 73: Data centre. Inside the data centre at Billings, Montana, where the signals from the 525 seismographs that compose the Large Aperture Seismic Array are electronically correlated and recorded.*

# 18 Out of this world

OTHELLO: It is the very error of the Moon;
        She comes more near the Earth than she was wont.
                      Shakespeare, *Othello*

*Fig. 67: Lunar seismograph stations and moonquakes. This sketch map shows the positions of the seismographs that are or have been operating on the moon and the epicentres of some of the moonquakes they have detected. By terrestrial standards 'normal' moonquakes are very deep indeed.*

Geophysicists studying the basic structure and tectonics of our planet have been known to complain that there is only one Earth. It is very difficult to know whether the things you have discovered are terrestrial accidents, or true of planets in general and therefore of prime importance. Since November 1969 when an American Apollo space mission successfully placed a seismograph on the Moon the situation has become a little better. There are now five stations operating (Figure 67, Plate 74).

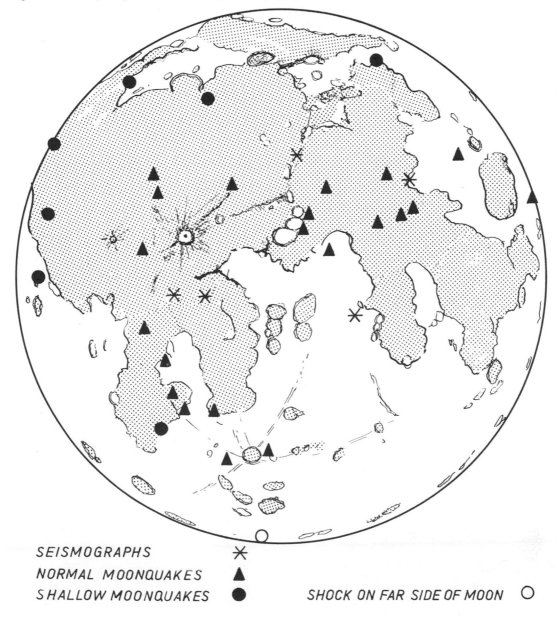

SEISMOGRAPHS                  ✳

NORMAL MOONQUAKES     ▲

SHALLOW MOONQUAKES    ●         SHOCK ON FAR SIDE OF MOON  ○

Before the first instrument was landed, seismological opinion about the existence of moonquakes (or *selenoseisms* if you insist upon a word in the classical tradition) was divided, but it was readily agreed that a seismograph on the Moon would yield a great deal of needed information. The impact of meteorites could probably be recorded, it would certainly be possible to record the impact of landing spacecraft, and if all else failed explosive charges could be detonated. In one way or another, knowledge of the Moon's interior would be forthcoming.

The first problem was to develop a seismometer that could withstand the shock of an unmanned landing. Seismologists took to dropping seismographs out of helicopters and even to firing them like circus artists from small cannon. Unfortunately the first attempts to land an instrument failed, and even when there was an astronaut on the spot the recordings looked so strange that he was accused of stumbling over something, but in the end things sorted themselves out.

There are interesting differences between earthquakes and moonquakes, and the internal structure and the wave-transmitting properties of the Moon have turned out to be rather different from those we expected. Compared with the Earth, the Moon is seismically quiet. Nearly all the shocks are very small. Over a year the total energy they release is barely sufficient to make a shock much bigger than magnitude 2, but they are fairly numerous and the recording stations are sensitive enough to pick up between 600 and 2 000 shocks a year, depending on the site. This does not include the very small 'thermal moonquakes' that accompany the abrupt temperature change at lunar sunrise and sunset. These tiny shocks seem to be the result of small-scale cracking and slumping of the surface.

Three larger kinds of disturbance are picked up. First there are the impacts of falling meteorites, though it has turned out that there are not nearly so many big ones as terrestrial meteor observations had suggested. Next there are the normal moonquakes, which turn out to originate at depths between 600 and 900 kilometres, and could not be regarded as 'normal' on Earth. These seem to come from a limited number of foci, perhaps fewer than fifty. The seismograms of different shocks from the same focus are almost identical with one another, and each focus seems to become active at some definite time of the month. Tidal forces apparently account for this. There are peaks of activity 14 days apart, and secondary peaks at intervals of 206 days, which would coincide with the Sun's contribution to the tidal forces.

The last type of moonquake is very shallow, and may result like terrestrial earthquakes from the release of crustal stress. So far only about a dozen of these have been observed, and there is no obvious pattern in their positions or times of occurrence (Figure 67).

Lunar seismograms are very different in appearance from those of earthquakes (Figure 68). The movements are much higher in frequency, and reverberations continue for a very long time. It is hard to pick out definite phases, and there are no clear surface-waves. The very dry condition of the rocks on the lunar surface is thought to be responsible, but we still have much to learn about wave propagation on the Moon.

The interior of the Moon, like that of the Earth, has three main divisions, but their properties are rather different. By using the records of artificial shocks, meteorite impacts, and the larger moonquakes, it has been possible to build up a travel-time curve for

P-waves for distances up to about 1 000km. The phases *PP* and *PPP* have also been identified (Figure 69).

Compared with the Earth's, the Moon's layers are comparatively irregular, and contain large inhomogeneities. The crust is about 60 kilometres thick, and within it the average *P*-velocity is about 6·7 km/sec. Higher velocities can be found not only in the basalts that form the floors of the great lunar seas (the *maria* as they are called), but also at the base of the crust where they may in some places amount to a kind of high-velocity layer. Below the crust the velocity rises to 8 km/sec., and remains fairly uniform to the base of the mantle, which extends to a depth of about 700 kilometres.

The core is not at all closely analogous to that of the Earth. Astronomical measurements have shown that the Moon's mean density is only 3·3, so that no great quantity of metal could exist. The lunar core does not seem to transmit *S*-waves, or at least does not transmit them well, but it appears to be solid, and the explanation seems to lie in its lack of strength. It might therefore be appropriate to describe it as a lunar asthenosphere, and the mantle above it as the lithosphere. Conditions at the boundary are complicated, and it may be far from smooth.

These lunar studies provide a first glimpse of the contributions that seismology can make to planetary astronomy. By the time this book

*Fig. 68: Moonquakes. Seismograms of normal and shallow moonquakes and of a meteorite impact. The two upper traces in each case are from long-period horizontal component seismographs, and the lower ones from long- and short-period verticals. Note the gradual build-up and slow decay of the vibrations. (After Nakamura et al.)*

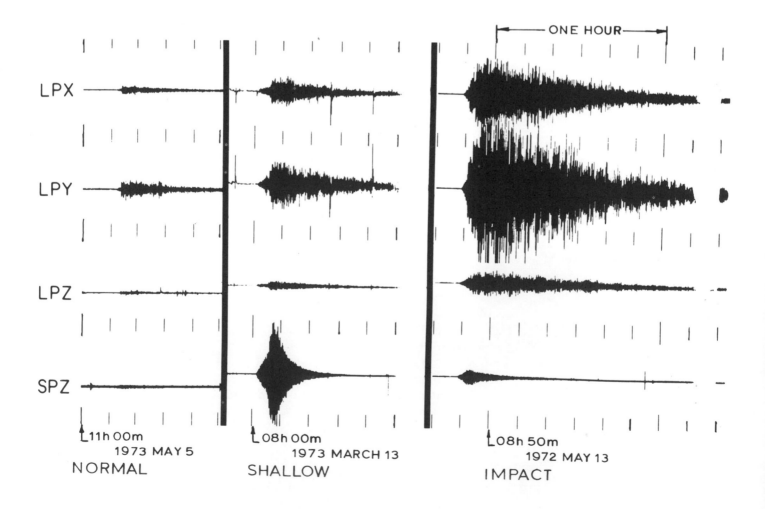

ONE HOUR

LPX

LPY

LPZ

SPZ

11h 00m
1973 MAY 5
NORMAL

08h 00m
1973 MARCH 13
SHALLOW

08h 50m
1972 MAY 13
IMPACT

is in print it seems likely that the two Viking missions will have landed seismographs on Mars. Getting their information back to Earth will be more difficult technically than getting it back from the Moon, but it is believed that the problems have been solved. Each of the stations will have a life-time of only 90 days, and the two of them will be running together for only half of that time. What we already know about Mars suggests that the structure and tectonics will be more Earth-like than those of the Moon, and it should not be long before marsquakes (*areoseisms*?) join the earthquakes and the moonquakes as subjects for seismological concern.

In November 1976 a seismometer placed on the Plains of Utopia by the Viking space-craft recorded what appears to be a shock of about magnitude 6.

*Fig. 69: Internal structure of the Moon. A cross-section showing the size of the lunar crust, mantle, and core, and the foci of normal and shallow moonquakes.*

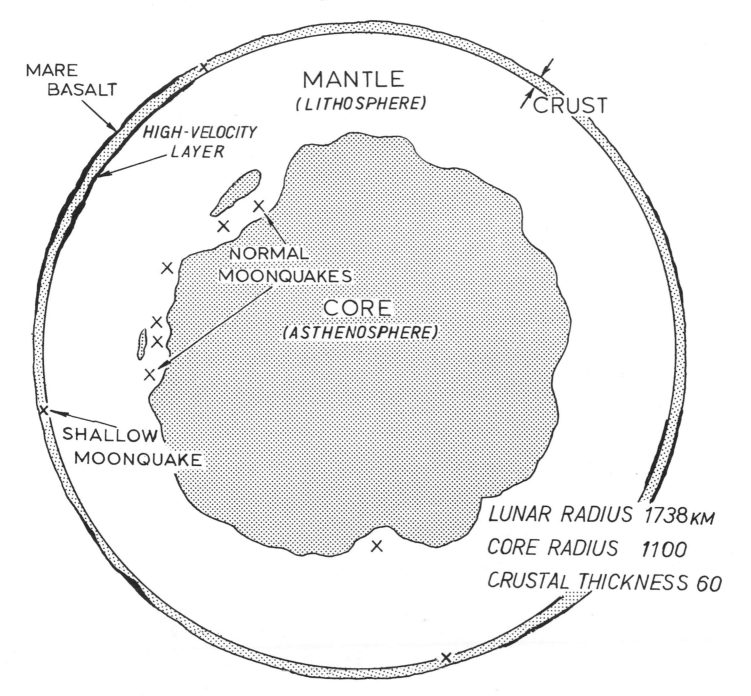

MARE BASALT

MANTLE (LITHOSPHERE)

CRUST

HIGH-VELOCITY LAYER

NORMAL MOONQUAKES

CORE (ASTHENOSPHERE)

SHALLOW MOONQUAKE

LUNAR RADIUS 1738 KM

CORE RADIUS 1100

CRUSTAL THICKNESS 60

# 19 More seismic geography

JACQUES: . . . strange places cramm'd
        With observation . . .
        Shakespeare, *As You Like It*

We have already described the distribution of the world's seismic belts and stable areas, and seen how both the broad pattern and the local character of the activity are explained by the plate-tectonic hypothesis. In most parts of the world I have visited, seismic and otherwise, the active regions best known to the general public seem to be California and Japan, perhaps because the more vigorously active countries are less developed, or because the work of their seismologists is less well publicised. Both these places, like New Zealand, lie on the margin of the Pacific Plate, but in the three cases the nature of the contact with the neighbouring plate is different, and the character of the seismicity differs accordingly. Let us examine it in more detail.

*Plate 75: San Andreas Fault. An aerial view of a section of the San Andreas Fault, showing how the spurs of the hills have been truncated by successive horizontal movements of the fault.*

Of the three, California is the simplest. Here the great San Andreas Fault (Plate 75) marks the contact between the Pacific and the American Plates. Periodical transcurrent movement along this fault (or one of the subsidiary faults related to it) gives rise to shallow earthquakes, but there is no subduction or overthrusting of either plate to produce deep-focus activity. The smaller shocks in particular are often very shallow, and as a consequence are felt only over a small area, even when people at the epicentre feel quite high intensities. Californians feel fewer shocks than New Zealanders, but the ones they do feel are more alarming! The pattern of epicentres (Figure 70) and the pattern of faults (Figure 71) are closely similar, explaining the early readiness of American seismologists to accept the elastic-rebound theory. By comparison, Japan and New Zealand offer complicated problems, but they are far more typical of the Pacific margin as a whole. The basic simplicity of the Californian pattern is not at all usual.

New Zealand's Alpine Fault, which follows the western slopes of the Southern Alps (Plate 76, Figure 76) offers many geological parallels to the San Andreas Fault of California, but its existence could not easily be deduced from maps of New Zealand earthquakes (Figures 72, 73 and 74). Although the level of activity varies, and some parts of the country may experience a temporary quiescence, shallow shocks are experienced in all parts of the two main islands. It

*Fig. 70: Earthquakes in California. This map shows the epicentres of the earthquakes that occurred over a period of about three months. The broken line shows the area within which the shocks could be reliably detected and located.*

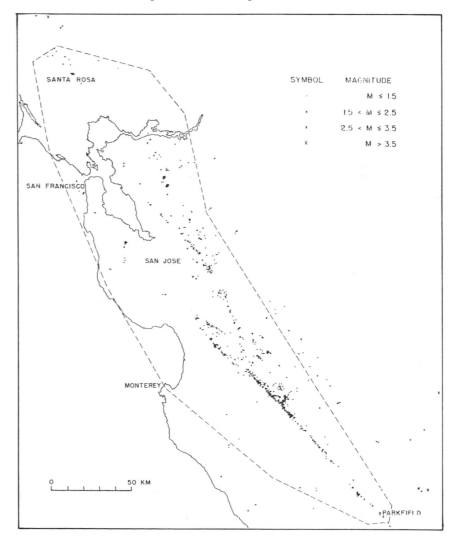

is nevertheless possible to distinguish two important groupings. The shocks of the Main Seismic Region (Figure 76) cover most of the North Island except the Northland Peninsula, and the northern parts of the South Island. Those of the Fiordland (or Southern) Region are concentrated in the south-western part of the South Island. Between the two lies the Central Seismic Region which is by no means inactive, but is less seismic than the other two regions.

There are no deep-focus shocks in the Central Region, but they occur in both the Main and Fiordland Regions. Those of the Main Region lie within a zone that crosses it from the Bay of Plenty to Nelson and Marlborough (Figures 74 and 75). With the exception of a small group of shocks that lie about 600 km below northern Taranaki, the deepest earthquakes are at the northern end of the zone. Going southwards, the maximum depth becomes less in a regular way, until the deep and shallow systems merge. This system of foci, which has sometimes been called the New Zealand Sub-Crustal Rift, is of the kind that many writers call a Benioff Zone, and is now considered by many seismologists to mark the position of the descending edge of the Pacific Plate.

The deep activity in Fiordland is much more tightly grouped than that in the north. The epicentres all lie close to Lake Te Anau, and the focal depths are about 100 or 120 km. These are the southernmost deep shocks to be found on the western side of the Circum-Pacific Belt.

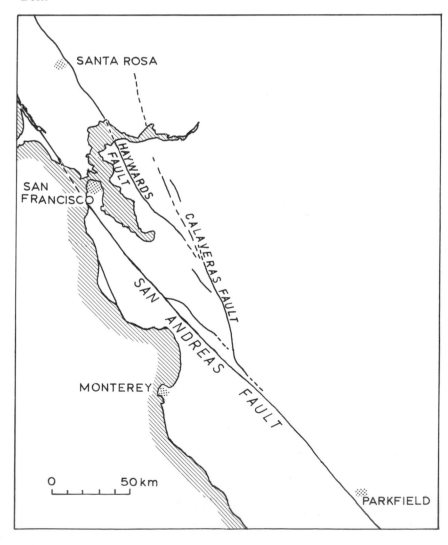

*Fig. 71: Faults in California. Major faults in the area shown in Figure 70. Earthquake activity in California closely follows the pattern of geological faults apparent at the surface.*

*Plate 76: The Alpine Fault, following the western side of the snow-covered Southern Alps in the South Island of New Zealand. This photograph, taken from an orbiting satellite, shows over 150km. of its length from the Grey River to the Franz Josef Glacier. The large lake at the northern end is Lake Brunner, and that at the south Lake Mapourika, with the Okarito and Saltwater Lagoons on the coast to the north of it.*

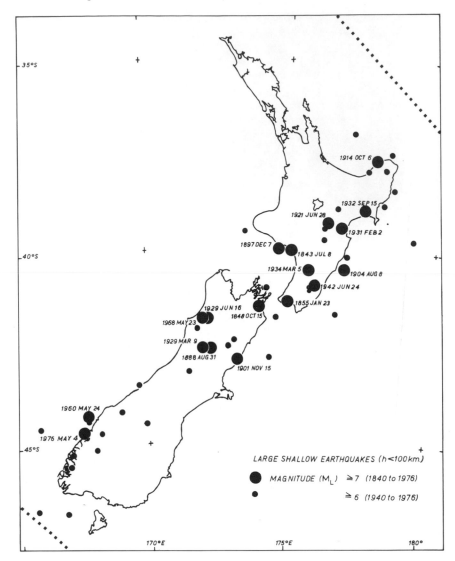

*Fig. 72: Large shallow earthquakes in New Zealand. The south western part of the South Island is very sparsely inhabited. The present distribution of magnitude 6 earthquakes suggests that the historical record of shocks in that part of the country is very incomplete. Magnitudes of shocks before 1929 have been estimated by comparing their felt effects with those of instrumentally recorded shocks.*

Considering the configuration of the earthquake activity and the position of the other geophysical features of the region (Figure 76), it appears that under the North Island the edge of the Pacific Plate is being thrust or pulled beneath the edge of the Indian Plate, while in the Fiordland Region, it is the Pacific Plate that is on top. The transition between the two arrangements, in which the Alpine Fault must play an important part, is naturally complex.

The arrangement of geophysical features in the Main Seismic Region is broadly that of an island arc. There are both active and recently extinct volcanoes, and the North Island is crossed by a major negative gravity anomaly. Off its east coast lies the submarine Hikurangi Trench. All of these features and the belt of deep earthquakes are roughly parallel and in the relative positions to be expected, though there are important variations in the finer detail. There is a narrow gap and an offset between the New Zealand deep-focus activity and the great system that continues the Circum-Pacific Belt north-eastwards to the Kermadec Islands and Tonga.

It is clear that the Fiordland system is oriented towards the Tasman Basin rather than towards the Pacific, but its geophysical features are less well marked. There are no active volcanoes, and older volcanism is represented only by the Otago Peninsula (close to

*Fig. 73: Shallow earthquakes in New Zealand. This map shows the activity in 1971 and 1972. The broad pattern persists from year to year, but the details change. The absence of a shock reaching magnitude 6 is unusual, and activity in the Central Region is somewhat above average. The absence of shocks in the Northland Peninsula and the south-east of the South Island, however, is normal, though neither of these regions is permanently without shocks.*

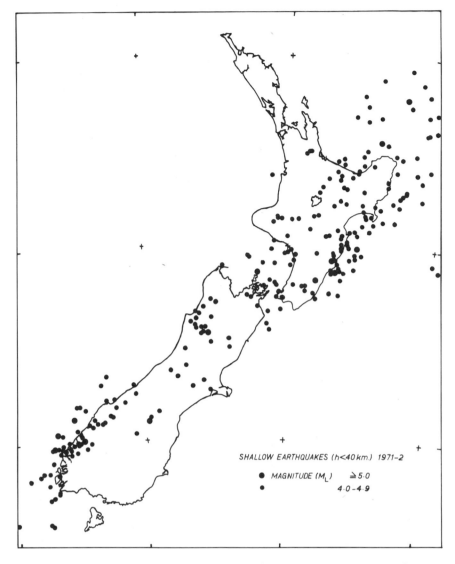

SHALLOW EARTHQUAKES (h<40km.) 1971-2

● MAGNITUDE ($M_L$) ⩾5·0

· 4·0-4·9

Dunedin) and the tiny Solander Island, in the western approaches to Foveaux Strait. Although there is deep water very close to the west coast there is no well-defined trench, and the arrangement of the gravity anomalies, positive and negative, is not quite that conventionally expected. Fiordland is a rugged area, covered with dense forest and for the most part without permanent inhabitants. Close seismograph stations have been established only within recent years, and other geophysical data are just becoming available.

The Northland Peninsula was until recently believed to be quite without earthquakes, but in November 1963 a small shock was felt near Kaitaia in the far north of the peninsula. On Christmas Eve a further shock, of about magnitude $5\frac{1}{4}$ did some minor damage. Since then there have been several smaller shocks in the same area, and in other places between there and Auckland. The publicity brought to light accounts of earthquakes felt in the Bay of Islands in 1914, and it is now clear that no part of New Zealand is without its earthquakes. Occurrences like this are a warning against too fine a division in seismic zoning schemes.

So far as we know, New Zealand is spared from the very largest earthquakes. Only two, the semi-legendary *Hao-whenua* in about 1460 and the south-west Wairarapa earthquake in 1855, seem likely to have had magnitudes as high as 8. Both the historical record and

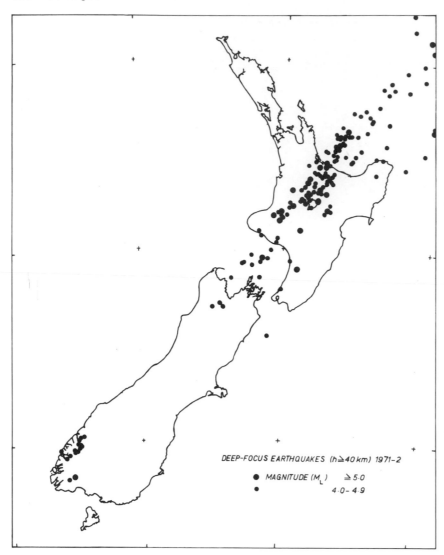

DEEP-FOCUS EARTHQUAKES (h≥40 km) 1971-2

● MAGNITUDE ($M_L$)    ≥ 5·0

· 4·0 - 4·9

*Fig. 74: Deep earthquakes in New Zealand. Epicentres of sub-crustal earthquakes in 1971 and 1972. The two separate systems of deep activity are clearly shown.*

the pattern of the smaller activity suggest that on the average shocks as big as these do not happen more than about once a century, but magnitude 7 earthquakes can be expected about once a decade. Fortunately, few of them have happened close to large towns. There is a list of these shocks and an epicentre map in the Appendix, and some of the larger or more interesting ones are described in the next chapter.

Japanese earthquakes arise from the relative movement of the Pacific and Eurasian Plates; but we find that as in New Zealand the meeting of the plates has produced a rather complicated structure. The line of seismicity that extends southwards from Kamchatka through the Kuril Islands and Hokkaido divides in central Honshu, and the inner branch that follows the main axis of Japan through Shikoku and Kyushu is a secondary one. The main activity turns abruptly to the south-east and follows a chain of small volcanic islets that includes the Bonin and Volcano groups. This change in direction is shared by the gravity anomalies, the volcanoes, and the submarine trench off eastern Japan (Figure 77). Geologically it is marked by a great volcanic depression known as the Fossa Magna, which crosses central Honshu and contains a number of important cones, including Mount Fuji. The deep-focus earthquakes of the outer system extend beneath Honshu and the Japan Sea to the Asian mainland, but in the

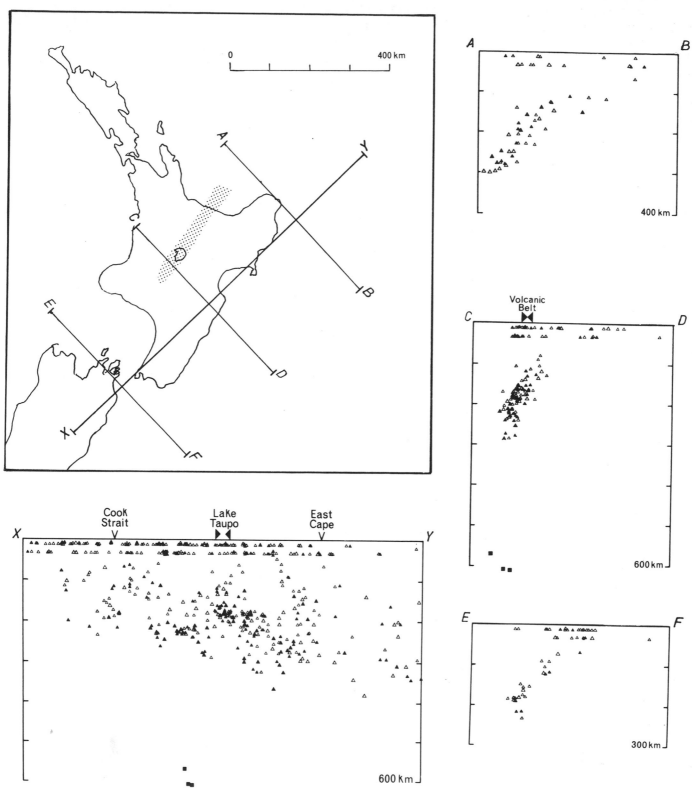

*Fig. 75: Deep earthquakes in New Zealand. These cross-sections of the Main Seismic Region show that the foci lie within a restricted volume that may indicate the extent of a down-going lithospheric slab. Note the compact group of isolated shocks at a depth of about 600 km. The shading on the map indicates the active volcanic region. (Cross-sections after Hamilton and Gale.)*

inner system there are breaks in both the line of volcanoes and the deep seismicity that last almost to Kyushu. In terms of plate tectonics, the inner and outer systems embrace a Philippines 'platelet' (Figure 53) or in older language, northern Japan has an arcuate and southern Japan a block-type structure.

Japan's long civilization has produced a very detailed historical record of its past earthquakes, though China can boast an even longer one. The earliest reliable record of a Japanese earthquake dates from A.D. 416 and, for central Japan at least, the record of large events becomes very complete after the great Nankaido shock in 684. Imamura, who has catalogued 66 destructive shocks between 1596 and 1935, considers that over that period shocks in even remote parts of the country were adequately covered.

There is doubt whether the Colombia-Equador earthquake on January 31, 1906 or the Sanriku shock off the east coast of Honshu on March 3, 1933, both of which Richter has assigned magnitudes of 8·9, was the largest since instrumental records have been available; but there is no doubt that from the human point of view the Chinese Tang Shan earthquake on July 27, 1976 was the greatest natural disaster in modern times. Only the sketchiest accounts of the catastrophe are yet available, but about half a millon people lost their lives. This is the highest death toll in any earthquake in the last four

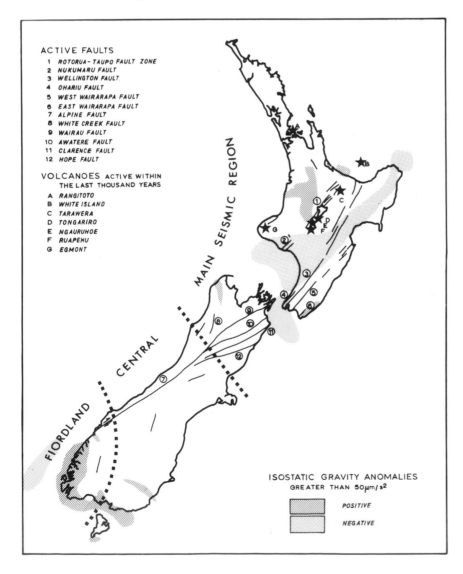

ACTIVE FAULTS

1 ROTORUA-TAUPO FAULT ZONE
2 NUKUMARU FAULT
3 WELLINGTON FAULT
4 OHARIU FAULT
5 WEST WAIRARAPA FAULT
6 EAST WAIRARAPA FAULT
7 ALPINE FAULT
8 WHITE CREEK FAULT
9 WAIRAU FAULT
10 AWATERE FAULT
11 CLARENCE FAULT
12 HOPE FAULT

VOLCANOES ACTIVE WITHIN THE LAST THOUSAND YEARS

A RANGITOTO
B WHITE ISLAND
C TARAWERA
D TONGARIRO
E NGAURUHOE
F RUAPEHU
G EGMONT

MAIN SEISMIC REGION

CENTRAL

FIORDLAND

ISOSTATIC GRAVITY ANOMALIES
GREATER THAN 50μm/s²

POSITIVE

NEGATIVE

*Fig. 76: Seismotectonic features of New Zealand. The relationship of the three seismic regions to the active volcanoes, major faults, and gravity anomalies. The close relationship between the earthquakes and the surface faulting found in California (Figures 70 and 71) is not present in New Zealand.*

*Plate 77: Regional uplift. White bands of dead barnacles and other marine growths record the uplifting of the island of Awa Shima and nearby parts of the coast of Honshu in the Niigata earthquake of 1964.*

centuries, and the second highest in all recorded history. The only comparable event of which we have an adequate account is the Kwanto earthquake on September 1, 1923, which almost completely destroyed Tokyo and Yokohama, two of the most densely populated cities in the world. Official figures record the deaths of nearly a hundred thousand people.

The Kwanto earthquake, which is usually called after the province most severely affected, was in fact centred about 80 km south-west of Tokyo near the island of Oshima in Sugami Bay, and many of the smaller towns about the bay were badly damaged by the tsunami that followed. In some of the smaller inlets it reached heights of up to twelve metres and there were many drownings; but the tsunami had its advantages: it extinguished many fires that would otherwise have been uncontrollable.

*Plate 78: Faulting and uplift. Displacement of the Hanning Bay Fault in the 1964 Alaskan earthquake. The white coating on the rocks at the left consists of the bleached remains of dead sea creatures lifted above water-level. The whole area has been raised, but the land on the left of the fault has come up some three metres more than that on the right.*

*Plate 79: Transcurrent faulting. Many photographs of distorted fence-lines have been published since this one was taken by Alexander McKay at Glynn Wye in north Canterbury in 1888, first establishing the importance of transcurrent movements. The displacement was about three metres.*

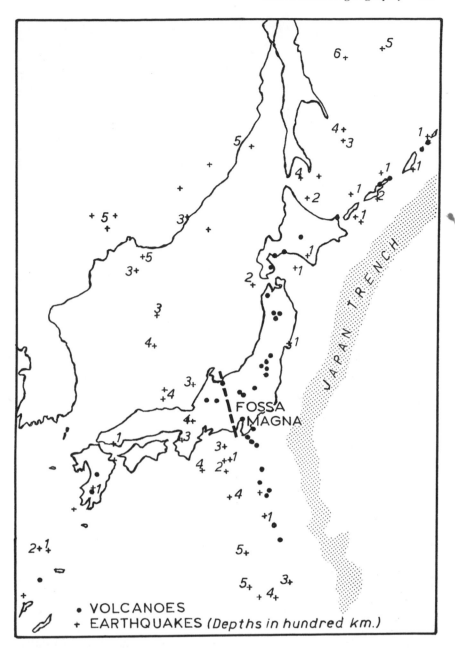

*Fig. 77: Japanese deep earthquakes. This map shows the relative positions of the deep earthquakes, the Japan Trench, the Fossa Magna, and the active volcanoes. Shallow earthquakes have not been shown.*

*Plate 80: Kwanto earthquake, 1923. This picture, taken from a military aeroplane, shows the many separate outbreaks of fire which gave rise to conflicting streams of refugees.*

*Plate 81: The ruins of Tokyo after the Kwanto earthquake and subsequent fire.*

*Plate 82: Refugees in a Tokyo park after the Kwanto earthquake.*

In Tokyo and Yokohama, the enormous death-toll was due to fire, and not to collapsing buildings. Japanese homes have traditionally been made of wood, with internal partitions of light sliding paper-covered frames. They are heated with portable charcoal braziers, which can easily tip and ignite the woven matting that covers the floors. In the hour that followed the earthquake, over a hundred fires had been located by the fire department, but with the telephone and alarm systems out of action and the streets becoming increasingly jammed with refugees there was little they could do. The streams of fugitives, many of them carrying inflammable belongings on handcarts, converged upon the bridges of the Sumida-gawa River, not realizing that the danger from which they were fleeing was equally serious on both sides. The bridges themselves caught fire, and no escape from the heat was to be found even in the river, down which flaming debris was drifting. Fire has been a complication in many earthquake disasters, to the extent that many Americans think of the destruction of San Francisco in 1906 as a great fire rather than an earthquake, but it did not match the horror and tragedy of the events in Tokyo in 1923.

The details of the ground movement in the Kwanto earthquake still puzzle seismologists, though we should not be surprised to find that a shock of magnitude 8·3 is a complex event, and some of the movements observed should undoubtedly be attributed to the larger aftershocks. Imamura believes that there was at least one very large one under the land to the north of the main epicentre.

Japanese seismologists carried out a very precise survey of the area affected (Figure 78). Assuming that trig stations some 80 kilometres to the north were still in their original positions, they found that the whole of the Boso Peninsula and the land about Sugami Bay had moved to the south east. On the peninsula the displacements were as great as four and a half metres, but they became progressively less inland, being less than a metre on the far side of Tokyo and eventually becoming undetectable. The island of Oshima, on the other hand, seemed to have moved nearly a metre to the north. As well as the horizontal movements, they also found an uplift of about two metres around the bay.

What happened beneath the waters of the bay has still to be sorted out. Some of the changes in depth reported by the Japanese naval party that prepared the new charts can possibly be explained by slumping, but the deepest part of the bay seemed to have become about 200 metres deeper, and there were other subsidences twice as big.

In the open ocean it is often reasonable to attribute apparent changes in depth to uncertainty in the position of the survey ships, but when 83 000 soundings in a land-locked bay are involved this seems less likely. The alternative is to assume movements larger than in any other known earthquake, and most seismologists assume some defect in the survey made before the earthquake.

In 1923 the school of seismological research established by Milne had lost something of its initial impetus, but as a result of the Tokyo disaster the Imperial Earthquake Research Institute was set up at Tokyo University, and a new period of vigorous Japanese research began. Californian research was a little slower to begin, but the report of the commission that investigated the San Francisco earthquake of 1906 and the elastic rebound theory put forward by Reid as a result are major seismological landmarks.

The San Francisco shock on April 18, which like the Kwanto earthquake had a magnitude of 8·3, occurred in a surprising year. In 1906 at least seven other earthquakes are believed to have reached magnitude 8. The Colombia-Equador shock on January 31 with a magnitude of 8·9 contends with the Sanriku earthquake in 1933 for the title of largest instrumentally recorded shock, and a Chilean shock on August 17 reached 8·6. It is not size alone that makes an earthquake remembered.

The great earthquake in 1906 is not the beginning of California's earthquake history. Shocks had been felt by explorers in the eighteenth century, and they were familiar to the fathers of the Spanish missions, several of which were seriously damaged. In 1812 forty people were killed when the church at San Juan Capistrano collapsed, and the year became known as the 'year of earthquakes'. There were large shocks near San Francisco in 1836 and 1838, and one near Fort Tejon in central California in 1852. The Owens Valley earthquake in 1872 was the first to become the subject of a geological report.

Relative movement along the Californian faults is carrying the western coast of the state northwards at an average rate of a few

Sumida-
gawa.

TOKYO

TOKYO BAY

YOKOHAMA

BŌSŌ
PENINSULA

ATAMI

SAGAMI BAY

ITO

EPICENTRE

ŌSHIMA

50 KILOMETRES

4 METRES
DISPLACEMENT

Fig. 78: Ground displacement in the
Kwanto earthquake. The arrows show the
direction of the permanent ground
movement revealed by comparison of
precise surveys made before and after the
shock. Their lengths are proportional to
the amount of the displacement. The
locations of a number of places mentioned
in the text have also been shown.

Fig. 79: Transform faulting. The
transverse fractures that break up the mid-
oceanic ridges are believed to be transform
faults. Most earthquakes occur on the
segment of the fault between the sections of
the ridge. Here the sense of the movement
is opposite to that which would be inferred
from the displacement of the ridge,
because of the spreading from its crest.

centimetres a year, a process that must eventually bring about a
*rapprochement* between the citizens of Los Angeles and those of San
Francisco, who live on opposite sides of the San Andreas Fault.

In size and extent the San Andreas is very similar to the Alpine
Fault in New Zealand, but instead of ending in opposing overthrusts,
the San Andreas Fault is related to a series of submarine fracture-
zones that had been puzzling geophysicists ever since they became
known in the 1950s. These too are transcurrent faults, but of a kind
that was called *transform faults* by Professor J. Tuzo Wilson, the
Canadian who succeeded in explaining them in 1965. Transform
faults occur where a mid-oceanic ridge has been fractured, and the
sections displaced laterally. The result is a fracture with different
rates of spreading at adjacent points on the opposite sides (Figure
79). The seismicity of mid-oceanic ridges is often associated with
these transverse fractures.

Considered as a disaster the San Francisco earthquake in 1906 falls
well short of the horror that occurred in Tokyo in 1923, but the
destruction of a great city by earthquake and fire is never a small
matter. It is estimated that some 700 people died and 28 000 lost their

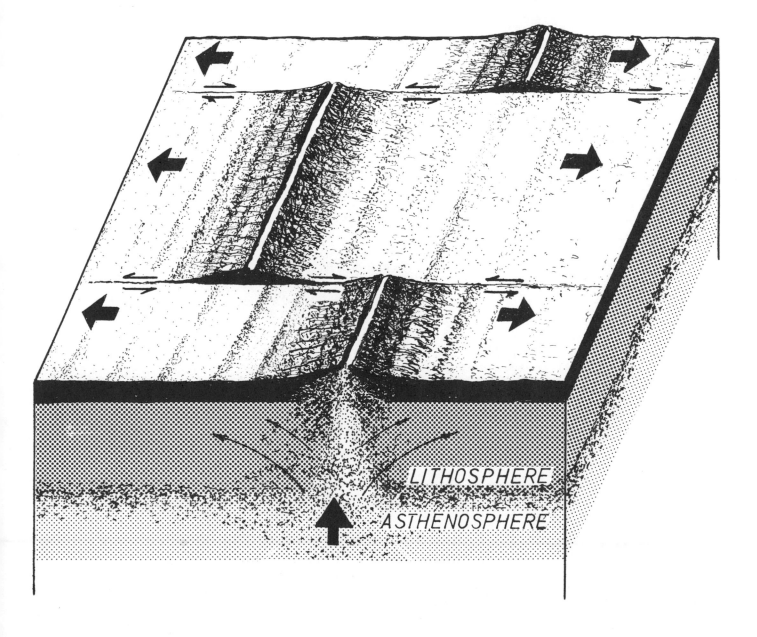

LITHOSPHERE

ASTHENOSPHERE

homes. The greatest damage was in the business area of the city, built mainly upon land reclaimed from the bay. The subsequent fire was confined to an area of just under ten square kilometres only by the decision to dynamite rows of buildings that were still standing. Many of the water-mains had been disrupted, and in the absence of isolating valves the pressure soon fell in the sections that had remained intact. The total value of the property lost has been put at about four million dollars.

The shock had a magnitude of 8·3. The value is particularly well known for so early a shock, as the Investigation Commission had the foresight to collect and publish seismograms from all over the world. In very large earthquakes it is probably misleading to talk about the epicentre, for the source must have an appreciable size, but it is usual to assign a point on the San Andreas Fault about 50 kilometres north-west of the city. The fresh fault breakage that resulted is the longest on record for a single shock, even if we accept the minimum estimate of 300 kilometres. In places the fault passes beneath the sea, and there are other observational difficulties. Richter suggests that the true value is nearer 430 kilometres. The amount of the displacement varies greatly, reaching a maximum of nearly five metres north of the Golden Gate, leaving aside an offset of seven metres in soft ground near Tomales Bay, which is probably a surface effect and not a true indication of the fault movement. The displacement is almost all horizontal. No change in level of more than a metre was reported anywhere, and in most places there was little or none.

The area of damage follows the fault for well over five hundred kilometres, but it is only about eighty kilometres wide. This unusually pronounced elongation is probably due in part to the extent of the faulting, but differences in geological foundation account for some of it.

# 20 Some famous earthquakes

> . . . The strong-based promontory
> Have I made shake, and by the spurs pluck'd up
> The pine and cedar:
>> Shakespeare, *The Tempest*

Earthquakes have always been the subject of rumour and exaggeration. That ancient gossip writer, Pliny, tells of twelve cities in Asia overthrown by earthquake; and Seneca records the birth of two new islands, Thereon and Therea. In 740 'The Citie of *Constantinople* was so wonderfully shaken with an Earthquake an whole yeare together, that the Emperour thereof, and all his people, were constreyned to dwell abroade in the fields vnder tents and pauilions, for feare that their houses & buildings would fall on their heads.'

The theoreticians of classical antiquity have not left seismology much of permanent value. Aristotle, who often has something interesting to say even when he is wrong, ascribes earthquakes to winds imprisoned in underground caverns, and so lays the basis for popular beliefs about earthquake weather.

Instrumental seismology begins in China, where Chang Heng devised a seismoscope in A.D. 132. It was a nice blend of artistry and practicality. Round the outside of a tall jar containing an inverted pendulum was a ring of carved dragons' heads, each holding a ball in its jaws. When the pendulum moved, one or more balls was dislodged and fell into the open mouth of a frog stationed below in a suitable place to swallow it.

It is not only the great disasters that are recorded in history.'Tis since the earthquake now eleven year,' says Juliet's nurse, and Shakespeare himself no doubt felt the earthquake of 1580. This shock forms the subject of a pamphlet by Thomas Twyne, which contains more good sense and accurate observation than the modern reader would expect from the title – 'A fhorte and pithie difcourfe concerning the engendring, tokens, and effects of all Earthquakes in Generall; Particularly applyed and conferred with that moft ftrange and terrible worke of the Lord in shaking the Earth, not only within the Citie of London, but alfo in moft partes of all Englande: VVhich hapned vpon VVenfday in Eafter weeke laft paft, which was the fixt day of April, almoft at fixe a clocke in the euening, in the yeare of our Lord GOD. 1580.'

Twyne's views upon the cause of earthquakes, like those that Shakespeare has put into the mouth of Hotspur, are basically Aristotelian, though he does not understate the part played by God's wrath. He is nevertheless a keen observer and an accurate reporter, and his account became a pattern for many that followed it, both in the Old World and the New.

We do not know the magnitude of the earthquake in the Shansi province of China in 1556, which is reliably supposed to have killed over 830 000 people. Although it is the worst seismic disaster on record, it is not likely to have been the largest known earthquake. That title is usually accorded the Lisbon earthquake of 1755, which possibly reached magnitude 9.

The epicentre of the Lisbon shock is believed to have been at sea, perhaps a hundred kilometres off the coast of Portugal. Because of the unusually widespread occurrences of seiches it has been difficult to establish the limits of the felt area. It was certainly more than 1 500 kilometres in radius, extending from the Azores to Italy, and from England to North Africa. Seiches were reported from as far away as Norway and Sweden, over 3 500 kilometres from the epicentre. We can safely dismiss statements that it was felt in the New World as reports of unrelated shocks.

The damage to Lisbon was very great. In 1755 the city had about 230 000 inhabitants, nearly 30 000 of whom were killed, according to conservative estimates. Great numbers of people were in the churches, for it was All Saints' Day, and the time of the first Mass. The shock was followed by a tsunami about seven metres in height, and by fire.

The disaster shocked all Europe, and the moralists and the wiseacres were not slow to make capital of it. Voltaire, in a preface to his *Poem on the Disaster of Lisbon* rebukes people who contended that 'The heirs of the dead would now come into their fortunes, masons would grow rich in rebuilding the city, beasts would grow fat on corpses buried in the ruins; such is the natural effect of natural causes'; but he secured the earthquake a more permanent place in literature by the reference in *Candide*.

'The earthquake is nothing new,' said Pangloss. 'The town of Lima in America experienced the same shocks last year. The same causes produce the same effects. There is certainly a vein of sulphur running under the earth from Lima to Lisbon.' Many of the learned men of the age would probably have agreed. The rest of the report is less factual, but reminds us again that in former times, natural disasters of this kind were more the occasion for examination of the national conscience than for investigation and taking practical measures against a recurrence. 'The University of Coimbra had pronounced that the sight of a few people ceremonially burned alive before a slow fire was an infallible prescription for preventing earthquakes; so that when the earthquake had subsided after destroying three-quarters of Lisbon, the authorities of that country could find no better way of avoiding total ruin than by giving the citizens a magnificent *auto-da-fé*.' This was no doubt as efficacious as the products of Joseph Addison's 'impudent mountebank, who sold pills which (as he told the country people) were very good against an earthquake'. It may be noted that the University of Coimbra is now equipped with seismographs.

It is not possible to give an account of every major earthquake from those times to the present, but a list of the more important ones is given in the Appendix. Europe has fortunately been free from further disasters on the scale of the Lisbon earthquake, whether in consequence of the *auto-da-fé* or not I venture no opinion. Other parts of the world have not fared so well. The New World was by no means earthquake free, and in the New England colonies, the settlers speculated on whether the 'electrical substance' drawn from the air by Mr Franklin's new lightning-rods might not be responsible.

It cannot be too often stressed that areas of minor seismicity are not free from the risk of larger shocks. Lisbon is not in a region of high activity, and the Mississippi Valley where the New Madrid earthquakes occurred in 1811 is even less active. The epicentral region was not densely settled at the time, but several of the shocks were of destructive intensity. Richter suggests that the largest of them, on December 16, was the largest known earthquake in what was then the territory of the U.S.A. It was felt in Boston, 1700 kilometres away, and in other places from Canada to New Orleans. Both its size and its location present a challenge to tectonic theory.

Another part of the United States not usually considered liable to earthquake is South Carolina, but Charleston was badly damaged in 1886. This shock was one of the first to be the subject of an extended geological report, and there are some excellent photographs (Plate 63).

Modern seismological observation, however, should begin with the visit of Robert Mallet to the area affected by the Italian earthquakes in 1857. In 1862 he published *The Great Neapolitan Earthquake of 1857; the first Principles of Observational Seismology*. These two volumes are finely illustrated with coloured lithographs, and are a seismological classic. Damaged towns and villages are described in detail. The direction of overthrow of buildings and monuments, the nature of the forces needed to produce the damage, and the patterns of isoseismals are all carefully discussed, and an attempt is made to frame general principles. Mallet was not content just to describe damage. He was also an experimenter. He investigated the speed at which earthquake waves could travel by using charges of gunpowder to generate a shock, observing their

*Plate 84: Raised beach terraces at Turakirae Head, east of the entrance to Wellington Harbour, preserve a long history of vertical movement of the coast, probably associated with ancient earthquakes. Sudden uplifts have left a succession of terraces, the edges of which are marked by lighter bands. The beach between the water-line and the first of these was first exposed in the West Wairarapa earthquake of 1855, and the next one above it in about 1460. The probable dates of the higher terraces are roughly 1100 B.C. and 2900 B.C. The slightly tilted steps on the more distant headland are the remnants of a still older beach, cut by the sea during the Pleistocene, at least 100 000 years ago.*

arrival by watching the surface of a shallow bowl of mercury. He was also responsible for coining many of our technical words, among them seismology, isoseismal, and seismic focus. The earthquake was not a big one, unless we measure its importance by the contribution to knowledge which resulted from it.

Members of Captain Cook's expedition to New Zealand felt an earthquake in the Marlborough Sounds, but the country's earthquake history begins in about 1460. Maori traditions give details of a large shock near Wellington about that time, accompanied by impressive coastal uplift. The present Miramar Peninsula ceased to be an island, and there was a further additon to the series of raised beach-terraces at Turakirae (Plate 84). Here a whole set of terraces records successive uplifts going back for at least 6 500 years.

Organized European settlement of New Zealand dates from 1840, when the newly-arrived colonists felt their first shock. Thinking that the natives were trying to pull down their houses, they sprang from their beds and seized swords and pistols to do battle with the adversary. Three years later a more severe shock struck Wanganui. Houses and a church were damaged and a Maori was buried in a landslide; but the seriousness of the earthquake problem was not realized until 1848 when the Marlborough earthquake on October 16 destroyed or damaged most of the buildings in Wellington (Plate 85). Three lives were lost when an aftershock brought down an already damaged wall.

This earthquake has often been credited with the formation of the prominent 'Earthquake Rent' that can be followed along the side of the Awatere Valley for a hundred kilometres. Of course no single earthquake was responsible for the Awatere Fault, and on this occasion it did not move at all. Historical research has recently come upon clear descriptions of fault movement in the Wairau Valley, parallel and to the north west of the Awatere, which was not explored until some years later.

So large a shock within ten years of the founding of the city should have warned the colonists that special building measures would be needed in their new home, but the warning went largely unheeded. They discussed whether the shock had been caused by gas becoming ignited in a cavern under Cook Strait, propped up their damaged buildings, and went on building new ones in the same style as the old. In 1855 the lesson was repeated.

The 1855 earthquake is the only New Zealand shock in historic times believed to have reached magnitude 8. It originated on the South-West Wairarapa Fault on the far side of the Rimutaka Mountains, about 25 kilometres east of the city. There was vertical movement of up to three metres, and possibly surface breakage over about 50 kilometres, as well as uplifting of the coast and the shores of Wellington Harbour. Except for the Indian shock in the Rann of Kutch in 1819, this was the first occasion on which faulting had been observed to accompany an earthquake, and it became well-known to geologists from an account published by Lyell in his *Principles of Geology*.

Wellington had grown rapidly since 1848 and many of the new buildings were destroyed. It was realized that timber structures had fared relatively well, and the city authorities became divided upon whether fire or earthquake was likely to prove the greater hazard in the future. Eventually they settled upon brick for the central city, though most Wellingtonians still choose to live in a wooden house.

There have since been several serious fires, but there was to be no more serious earthquake damage in the city until the Masterton earthquakes of 1942.

Christchurch, like Wellington, has experienced large earthquakes, though there has never been an important epicentre quite so close. One of the more amusing aspects of Christchurch's troubles has been the difficulty of providing the cathedral with a fitting spire. The upper portion has been destroyed several times, in spite of a number of ingenious expedients, such as mounting the cross on top to swing like a pendulum, and having it consecrated by a bishop hauled to the top in a bosun's chair. Nevertheless, the present arrangement, in which the upper part is of wood, has maintained a suitable architectural composure for many years. The greatest of the Canterbury shocks occurred in 1901 near Cheviot, or Mackenzie as the township was then called. The government geologist of the time, Alexander McKay, published a very readable account of this shock. It begins with a summary of the views then commonly held concerning the cause of earthquakes, reviews the earlier earthquake history of the

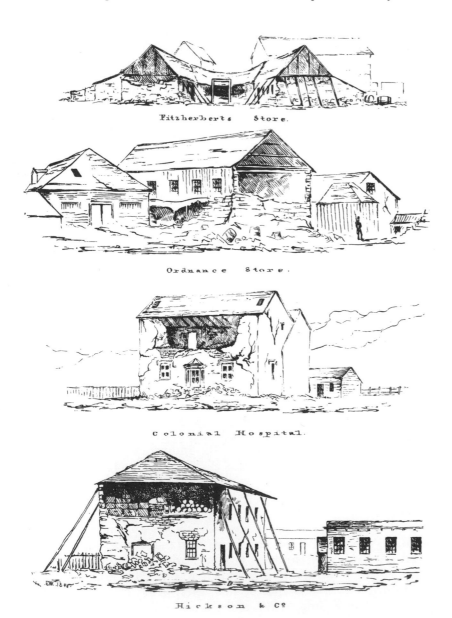

*Plate 85: Marlborough earthquake, 1848. These sketches of damaged buildings in Wellington are the earliest pictorial record of the effects of earthquakes in New Zealand.*

district, describes the damage he observed, reports the opinions of the local farmers, and concludes with an anecdote about a horse which died of fright.

The main shock was on 16th November, and on the 20th, McKay left Wellington for Christchurch, where he examined the cathedral spire, noticed that there had been a slight shift, and that 'some repairs had been effected'. The journey to Cheviot involved both rail and coach, as the train did not then run beyond Amberley; but he arrived at 4 p.m., just in time for an aftershock, which he did not feel. He remarks with some asperity upon the 'eagerness of the Press after the smallest item that deals with what is called "stricken Cheviot"', for he seems to have been deeply impressed by a common aspect of moderate earthquake damage. It is not obvious except at close range. From about a kilometre away 'the township looked the very ideal of a country town, in nothing peculiar save that it was smokeless because there were no chimneys'. When he entered the town, however, he found that the streets were littered with glass from broken windows, and most of the inhabitants, having pitched tents in the paddocks and harnessed the buggy for a quick retreat, had gathered at the post office to discuss the last aftershock.

The damage he found was of the kind usual with wooden buildings. They had moved from their foundations, the chimneys had fallen – in many cases through the roof – and contents were badly disarranged. Superficial cracks and slumps appeared along the roads. On the following day, 'a strong nor'-wester continued to blow, which made it impossible to do any photography, and rendered work of any kind very unpleasant'.

He records one of the earliest instances which has come to my notice of the direction of approach of an earthquake wave being determined by two people in telephone communication, one feeling the shock before the other. In this case it gave clear evidence that the shock originated to the north of Parnassus, a conclusion McKay had reached on other grounds. This was at variance with local opinion in Cheviot, which held that the shock had come from the east, or from the sea. These were honest opinions, but there were also some tall stories current. Mount Cookson, a limestone formation, was reported to be in eruption; and the bed of the Waiau River had been seen to open, first engulfing the water, and then as it closed again, forcing it to discharge in spouting columns which played to a height of ten metres! This story could have some foundation in the formation of sand craters.

The two earthquakes that have remained uppermost in the minds of the New Zealand public are the Murchison (or Buller) earthquake of 1929, and the Hawke's Bay earthquake in 1931. The Murchison earthquake, in which 17 people died, was the first New Zealand shock in which there had been a large loss of life.

Murchison, from which the shock has taken its name, is a small settlement of only 300 people built on narrow river-flats where the steeply-gorged Buller River is joined by two tributaries. The valley is nowhere more than a kilometre wide, and the hills rise abruptly at its sides for twelve or fifteen hundred metres. It is one of the wettest parts of New Zealand, the shock occurred in mid-winter, and the weather had been exceptionally bad. The conditions were favourable for landslides, and many spectacular slips occurred, cutting roads and damming rivers. Many casualties were the result of the landslides, and others occurred in the flooding that followed the bursting of the temporary dams.

The hardships faced by the survivors are the material from which legends are made. The townships of Westport and Nelson, from which Murchison generally obtained its supplies, had themselves been damaged, and the roads were cut. The Public Works Department did what it could to shelter the homeless in sodden marquees put up in the school grounds, but it was five days before the road to Nelson could be opened again. No sooner had the town been evacuated and left in the care of a few watchmen than the real refugees began arriving from the remoter valleys.

Hoping to find shelter in Murchison, more than thirty women and children, sick and elderly, had made their way over thirty kilometres of landslides, and through bush so thick that tracks had to be cut.

Karamea had been completely forgotten. The tiny settlement had not been seriously damaged, but the road to Westport which was its only link with the outside world was cut in so many places by slips and washouts that it no longer existed, and food was running desperately short. A settler along the road walked the fifty kilometres to Westport in search of help, but it was not to arrive until a pioneer aviator was able to land his Tiger Moth on the beach fully two weeks later.

The earthquake, which had a magnitude of 7·8, was felt in all parts of New Zealand. Two members of the Geological Survey, M. L. Ongley and H. E. Fyfe, who made an exhaustive field study of the epicentral region found that the whole region had been uplifted, but that the eastern side had moved more than the western, causing a rift along the White Creek Fault, a feature that had previously been regarded as inactive. Where the fault crossed the main road, it left a vertical barrier five metres high.

*Plate 86: Landslide. One of the many large landslides triggered by the Inangahua earthquake. This one temporarily dammed the Buller River, creating a further hazard for places down stream.*

This shock seems to have been an unusually noisy one. The sounds may have been intensified by concentration in the narrow valleys, but they also travelled more than 100 kilometres through the high atmosphere and descended again in Taranaki. Weather conditions at other places at the same distance were not suitable for hearing them, but close to the epicentre noises like rolling thunder and bursts of artillery fire accompanied the aftershocks for many weeks.

New Zealand was badly shocked by the Murchison earthquake, but the Hawke's Bay earthquake that followed two years later was an even more serious disaster (See Plates 3 and 45). This time the towns of Napier, Hastings, Gisborne, and Wairoa – in all about 30 000 people – lay within the area of destruction. Of these people 256 were killed. The business areas of Napier and Hastings were almost totally destroyed, and fires completed the work of the earthquake.

The shock, on the morning of February 3rd, 1931 (local time) was centred within about 25 kilometres of Napier, and had a magnitude of 7·9. There was only minor faulting, but a tract of land some 90 kilometres long and 15 kilometres wide was raised by amounts up to 3 metres. Near Napier itself the rise was about two metres, draining large areas of the Ahuriri Lagoon and providing New Zealand with another fourteen square kilometres of territory, on which the city has since built its aerodrome.

About two weeks after the main shock a remarkable event occurred at Sponge Bay, near Gisborne. Men working on the beach saw a boulder bank rise from the sea, without previous warning, and without any tremors they could feel. The top of the bank is more than two metres above sea level, and its area is nearly a hectare.

Since 1931 New Zealand has not had an earthquake as big as those in Murchison and Hawke's Bay. On June 24th, 1942 a shock of magnitude 7 with an epicentre near Masterton badly damaged older buildings in an area that extended to the city of Wellington. There were no deaths, and only minor injuries, but the necessary repairs were a severe burden on the manpower of a country that was then at war. This shock resulted in the introduction of the Earthquake and War Damage Insurance scheme.

On May 24th, 1968 there was a magnitude 7 earthquake at Inangahua, about 35 kilometres from Murchison, which again brought down major landslides, one of which caused two deaths (Plate 86; see also Plate 65). An isoseismal map for this shock was given in Chapter One. The improved seismograph network, and the fact that parties of geologists and portable stations to record the aftershocks could be rushed into the area within a few hours of the event have made this the best studied New Zealand earthquake. The area is not densely populated, but there was serious damage to houses, bridges, railway lines, and underground pipes. In the month that followed the main shock there were fifteen aftershocks of magnitude 5 or more.

# 21 Some recent earthquakes

. . .Is this the scene
Where the old Earthquake-daemon taught her young
Ruin? Were these her toys?

P. B. Shelley, *Mont Blanc*

The year 1960 is among the most tragic in recent earthquake history, not only because of the catastrophic effects of the magnitude 8·5 Chilean earthquake in May, and the disastrous tsunami that followed it, but because of the disproportionately severe consequences of several earthquakes of moderate size that occurred in countries whose traditional building methods are faulty. On 21st February, a magnitude 5·5 earthquake killed forty-seven people in the Algerian village of Melousa, and on 24th April, 450 inhabitants of Lar and nearby villages in Iran were buried beneath the ruins of buildings destroyed by a shock whose magnitude was only $5^3/_4$, among them two hundred children parading in a festival procession through the narrow streets. A shock of the same magnitude that struck Agadir on the night of 29th February levelled the old city to the ground, and destroyed about half the buildings in the modern business centre. Over a third of its population was killed. Another third was injured. So many dead lay beneath the fallen masonry that orderly identification and reinterment was out of the question. The area was bulldozed flat and abandoned.

It can be argued that the Agadir earthquake was something of a freak. The last time a major earthquake occurred in this part of Morocco was in 1731, and the event appears to have been forgotten. More recent minor shocks were dismissed as of no importance. It had certainly never been suggested that Agadir lay in a major seismic zone, and even now many seismologists would feel that something larger than a magnitude $5^3/_4$ earthquake is needed before a place can be admitted to that category. After all, a shock of that size happens somewhere on Earth every three or four days. The other unusual circumstances are the shallow focal depth, estimated from the limited extent of the damaged area to be only 3 or 4 kilometres, and the fact that the epicentre lay within a kilometre or two of the town. When the radius of the area of damaging intensities is so small, it seems particularly unfortunate that this area should contain a city, and that the buildings of that city should be so poorly constructed.

What sort of place was Agadir, and how far was the disaster avoidable? The origins of the city are lost in antiquity. In the sixteenth century the Sherif Moulay Mohammed wrested it from the Portuguese and built the Kasbah; but after the earthquake of 1731 it suffered a decline until the early years of the present century when the natural advantages of its safe anchorage and the attractiveness of its fine sandy beaches were again recognized. Its importance as a port and a tourist centre increased, and in the expanding industrial area sixty canneries prepared sea-foods and agricultural produce for export.

It need not surprise us that the buildings of the Moroccan quarter fared badly. The old stone masonry was held together with a mortar of mud and sand, and roofed with anything from timber and corrugated iron to reinforced concrete slabs. The fate of so many attractive modern-looking hotels, apartment blocks and public buildings is more disturbing; but in most cases the appearance of quality was confined to the smooth outer plaster skin. Behind lay unreinforced stone masonry and inadequate mortar. The few reinforced-concrete buildings fared better. Although most of them lacked adequate cross-bracing, they did not collapse completely like the unbonded masonry.

Unlike Morocco, Chile is a country with a long history of large earthquakes. The epicentre of the magnitude $8\frac{1}{2}$ earthquake on 22nd May was in the south of the Arauco peninsula. It was almost immediately followed by great numbers of aftershocks, some of them large, spread over almost the whole length of the country; and it is not always clear which shock was responsible for any particular damage. The cities of Concepción and Valdivia were badly shaken, but many of their newer buildings conformed with effective codes imposed after a large earthquake in 1939, and performed well. Older masonry structures dating from before the introduction of the code were less fortunate.

Most of the phenomena associated with large earthquakes were observed in Chile — ground uplift in some regions, subsidence and consequent inundation in others, seiches in the lakes, landslides that dammed rivers, and mysterious lights in the air. Water-saturated clay soils flowed from beneath buildings, leading to their collapse, and blocking waterways, streams, and harbours. Two days after the shock the volcano Puyehue, 650 kilometres south of Concepción, erupted for the first time since 1905. Almost the only earthquake phenomenon that was not observed was surface faulting, though this has not stopped geologists from publishing maps showing a 'probable causative fault' in the sea.

The tsunami that followed was the most serious for many years. Not only were many of the coastal towns of Chile itself inundated,

*Fig. 80: Alaskan uplift and subsidence. The zones of uplift and subsidence in the great earthquake of March 27th, 1964, as mapped by Dr George Plafker of the U.S. Geological Survey. Surface faulting was observed only at the southern end of Montague Island. The area in which aftershocks occurred is almost identical with the zone of uplift.*

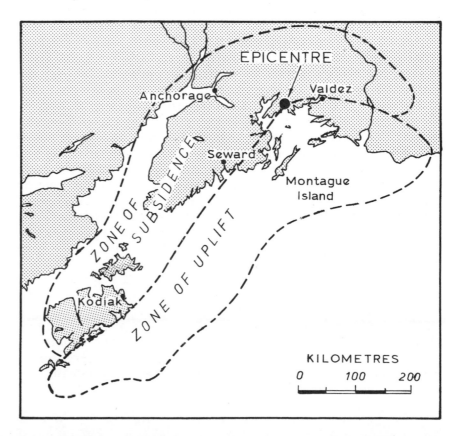

but the wave crossed the Pacific and caused damage around its entire perimeter. In Hawaii there were sixty-one deaths, in spite of the fact that the authorities had advised evacuation of the danger areas. Japan also suffered many casualties and extensive damage to coastal property and port installations. In New Zealand there was only minor damage.

Poor buildings of the type that made the Lar, the Agadir, and the Melousa earthquakes so disastrous were also to be found at Buyin-Zara. This region of Iran experienced a larger shock, of about magnitude 7, and the casualties were proportionately higher. Some twelve thousand villagers and much of their livestock were killed. Dr N. N. Ambraseys, who visited the area under UNESCO auspices, reports that those seismologists who had studied the area considered it to be 'the least seismic in the country', and that even the oldest villagers had never felt a shock strong enough to alarm them. The survival of old buildings and bridges in the area showed that nothing approaching the severity of the present shock could have occured since 1630. Most of the buildings were made of adobe-brick, and few survived the shaking. No major cities lie close to the epicentre, but the intensity in Teheran was great enough to crack plaster and to cause panic. People leapt from first-storey windows, lost control of vehicles, and fled from homes and places of entertainment.

This earthquake was accompanied by conspicuous faulting extending for over a hundred kilometres, probably occurring in at least two stages. Seiches, changes in the flow of springs and wells, and small mud-fountains were also reported. There is an apparently well-authenticated report of 'earthquake lights'. Thirty-nine people reported an orange-red glow over Rudak, a region in which there is no electricity supply. The glow was followed by a sound like a low-flying aeroplane. The Chilian apparition already mentioned was described as bluish-green.

The magnitude 6 earthquake at Skoplje, in Yugoslavia, on 26th July, 1963, provides yet another instance of the disastrous consequences of a moderate earthquake in a city that had chosen to ignore obvious precautions. Moderate earthquakes are not uncommon in other parts of Macedonia, and historical records show that Skoplje itself was destroyed twice before, in A.D. 518, and again in 1555. Many of the damaged buildings were new; but although the regulations specified anti-seismic precautions, it appears that they had frequently been waived as a natural result of impatience to repair the ravages of war, and to house the people of a rapidly-growing city with as little delay as possible. The gamble did not come off (Plates 49 and 50). Some of the building failures in the new areas were as spectacular and disastrous as those in the Old City, where many picturesque one-storey adobe houses and shops with tile roofs dating back several centuries managed to survive. On the other hand, there were only minor breaks in the water and sewerage systems. Poor foundations were an important factor in the disaster. The city lies on the late Tertiary sands and gravels of the Vardar basin, varying in thickness from three metres to eighty or more.

A surprising feature of the Skoplje earthquake was that no fire followed it. It seems that the greater use of electricity for domestic heating and cooking is at last reducing what was once the greatest of earthquake hazards. On the other hand, it must be remembered that the shock took place at a quarter past five on a summer morning.

On 27th March, 1964, an earthquake of magnitude $8\frac{1}{2}$ occurred at the northern end of Prince William Sound, Alaska. Although some faulting was observed on Montague Island, the enormous extent of the areas of uplift and subsidence is by far the most striking geological consequence of the shock. The area of aftershocks, which extends from near Valdez to the southernmost tip of Kodiak Island is almost exactly the size and shape of the South Island of New Zealand (Figure 80). Several of these aftershocks had magnitudes of 6 or more, and were therefore considerable earthquakes in their own right.

The wide publicity given to the effects of this earthquake upon the city of Anchorage has diverted attention from the fact that the epicentre was 130 kilometres away, and that other cities, such as Valdez and Seward, though just as close, were much less severely damaged. Much of Anchorage was built upon a thick tongue of old glacial moraine. Layers of sand and gravel underlain by ninety metres or so of unstable clay and poised above a steep submarine slope were held together by permafrost. It is not surprising that such a material proved unable to withstand shaking.

The chief engineering lessons from this shock are not to be found in the prestressed concrete flats that collapsed because of inadequate anchoring of the tensioning cables, or in the buildings that lost precast decorative panels inadequately tied to their facades, but in the many structures, ranging from small wooden houses to large city buildings, that remained in one piece after their foundations had

*Plate 87: Superficial slumping. Much of the damage at Niigata, like that at this railway-station, was due to consolidation or slumping of poorly-compacted ground.*

failed completely, leaving them bridging gaping chasms, or tilted at improbable angles (Plate 57). Ordinary well-constructed buildings have a surprising resistance to shaking, but no building can be safer than the site on which it stands. Much of the effort now directed to discussing differences in the frequency of earthquake occurrence would be better directed to the adequate study of differences in foundation characteristics. This lesson was to be repeated three months later in Japan.

Niigata is a city of about 340 000 inhabitants, situated on a low-lying sandy area at the mouth of the Shinano River, on the west coast on northern Honshu, the largest island of Japan. Just after 1 p.m. on 16th June, 1964, an earthquake of magnitude $7^3/_4$ occurred at sea about 70 kilometres north of the city. Casualties were few – twelve dead in Niigata itself, and as many more in nearby townships and the surrounding countryside. Most of the larger buildings were modern structures of reinforced concrete. They survived the shaking, but were badly damaged by the behaviour of the poor foundations.

About a third of the city subsided, by as much as two metres in places, as a result of compaction of the sand being shaken. Simultaneously, ground water was expelled through 'sand volcanoes', around the edges of heavy buildings, and through large fissures, so that pedestrians found themselves up to their knees in swirling muddy water. Flooding of this kind was worsened by a combination of high tide, and a small tsunami (Plate 33). These halted the normal flow of the river, which burst its banks and turned the streets within half a kilometre into temporary channels, in some of which the current was strong and deep enough to float motor vehicles. Bridge spans collapsed when the piers moved as a result of foundation failure (Plate 66), the runways of the aerodrome were cracked and under water, and the seventy tanks of the oil refinery caught fire. The fire spread to neighbouring houses, and destroyed 300 of them. Its cause is unknown. No outbreaks occurred elsewhere in the city. Electricity, water-supply, sewerage, and other city services were disrupted.

Apart from the flooding, which in some areas had not subsided after three days, the most spectacular effect was the tilting of many large and otherwise undamaged buildings. One of a group of eight similar four-storey reinforced-concrete apartment buildings overturned almost completely (Plates 70 and 88), and all of them sank some distance into the ground (Plate 62). The overturning took place slowly, and a newspaper report has it that a woman hanging out washing on the roof of the tilted building was able to ride down gently and to step off at ground level.

There has been no greater disaster in the Southern Hemisphere than the Peruvian earthquake of May 31st, 1970. The magnitude of the shock was 7·7, and the epicentre was about 25 kilometres off the coast to the west of Chimbote, a coastal port with a population of about 120 000. There are modern reinforced concrete buildings in Chimbote, and steel-framed factories, but the prevailing form of construction is adobe, which is used for most of the houses, some of which are two storied.

In the towns and villages over a radius of about a hundred kilometres, the adobe collapsed. Many of the better buildings were on poor foundations, and there was widespread liquefaction of the soil. It comes as no surprise that nearly 500 people died in Chimbote, but the total estimated loss of 70 000 lives, 50 000 injured, and 800 000 left homeless is staggering. The reason was the debris avalanche of Huascaran.

*Plate 88: Improvisation. Realizing that their toppled apartment block is still in one piece, these Niigata citizens decided to return home and live on the walls.*

*Plate 89: Restoration. After the Liaoning earthquake, Chinese farmers begin the task of clearing the ejected mud and rubble from their roads and fields.*

*Plate 90: The Huascarán avalanche. The Plaza de Armas in Yungay before and after the catastrophic lahar triggered by the Chimbote earthquake in 1970. Only the palm trees remain to mark the former position of the town.*

Nevado de Huascarán is an Andean peak 6 768 metres high lying just over a hundred kilometres due east of Chimbote. From its sheer western face an enormous mass of rock capped with ice and snow broke away and swept down the Llanganuco Valley towards the town of Yungay and the village of Ranrahirca. There had been avalanches before, even without the stimulus of an earthquake. In 1962 one of them had almost wiped out Ranrahirca, but Yungay was considered safe, for between it and the path of the avalanche there ran a spur some 250 metres high. In 1970 it was not enough; a lobe of the debris swept over the ridge.

Yungay had been a picturesque place with a handsome square and a cathedral. All that remained of it was a small part of the cathedral wall and four palms that had stood in the square. Of the 18 000 inhabitants, 15 000 were missing. In less than five minutes the debris had fallen three kilometres and swept forwards twelve. In Yungay, Ranrahirca, and other villages in its path, twenty-five or thirty thousand people lost their lives (Plate 90).

The Yungay avalanche was a giant lahar. Its highly fluid character is clear from the mud splashed on to the valley walls, from its great speed, and its ability to cross the dividing ridge. At the start it was probably ten or fifteen metres thick, but it quickly thinned as it travelled, and only three metres of debris were left in the Yungay town square. In it were huge boulders, some weighing as much as a hundred tons.

It is well to close with this reminder that we have not yet solved the whole earthquake problem. We have the examples of Yungay, Niigata, and Anchorage to show that even if buildings designed in accordance with a modern building code will not shake to pieces, the siting of our cities, towns and individual buildings is still in need of study.

*Plate 91: Lahar debris. A close-up view of some of the material that composed the Huascarán avalanche.*

*Plate 92: What now? After the Niigata earthquake, homeless citizens confront the blaze of the fuel storage depot.*

Specialized structures like dams and bridges and ever taller buildings continue to challenge the seismic engineer, and a host of secondary problems remain unsolved. Most of our water, electricity, and drainage systems are vulnerable at one point or another, and so are our roads, railways, docks, and aerodromes.

In many parts of the world, seismic zoning is leading to improved building codes. In others, as is unfortunately true of my own country, ill-informed pressure groups are able to use it as an excuse for relaxing existing precautions. The earthquakes at Niigata, Agadir, and Buyin-Zara all occurred in regions supposed (on inadequate grounds) to be safer than regions a few hundred kilometres away. The precautions taken by a wise community will not only provide a degree of resistance adequate for the prevailing level of activity, but must also provide for the infrequent large earthquake that is possible in regions of minor seismicity, or which falls outside the known limits of an active area.

# Appendix

If a man will begin with certainties, he shall end in doubts;
but if he will be content to begin with doubts, he shall end
in certainties.

Francis Bacon, *The Advancement of Learning*

## Facts and figures

In bringing this survey of present-day seismology to a close I am
conscious of how much has been left out. There is nothing about
laboratory experiments on the behaviour of materials under high
temperature and pressure, the ramifications of modern tectonic
theory have barely been sketched in, and whole regions of the Earth
seem to have been dismissed with little more than a mention.

But I hope it is possible to see what seismology is about, and how
many branches of physical and geological knowledge can be brought
to bear upon it. Few of us who claim to be seismologists can discuss
more than a handful of specialist problems with any authority.

This final section of the book brings together some tables of figures
and lists of historical events which the reader may care to have for
reference, and lists a few of the books that may help the student who
wishes to go further.

## The size of the Earth

More than two hundred years ago French scientists began a battle to
establish an international standard of length based upon the size of
the Earth. The *metre* was intended to be one ten millionth part of the
distance from the equator to the pole, which they established by
carrying out a heroic series of geodetic measurements between about
1790 and 1820. They incidentally laid the foundation of modern
gravity observation.

International agreement to adopt the metre and its associated
standard of mass the kilogram has now been reached, and most
countries have either made the change to the units of the Système
International or are in the course of doing so. S.I. units have
therefore been used throughout this book, but the accompanying
official recommendations concerning preferred multiples (which
would deprive us of so useful a unit as the centimetre) have been
passed over whenever popular usage seemed likely to part company
from official edict. My most wilful offence has been to use 'ton' to
mean metric ton throughout. When tons avoirdupois no longer
appear in the problems of school arithmetics, and short tons and long
tons have vanished from commerce, the form *tonne* should become
as rare in English as *gramme* is now.

Geophysicists, who saw no reason to express densities in four figures when they needed only two or three, have decided to adopt the
allowed unit *megagrams per cubic metre* ($Mg\ m^{-3}$), which yields
exactly the same numbers as their old *grams per cubic centimetre*.
Thus, honour is preserved on both sides, and the old advantage that
densities and specific gravities taking water as 1 are expressed by the
same numbers is still retained.

| | |
|---|---|
| Polar diameter of the Earth | 12 714 km |
| Equatorial diameter | 12 757 |
| Mean radius | 6 371 |
| Radius of the core | 3 473 |
| Radius of the inner core | 1 250 |
| Depth to the core | 2 898 |
| Depth to the inner core | 5 121 |
| Mass of the Earth | $5.98 \times 10^{24}$kg |
| Volume of the Earth | $1.083 \times 10^{21}$m$^3$ |
| Mean density of the Earth | $5.517$ Mg m$^{-3}$ |

## The geological column

| Years ago | Era | Period | Duration (years) |
|---|---|---|---|
| | Quaternary | Recent | 25 000 |
| | | Pleistocene | 2 million |
| 2 million | | | |
| | Tertiary or Cainozoic | Pliocene | 10 million |
| | | Miocene | 13 million |
| | | Oligocene | 15 million |
| | | Eocene | 20 million |
| | | Palaeocene | 10 million |
| 70 million | | | |
| | Secondary or Mesozoic | Cretaceous | 65 million |
| | | Jurassic | 45 million |
| | | Triassic | 45 million |
| 225 million | | | |
| | Primary or Palaeozoic | Permian | 45 million |
| | | Carboniferous | 80 million |
| | | Devonian | 50 million |
| | | Silurian | 40 million |
| | | Ordovician | 60 million |
| | | Cambrian | 100 million |
| 600 million | | | |
| | Pre-Cambrian or Eozoic | Pre-Cambrian | |

Age of Earth's crust: 4 500 million years.

## Felt intensity scales

The version of the modified Mercalli scale given below is an abridged one intended only to give an indication of the main features of scales of this kind. There are strong arguments for using intensity scales adapted to local needs, and any reader who is called upon to make a practical assessment of damage is advised to look at the versions given by Richter (*Elementary Seismology,* pp 136 - 139) and Eiby (*New Zealand Journal of Geology and Geophysics 7*: 108 - 133, 1963). The most accessible English version of the MSK scale is probably that given by Båth (*Introduction to Seismology,* pp 125 - 128).

*I*. Not felt except by a very few under especially favourable circumstances.

*II*. Felt only by a few persons at rest, especially on the upper floors of buildings. Delicately suspended objects may swing.

*III*. Felt quite noticeably indoors, especially on the upper floors of buildings, but many people do not recognize it as an earthquake. Standing motor-cars may rock slightly. Vibration like the passing of a truck. Duration estimated.

*IV*. During the day, felt indoors by many, outdoors by few. At night, some awakened. Dishes, windows, doors disturbed; walls make cracking sound. Sensation like heavy truck striking the building. Standing motor-cars rocks noticeably.

*V*. Felt by nearly everyone; many awakened. Some dishes, windows, etc., broken; a few instances of cracked plaster; unstable objects overturned. Disturbance of poles, trees, and other tall objects sometimes noticed. Pendulum clocks may stop.

*VI*. Felt by all; many frightened and run outdoors. Some heavy furniture moved; a few instances of fallen plaster or damaged chimneys. Damage slight.

*VII*. Everybody runs outdoors. Damage negligible in buildings of good design and construction; slight to moderate in well-built ordinary structures; considerable in poorly built or badly designed structures; some chimneys broken. Noticed by persons driving motor-cars.

*VIII*. Damage slight in specially designed structures; considerable in ordinary substantial buildings with partial collapse; great in poorly built structures. Panel walls thrown out of frame structures. Fall of chimneys, factory stacks, columns, monuments, walls. Heavy furniture overturned. Sand and mud ejected in small amounts. Changes in well water. Disturbs persons driving motor-cars.

*IX*. Damage considerable in specially designed structures; well-designed frame structures thrown out of plumb; great in substantial buildings, with partial collapse. Buildings shifted off foundations. Ground cracked conspicuously. Underground pipes broken.

*X*. Some well-built wooden structures destroyed; most masonry and frame structures destroyed with foundations; ground badly cracked. Rails bent. Landslides considerable from river banks and slopes. Shifted sand and mud. Water splashed (slopped) over banks.

*XI*. Few if any (masonry) structures remain standing. Bridges destroyed. Broad fissures in ground. Underground pipe-lines completely out of service. Earth slumps and landslips in soft ground. Rails bent greatly.

*XII*. Damage total. Waves seen on ground surfaces. Lines of sight and level distorted. Objects thrown upwards into the air.

## Magnitudes and energies

The magnitude of an earthquake is a measure of the total energy radiated in the form of elastic waves, but this is not strictly speaking the full total of the energy released, for the elastic rebound process is a far from efficient generator of waves. Part of the stored elastic strain is converted into heat. Evidence of this may appear in metamorphism of rocks close to the surface of the fault break, or as a rise in the temperature of the ground water in nearby wells and springs. How much of the total energy becomes heat is very difficult to estimate.

In scientific terms, energy is power to do work, whether it takes the form of heat, or electricity, or elastic waves, or anything else. Energy is measured in joules. Formally a joule (J) is the work done when a force of one newton (N) is displaced through a distance of one metre in the direction of the force; and a newton is the force which, applied to a mass of one kilogram, will give it an acceleration of one metre per second per second ($1$ m s$^{-2}$).

The relationship between the energy of the elastic waves in joules and the numbers of the magnitude scale is not beyond argument, but most seismologists now use an equation derived by Markus Båth:

Log $E = 5 \cdot 24 + 1 \cdot 44 M_S$ (joules).

Magnitudes on the $M_L$ and $m_B$ scales must first be converted using the equations:

$m = 1 \cdot 7 + 0 \cdot 8\ M_L - 0 \cdot 01\ M_L{}^2$, and
$m = 0 \cdot 56\ M_S + 2 \cdot 9$.

The domestic unit of electric power, the kilowatt (kW) is equal to 1 000 joules per second. Båth has pointed out that the annual power consumption of Uppsala, his home city, which has about 100 000 inhabitants who use some 290 million units a year, could be supplied by appropriately harnessing an earthquake of magnitude $6 \cdot 8$. One of magnitude $8^3/_4$ would keep them going for over six hundred years, but they would get through a magnitude $1^1/_2$ in well under a second!

Attempts have sometimes been made to compare earthquakes with nuclear bombs, but it cannot be done very exactly and the appropriate conversion factors are still being discussed over international conference tables. The kind of rock in which the bomb is exploded has a lot to do with the efficiency of the wave generation. According to American sources you need to explode 10 kilotons in alluvium to get the effect of 1 kiloton in hard rock. Soviet experts have claimed that they get the equivalent of a shock of magnitude $4 \cdot 6$ to $4 \cdot 8$ from a 1 kiloton bomb, while the Americans say that 2 kilotons are needed to reach magnitude $4 \cdot 0$. The data in the following table are therefore presented with some diffidence.

| $M_S$ | Joules | |
|---|---|---|
| 0 | $1 \cdot 7 \times 10^5$ | Values for very small shocks are unreliable |
| 1 | $4 \cdot 8 \times 10^6$ | |
| 2 | $1 \cdot 3 \times 10^8$ | |
| $2^1/_2$ | | Smallest felt earthquakes |
| 3 | $3 \cdot 6 \times 10^9$ | |
| 4 | $1 \cdot 0 \times 10^{11}$ | |
| 5 | $2 \cdot 7 \times 10^{12}$ | Smallest damaging shocks Dunedin earthquake, 1974 |
| $5^1/_2$ | | Bikini bomb |
| $5 \cdot 9$ | | Agadir earthquake, 1960 |
| 6 | $4 \cdot 4 \times 10^{13}$ | Skoplje earthquake, 1963 |
| $6^1/_2$ | | 'Nominal' (20 kiloton) atom bomb |
| $6 \cdot 8$ | | San Fernando earthquake, 1971 |
| 7 | $2 \cdot 1 \times 10^{15}$ | Inangahua earthquake, 1968 |
| $7 \cdot 8$ | | Buller earthquake, 1929 |
| $7 \cdot 9$ | | Hawke's Bay earthquake, 1931 |

| | | |
|---|---|---|
| 8 | $5.7 \times 10^{16}$ | A 5 megaton bomb? |
| | | Aleutians underground test, 1971 |
| 8.3 | | San Francisco earthquake, 1906 |
| 8.4 | | Chile, 1960; Alaska, 1964 |
| 8.9 | | Largest recorded shocks: |
| | | Colombia, 1906; Sanriku, 1933 |
| 9 | $1.6 \times 10^{18}$ | A 300 megaton bomb? |

**Earthquake statistics**

The following table is based on data for the 47 years from 1918 to 1964, compiled by S. J. Duda:

| Magnitude | Number of shocks per decade | Energy release per decade |
|---|---|---|
| 8.5 – 8.9 | 3 | $156 \times 10^{16}$ joules |
| 8.0 – 8.4 | 11 | 113 |
| 7.5 – 7.9 | 31 | 80 |
| 7.0 – 7.4 | 149 | 58 |
| 6.5 – 6.9 | 560 | 41 |
| 6.0 – 6.4 | 2 100 | 30 |

Smaller shocks are very numerous and the data are less reliable. Gutenberg and Richter place the number of earthquakes per year above magnitude 5.0 at a little under a thousand, and that above 3.0 at about fifty thousand.

Because tectonic regions differ so greatly in size, it is difficult to compare the seismicity of one country with that of another, but the following table compiled by Markus Båth may be helpful. Nearly all the seismic energy is released in the larger shocks, so he has considered only the shocks of magnitude 7.9 or more, for the years 1904 – 1964.

| Region | Percentage of total seismic energy release | Energy per degree along the belt |
|---|---|---|
| Alaska | 4.3 | $6.1 \times 10^{16}$ joules |
| Western North America | 1.0 | 0.8 |
| Mexico – Central America | 4.2 | 2.3 |
| South America | 16.4 | 6.4 |
| S. W. Pacific – Philippines | 26.5 | 7.0 |
| Ryukyu – Japan | 15.8 | 13.5 |
| Kuril Islands – Kamchatka | 5.8 | 7.0 |
| Aleutian Islands | 3.0 | 2.9 |
| Central Asia – Turkey | 16.9 | 5.6 |
| Indian Ocean | 4.5 | – |
| Atlantic Ocean | 1.6 | – |

The total energy released within the stated limits of time and magnitude was $2.4 \times 10^{19}$ joules. About 77 percent of it was released in circum-Pacific areas.

## Historical earthquakes 1500 — 1902

The following list covers the period in which reliable information is available down to the general availability of instrumental records. It has been drawn mainly from John Milne's *Catalogue of Destructive Earthquakes*. All European earthquakes of Milne's Class III (which destroy towns and devastate districts) are included. Outside Europe, I have listed a selection of Class III shocks likely to be mentioned by general writers. To these are added some less intense shocks of special seismological interest, or connected with other historical events.

Dates may differ by one day from those in other accounts, as it is not always certain whether writers are using local time or Greenwich time for their records. They have all been given in the present calendar, as the change from 'Old Style' took place at different times in different countries.

The names printed in capitals are often used for convenience as 'proper names' of the earthquakes to which they refer, but it is usual to state the year as well in order to avoid ambiguity.

| | | |
|---|---|---|
| 1505 | July 6 | Persia, Afghanistan |
| 1509 | Feb. 25 | Calabria, Sicily |
| 1509 | Sept. 14 | Turkey |
| 1510 | Jan. 10 | Bavaria |
| 1511 | Mar. 26 | Adriatic |
| 1514 | Apr. 16 | Zante, Greece |
| 1531 | Jan. 26 | Spain, Portugal |
| 1549 | | Persia |
| 1556 | Jan. 24 | Austria, Bavaria |
| 1556 | Jan. 26 | SHANSI, China |
| 1590 | Sept. 15 | Central Europe |
| 1596 | | Nizhni Novgorod |
| 1609 | July 15 | Kansu, China |
| 1612 | Nov. 8 | Southern Europe |
| 1618 | Aug. 25 | Switzerland |
| 1622 | Oct. 25 | Kansu, China |
| 1638 | Mar. 27 | Italy, Greece |
| 1658 | Aug. 20 | Philippines |
| 1663 | Feb. 5 | St. Maurice, Canada |
| 1670 | Jan. 17 | Central Europe |
| 1679 | June 4 | Caucasia |
| 1687 | Oct. 20 | Lima, Peru |
| 1688 | Apr. 11 | Italy |
| 1688 | June 5 | Italy |
| 1688 | July 10 | Asia Minor |
| 1692 | June 7 | Jamaica |
| 1693 | Jan. 9 | Italy, Sicily |
| 1693 | June 11 | Malta |
| 1703 | Jan. 14 | Italy |
| 1703 | Dec. 31 | ODOWARA, Japan |
| 1706 | Apr. 10 | Iceland |
| 1710 | May-June | Algiers |
| 1718 | Dec. 10 | Cyprus |
| 1719 | May 25 | Turkey |
| 1721 | Apr. 26 | Persia |
| 1727 | Nov. 18 | Persia |
| 1728 | Nov. 28 | Philippines |
| 1730 | July 8 | Chile |
| 1730 | Dec. 30 | Hokkaido, Japan |

| 1737 | Oct. 11 | Calcutta |
|------|---------|----------|
| 1741 | Apr. 24 | Italy |
| 1751 | May 24 | Chile |
| 1755 | Nov. 1 | LISBON, Portugal |
| 1757 | July 9 | Azores |
| 1759 | Oct. 30 | Asia Minor |
| 1763 | July 29 | Hungary |
| 1766 | Oct. 21 | Venezuela |
| 1767 | July 11 | Zante, Greece |
| 1773 | June 3 | Guatemala |
| 1783 | Feb. 5 | Calabria, Italy |
| 1786 | Feb. 5 | Greece |
| 1786 | Mar. 9 | Southern Italy |
| 1789 | Sept. 30 | Perugia, Italy |
| 1790 | Apr. 6 | Transylvania |
| 1791 | Nov. 2 | Greece |
| 1796 | Feb. 26 | Asia Minor |
| 1797 | Feb. 4 | Ecuador, Peru |
| 1799 | July 28 | Italy |
| 1802 | Oct. 26 | Eastern Europe |
| 1805 | July 26 | Italy |
| 1810 | Feb. 16 | Candia, Greece |
| 1811 | Dec. 16 | NEW MADRID, U.S.A. |
| 1812 | Mar. 26 | Venezuela, Colombia |
| 1819 | June 16 | KUTCH, India |
| 1822 | Nov. 20 | VALPARAISO, Chile |
| 1823 | Mar. 5 | Southern Italy, Sicily |
| 1823 | May 7 | Central America |
| 1825 | Jan. 19 | Greece |
| 1827 | Sept. | Lahore, India |
| 1828 | Mar. 7 | Siberia |
| 1829 | May 5 | Turkey |
| 1832 | Mar. 8 | Calabria, Italy |
| 1833 | Aug. 26 | North India, Tibet |
| 1835 | Feb. 20 | CONCEPCIÓN, Chile |
| 1840 | July 2 | Armenia |
| 1846 | Aug. 14 | Central Italy |
| 1847 | July 31 | Nicaragua |
| 1847 | Oct. 8 | Chile |
| 1847 | Nov. 16 | Java, Sumatra |
| 1848 | Oct. 15 | MARLBOROUGH, New Zealand |
| 1853 | Apr. 21 | Sheraz, Persia |
| 1853 | Aug. 18 | Greece |
| 1855 | Jan. 23 | WELLINGTON, New Zealand |
| 1856 | Oct. 12 | Mediterranean |
| 1857 | Jan. 8 | Southern California |
| 1857 | Dec. 16 | The NEAPOLITAN, Italy |
| 1858 | Sept. 20 | Greece, Turkey |
| 1859 | Mar. 22 | Ecuador |
| 1860 | Dec. 3 | Central America |
| 1861 | Feb. 16 | S. W. Sumatra |
| 1864 | Jan. 12 | Chile |
| 1867 | Jan. 2 | Algiers |
| 1868 | Aug. 13 | CHILE-BOLIVIA |
| 1868 | Aug. 16 | Ecuador |
| 1870 | Oct. 5 | Mangone, Italy |
| 1872 | Mar. 20 | OWENS VALLEY, California, U.S.A. |

| 1875 | Mar. 28 | New Caledonia |
| 1875 | May 18 | Colombia, Venezuela |
| 1877 | May 9 | IQUIQUE, Chile |
| 1879 | Oct. 18 | S. Hungary, Roumania |
| 1880 | Feb. 22 | YOKOHAMA, Japan |
| 1880 | July 18 | Philippines |
| 1882 | Sept. 7 | Central America |
| 1883 | May 3 | Tabriz, Persia |
| 1883 | July 28 | Cassamicciola, Italy |
| 1883 | Aug. 27 | KRAKATOA (Eruption) |
| 1883 | Oct. 15 | Greece |
| 1885 | Mar. 27 | Greece |
| 1885 | Aug. 2 | Russian Turkestan |
| 1886 | Aug. 27 | Greece |
| 1886 | Aug. 31 | CHARLESTON, S. Carolina, U.S.A. |
| 1889 | July 28 | Kumamoto, Japan |
| 1891 | Oct. 28 | MINO-OWARI, Japan |
| 1893 | Jan. 31 | Greece |
| 1893 | Apr. 17 | Greece |
| 1894 | July 10 | Turkey |
| 1895 | Jan. 7 | Khorasan, Persia |
| 1895 | May 13 | Greece, Turkey |
| 1896 | June 15 | SANRIKU, Japan |
| 1896 | Aug. 26 | Iceland |
| 1897 | June 12 | ASSAM, India |
| 1897 | Sept. 21 | Philippines |
| 1898 | July 2 | Hungary |
| 1899 | Jan. 22 | S. W. Greece |
| 1899 | Sept. 10 | YAKUTAT BAY, Alaska |
| 1899 | Sept. 30 | CERAM, E. Indies |
| 1900 | Mar. 22 | Japan |
| 1900 | Oct. 9 | Alaska |
| 1902 | Apr. 19 | Central America |
| 1902 | Aug. 21 | Philippines |
| 1902 | Dec. 16 | Turkestan |

## Important earthquakes since 1903

This list begins in 1903 because that is the first year for which reasonably accurate and complete instrumental magnitudes are available. It contains all shocks with magnitudes of 8·0 or more, and a selection of smaller shocks that have been the subject of important researches, or have attracted unusual public attention.

From 1903 to 1954 the magnitudes quoted are those given in Gutenberg and Richter's *Seismicity of the Earth*, with appropriate amendments taken from Richter's *Elementary Seismology*. From 1955 to 1965 they are from Rothé's *La Séismicité du Globe* and should be completely consistent with the earlier figures. For later shocks, no authoritative listing of magnitudes exists. Reference has been made to Båth's *Introduction to Seismology*, to values of $M_S$ quoted in the *Regional Catalogue* of the International Seismological Centre, and to monographs on the individual earthquakes. Where appropriate the statistical corrections derived by Rothé have been applied.

| Date | Epicentral region | Magnitude | Focal Depth |
|---|---|---|---|
| 1903 Jan. 4 | Tonga | 8± | 400 km |
| Jan. 14 | Mexico | 8·3 | |
| Feb. 27 | Java | 8·1 | |
| June 2 | Aleutians | 8·3± | 100 km? |
| Aug. 11 | Thessaly, Greece | 8·3 | 100 km |
| 1904 June 7 | Sea of Japan | 7·9 | 350 km |
| June 25 | Kamchatka | 8·3 | |
| June 25 | Kamchatka | 8·1 | |
| Aug. 27 | KOLYMA, Siberia | 8·3 | |
| Dec. 20 | Costa Rica | 8·3 | |
| 1905 Jan. 22 | Celebes | 8·4 | 90 km |
| Apr. 4 | KANGRA, India | 8·6 | |
| July 9 | S. W. of Lake Baikal | 8·4 | |
| July 23 | S. W. of Lake Baikal | 8·7 | |
| Sep. 8 | CALABRIA, Italy | 7·9 | |
| 1906 Jan. 21 | HONSHU, Japan | 8·4 | 340 km |
| Jan. 31 | Colombia-Equador | 8·9 | |
| Mar. 16 | KAGI (Chia-i), Taiwan | 7·1 | |
| Apr. 18 | SAN FRANCISCO, California | 8·3 | |
| Aug. 17 | Aleutians | 8·3 | |
| Aug. 17 | Chile | 8·6 | |
| Sep. 14 | New Guinea | 8·4 | |
| Dec. 22 | SIKIANG, China | 8·3 | |
| 1907 Jan 14 | KINGSTON, Jamaica | – | |
| Apr. 15 | Mexico | 8·3 | |
| May 25 | Sea of Okhotsk | 7·9 | 600 km |
| Oct. 21 | KARATAG, Tadzhikstan | 8·1 | |
| 1908 Mar. 26 | Mexico | 8·1 | 80 km ± |
| Dec. 28 | MESSINA, Sicily | 7½ | |
| 1909 Feb. 22 | Fiji | 7·9 | 550 km |
| Mar. 13 | Honshu, Japan | 8·3 | 80 km |
| July 7 | Hindu Kush | 8·1 | 230 km ± |
| 1910 Apr. 12 | Ryukyu Is. | 8·3 | 200 km |
| June 16 | Loyalty Is. | 8·6 | 100 km |
| 1911 Jan. 3 | TYAN SHAN, Turkestan | 8·7 | |
| Feb. 18 | FERGHANA, Pamir | 7¾ | |
| June 15 | Ryukyu Is. | 8·7 | 160 km |
| 1912 Aug. 9 | Sea of Marmara | 7·8 | |
| 1913 Mar. 14 | Molucca Is. | 8·3 | |
| 1914 Nov. 24 | Mariana Is. | 8·7 | 110 km |
| 1915 Jan. 13 | AVEZZANO, Italy | 7½ | |
| May 1 | Kamchatka | 8·1 | |
| Oct. 3 | NEVADA, U.S.A. | 7¾ | |
| 1916 Jan. 13 | New Guinea | 8·1 | |
| 1917 Jan. 30 | Kamchatka | 8·1 | |
| May 1 | Tonga | 8·6 ± | |
| June 26 | SAMOA | 8·7 | |
| 1918 Aug. 15 | Caroline Is. | 8·3 | |
| Sep. 7 | Kuril Is. | 8·3 | |
| Nov. 18 | Banda Sea | 8·1 | 190 km |
| 1919 Jan. 1 | Tonga | 8·3 | 180 km |
| Apr. 30 | Tonga | 8·4 | |

| | | | | |
|---|---|---|---|---|
| 1920 | June 5 | Taiwan | 8·3 | |
| | Sep. 20 | Fiji | 8·3 | |
| | Dec. 16 | KANSU, China | 8·6 | |
| 1921 | Nov. 15 | Hindu Kush | 8·1 | 215 km |
| | Dec. 18 | Peru | 7·9 | 650 km |
| 1922 | Nov. 11 | ATACAMA, Chile | 8·4 | |
| 1923 | Feb. 3 | Kamchatka | 8·4 | |
| | Sep. 1 | KWANTO, Japan | 8·3 | |
| 1924 | Apr. 14 | Philippines | 8·3 | |
| | June 26 | S. W. of Macquarie Is. | 8·3 | |
| 1925 | Mar. 1 | QUEBEC, Canada | 7·0 | 60 km |
| | Mar. 16 | Yunnan, China | 7·1 | |
| | June 28 | MONTANA, U.S.A. | 6¾ | |
| 1926 | June 26 | RHODES, Dodecanese Is. | 8·3 | 100 km |
| 1927 | Mar. 7 | TANGO, Japan | 7·9 | |
| | May 22 | KANSU, China | 8·3 | |
| 1928 | Mar. 9 | Indian Ocean | 8·1 | |
| | Dec. 1 | Chile | 8·3 | |
| 1929 | Mar. 7 | Aleutians | 8·6 | |
| | May 1 | SHIRWAN, Iran | 7·1 | |
| | June 16 | BULLER (Murchison), N.Z. | 7·6 | |
| | June 27 | South Sandwich Is. | 8·3 | |
| 1930 | Nov. 20 | IZU, Japan | 7·1 | |
| 1931 | Feb. 2 | HAWKES BAY, N.Z. | 7·9 | |
| | Oct. 3 | Solomon Is. | 8·1 | |
| 1932 | May 14 | Celebes | 8·3 | |
| | May 26 | Tonga-Kermadec Trench | 7·9 | 600 km |
| | June 3 | Mexico | 8·1 | |
| 1933 | Mar. 2 | SANRIKU, Japan | 8·9 | |
| 1934 | Jan. 15 | BIHAR, India | 8·4 | |
| | June 29 | Celebes | 6·9 | 720 km |
| | July 18 | Santa Cruz Is. | 8·1 | |
| 1935 | Apr. 20 | Taiwan | 7·1 | |
| | May 30 | QUETTA, Baluchistan | 7½ | |
| | Dec. 28 | Sumatra | 8·1 | |
| 1937 | Apr. 16 | Tonga | 8·1 | 400 km |
| 1938 | Feb. 1 | Java | 8·6 | |
| | Nov. 10 | BEHRING SEA | 8·7 | |
| 1939 | Jan. 25 | Chile | 8·3 | |
| | Apr. 30 | Solomon Is. | 8·1 | |
| | Dec. 21 | Celebes | 8·6 | 150 km |
| | Dec. 26 | ANATOLIA | 7·9 | |
| 1940 | May 24 | Peru | 8·4 | |
| 1941 | June 26 | Burma | 8·7 | |
| | June 27 | Central Australia | 6¾ | |
| | Nov. 25 | West of Portugal | 8·4 | |
| 1942 | May 14 | Equador | 8·3 | |
| | Aug. 6 | Guatemala | 8·3 | |
| | Aug. 24 | Brazil | 8·6 | |
| | Nov. 10 | South of Africa | 8·3 | |
| 1943 | Apr. 6 | Andes | 8·3 | |
| | May 25 | Philippines | 8·1 | |
| | June 30 | Celebes Sea | 6·8 | 700 km |
| | July 23 | Java | 8·1 | 90 km |
| | Sep. 6 | Macquarie Is. | 7·8 | |
| | Sep. 10 | TOTTORI, Japan | 7·4 | |

| | | | | |
|---|---|---|---|---|
| 1944 Dec. 7 | Honshu, Japan | 8·3 | |
| 1945 Jan. 12 | MIKAWA, Japan | 7·1 | |
| Nov. 27 | Indian Ocean | 8·3 | |
| 1946 Aug. 4 | West Indies | 8·1 | |
| Nov. 10 | ANCASH, Peru | 7·3 | |
| Dec. 20 | Shikoku, Japan | 8·4 | |
| 1948 Jan. 24 | Philippines | 8·3 | |
| June 28 | FUKUI, Japan | 7·3 | |
| Oct. 5 | ASHKHABAD, Turkestan | 7·3 | |
| 1949 July 10 | TADZHIKSTAN | 8·0 | |
| Aug. 22 | S. Alaska | 8·1 | |
| 1950 Feb. 28 | Hokkaido, Japan | 7·9 | 340 km |
| Aug. 15 | ASSAM | 8·7 | |
| Nov. 2 | Banda Sea | 8·1 | |
| Dec. 2 | New Hebrides | 8·1 | |
| Dec. 9 | Andes, Argentina | 8·3 | 100 km |
| 1952 Mar. 4 | Hokkaido, Japan | 8·6 | |
| July 21 | KERN COUNTY, California | 7·7 | |
| Nov. 4 | Kamchatka | 8·4 | |
| 1953 Mar. 18 | N. W. ANATOLIA | 7·2 | |
| Nov. 25 | Honshu, Japan | 8·0 | |
| 1954 July 6 | FALLON, Nevada, U.S.A. | 6·6 | |
| Sep. 9 | ORLEANSVILLE, Algeria | $6^{3}/_{4}$ | |
| Dec. 16 | Nevada, U.S.A. | 7·1 | |
| 1955 Feb. 18 | QUETTA, Pakistan | $6^{3}/_{4}$ | |
| April 1 | LANAO, Philippines | 7·6 | 55 km |
| 1956 June 9 | KABUL, Afghanistan | 7·7 | |
| July 9 | SANTORIN, Greece | 7·7 | |
| 1957 Mar. 9 | Andreanof Is. | 8·0 | |
| Apr. 14 | S. of Samoa | 8·0 | |
| Jul. 28 | GUERRERO, Mexico | 7·8 | |
| Dec. 4 | Outer Mongolia | 8·3 | |
| Dec. 13 | Iran | 7·2 | |
| 1958 July 10 | S. E. Alaska | 7·9 | |
| Nov. 6 | Kuril Is. | 8·7 | 75 km |
| 1959 Jan 2 | Brittany | 5·2 | |
| May 4 | Kamchatka | $8^{1}/_{4}$ | 60 km |
| Aug. 18 | HEBGEN LAKE, Montana, U.S.A. | 7·1 | |
| 1960 Feb. 21 | MELOUSA, Algeria | $5^{1}/_{2}$ | |
| Feb. 29 | AGADIR, Morocco | 5·8 | |
| Apr. 24 | LAR, Iran | $5^{3}/_{4}$ | |
| May 22 | Arauco, CHILE | 8·4 | |
| 1961 June 1 | Ethiopia | $6^{3}/_{4}$ | |
| June 11 | LAR, Iran | $6^{3}/_{4}$ | |
| Aug. 31 | Peru-Brazil border | $7^{3}/_{4}$ | 629 km |
| 1962 Sep. 1 | BUYIN-ZARA, Iran | $7^{1}/_{2}$ | |
| 1963 Feb. 21 | BARCE, Libya | – | |
| July 26 | SKOPLJE, Yugoslavia | 6·0 | |
| Oct. 13 | Kuril Is. | $8^{1}/_{4}$ | 60 km |
| 1964 Mar. 27 | ANCHORAGE, Alaska | 8·4 | |
| June 16 | NIIGATA, Honshu, Japan | $7^{1}/_{2}$ | |

| | | | |
|---|---|---|---|
| 1965 Mar 28 | | Chile | $7\frac{1}{2}$ |
| 1966 Aug 19 | | VARTO, Turkey | 6·9 |
| 1967 Jul 30 | | CARACAS, Venezuela | 7·1 |
| 1968 Jan15 | | Sicily | 6·1 |
| | May 16 | TOKACHI, Japan | 7·9 |
| | Aug 1 | CASIGURAN, Philippines | 7·7 |
| | Aug 31 | DASHT-E-BAYAZ, Iran | 7·2 |
| | Oct 14 | MECKERING, W. Australia | 7·2 |
| 1969 Feb 28 | | Off coast of Portugal | 7·9 |
| | Jul 25 | E. China | 6·1 |
| 1970 Mar 28 | | GEDIZ, Turkey | 7·4 |
| | Apr 7 | Luzon, Philippines | 7·7 |
| | May 31 | CHIMBOTE, Peru | 7·7 |
| 1971 Jan 10 | | West Irian | 8·0 |
| | Feb 9 | SAN FERNANDO, California | 6·8 |
| | May 12 | BURDUR, Turkey | 6·8 |
| | May 22 | BINGÖL, Turkey | 6·7 |
| | Jul 9 | ILLAPEL, Chile | 7·7 |
| | Jul 14 | Solomon Islands | 8·1 |
| 1972 Jan 25 | | Taiwan | $7\frac{1}{2}$ |
| | Jul 30 | S. E. Alaska | 7·6 |
| | Dec 23 | MANAGUA, Nicaragua | 6·2 |
| 1973 Jan 30 | | MICHOACAN, Mexico | $7\frac{1}{2}$ |
| | Jun 17 | Hokkaido | 7·7 |
| 1974 Oct 3 | | Peru | 7·6 |
| | Dec 28 | PATTAN, W. Pakistan | 6·2 |
| 1975 Feb 4 | | LIAONING, China | 7·4 |
| | Feb 11 | GUATEMALA | $7\frac{1}{2}$ |
| | May 26 | N. Atlantic | 7·9 |
| | Jul 20 | Solomon I. | 7·9 |
| | Sep 6 | LICE, Turkey | 6·7 |
| | Oct 11 | S. of Tonga | 7·8 |
| 1976 Jan 14 | | Kermadec Is. | 8·0 |
| | May 6 | FRIULI, N. Italy | $6\frac{1}{2}$ |
| | Aug. 16 | Mindanao | 7·9 |
| | Jul 27 | TANG SHAN, China | 8·0 |

## New Zealand earthquakes

This list is included not only because of its obvious interest to New Zealanders, but because there are few other regions of moderate seismicity for which data are available to compile such a list. The epicentres of the larger shocks have been shown in Figure 72. The list includes all earthquakes believed to have reached magnitude 7 and a selection of other shocks that have attracted public interest or occurred in unusual places. Data for historical shocks are based upon information collected for the author's *Descriptive Catalogue of New Zealand Earthquakes* of which only the sections covering the years 1460 to 1854 have so far been published. Magnitudes of early shocks have been assigned on the basis of their felt effects. Instrumental data are taken from the annual *New Zealand Seismological Reports* and from special studies of individual shocks. In the period from 1860 to 1940 minor revision of some epicentres and magnitudes has still to be carried out. New Zealand dates have been used.

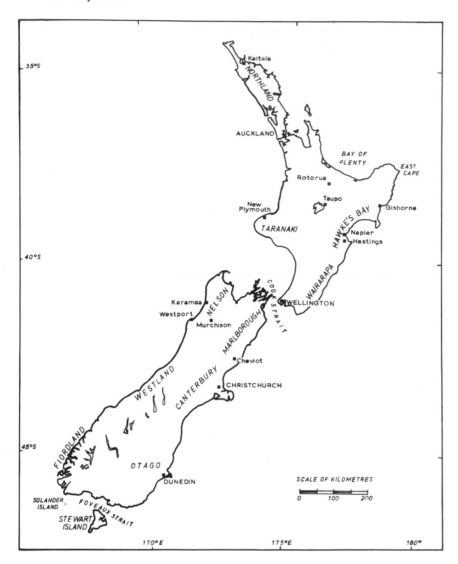

*Fig. 81: New Zealand showing the principal place-names mentioned in the text. Geological faults and active volcanoes are identified in Figure 76.*

Latitudes and longitudes of major epicentres are given, but readers unfamiliar with New Zealand geography may find Figure 81 helpful. All place-names used in the main text have been included.

1460±: Wellington. Possibly magnitude 8. Known in Maori tradition as *Hao-whenua*, the land swallower.

1773 May 11: Queen Charlotte Sound. Captain Furneaux of the *Adventure* records that his shore-party 'felt some two shocks of an earthquake but received no kind of damage'. The first New Zealand shock reported by a European observer.

1826: Fiordland. Uncertain traditions based upon the reports of sealers and whalers strongly suggest that a very large earthquake occurred about this time.

1843 Jul. 8: Wanganui. Magnitude not less than $7\frac{1}{2}$. Building damage and large landslides, resulting in two deaths.

1848 Oct. 16: N. E. Marlborough. Magnitude 7·1. Intensities reached MM X in the lower Wairau Valley, and there was serious damage to buildings in Wellington. Sometimes mis-called the Awatere Earthquake in spite of contemporary reports describing faulting in the Wairau. It is also mis-dated by up to three days because of confusion with aftershocks. Three deaths in the large aftershock on October 19.

1853 Jan. 1: New Plymouth. Magnitude about 6½. The strongest known shock in this part of New Zealand. Fallen chimneys and other minor damage to buildings and goods.

1855 Jan. 23: S.W.Wairarapa. Probably magnitude 8·1. Extensive faulting and coastal uplift. Destructive in Wellington, severely damaging in Wanganui. Five deaths.

1863 Feb. 23: Hawke's Bay. Building damage and ground fissures at Napier. Felt over most of the country. Information still very incomplete.

1876 Feb. 26: Oamaru. Some damage to buildings. Unusually large for this part of New Zealand.

1886 Jun. 9: Tarawera eruption. New Zealand's greatest volcanic disaster. Earthquakes were felt, but there is little evidence that they were severe.

1888 Sep. 1: North Canterbury. Magnitude about 7. Faulting at Glynn Wye provided one of the earliest observations of transcurrent movement.

1891 Jun. 23: Mouth of the Waikato River. Magnitude probably well over 6. An unusual location. Damaging in Raglan and Kawhia. Chimneys overthrown in Auckland.

1895 Aug. 18: Taupo. Magnitude over 6. Damage to buildings. Landslides and fissures. Possible surface faulting.

1897 Dec. 7: Wanganui. Magnitude 7. Damaging in Wanganui. Felt from Auckland to Timaru.

1901 Nov. 17: Cheviot. Magnitude 7. Damage and landslides in North Canterbury. One death.

1904 Aug. 9: Off Cape Turnagain. Magnitude 7½. Damage at Castlepoint.

1914 Oct. 7: East Cape Peninsula. Magnitude 7 to 7½. Damaging intensities in the eastern Bay of Plenty. One death.

1914 Nov. 22: East Cape Peninsula. Magnitude 6½ to 7. Felt over the whole North Island and south to Oamaru, but little damage reported. Possibly deep.

1917 Aug. 6: North Wairarapa, 40°·8S, 176°·0E. Magnitude above 6. Felt from Auckland to Cheviot.

1921 Jun. 19: Hawke's Bay, 30°·3S, 176°·4E. Magnitude 7. Focal depth about 80 km. Felt from Auckland to Dunedin. Minor damage over much of Hawke's Bay.

1922 Jun. 19: Taupo District. Many aftershocks. Often described as an earthquake swarm. Surface faulting and subsidence to the north west of Lake Taupo.

1922 Mar. 9: Arthur's Pass, 42°·5S, 172°·0E. Magnitude 6·9. Epicentre in thinly settled mountainous country. Felt over the whole country except the Northland Peninsula.

1929 Jun. 16: Buller, 41°·8S, 172°·2E. Magnitude 7·8. Destructive in the Murchison district, with numerous landslides and faulting. 17 deaths.

1931 Feb. 3: Hawke's Bay, 39°20'S, 176°40'E. Magnitude 7·9. Destructive. Intensity reached MM XI at Napier. Regional uplift. Minor faulting. 256 deaths.

1931 May 5: Poverty Bay. Magnitude above 6. Damage in the Gisborne area.

1932 Sep. 16: Wairoa, 38°·9S, 177°·55E. Magnitude 6·8. Damage in Gisborne and Wairoa.

1934 Mar. 5: Pahiatua, 40°·5S, 175°·6E. Magnitude 7·6. Damage in southern Hawke's Bay and northern Wairarapa. One death.

1942 Jun. 24: Southern Wairarapa, 40°·9S, 175°·9E.Magnitude 7·0. Damaging in the Wairarapa and Wellington.

1942 Aug. 1: Southern Wairarapa, 40°·95S, 175°·8E. Magnitude 7·1. Because of its greater focal depth (55 km) intensities were substantially lower than on Jun. 24.

1950 Feb. 5: South of the South Island 48°·5S, 164° E. Magnitude 7. Felt in parts of Otago and Southland.

1950 Aug. 5: South of the South Island 50° S, 164° E. Magnitude 7·3. Felt about Foveaux Strait.

1953 Sep. 29: Bay of Plenty, 37°·3S, 176°·8E. Magnitude 7·1 Focal depth 300 km. Very widely felt, with only minor damage.

1955 Jun. 12: Seaward Kaikouras, 42°·8S, 173°·3E. Magnitude 5·1. Minor damage in Cheviot district.

1958 Dec. 10: Bay of Plenty, 37°·2S, 176°·9E. Magnitude 6·9. Focal depth 330 km. Isolated damage to chimneys as far from the epicentre as Blenheim.

1960 May 24: Fiordland, 44°·2S, 167°·7E. Magnitude 7·0. Epicentral region sparsely inhabited. Minor damage to goods and plaster near Lake Wanaka. Not felt in the North Island.

1962 May 10: Wesport, 41°·65S, 171°·32E. Magnitude 5·9. Damage to chimneys, brick, and plasterwork, valued at $250 000. No casualties.

1963 Dec. 23: Northland, 35°·1S, 173°·5E. Magnitude 5·2. Damaged chimneys, house foundations, water-tanks and stacked goods in the area east of Kaitaia. Earthquakes in the Northland peninsula are rare. Before this event the region was considered aseismic.

1966 Mar. 5: Gisborne, 38°·52S, 177°·85E. Magnitude 6·2. Damage to older buildings on poor ground. Many cracked chimneys. Some gas and water mains broken.

1966 Apr. 23: Cook Strait, 41°·64S, 174°·52E. Magnitude 6·1. Damage to chimneys and household goods in Seddon.

1968 May 24: Inangahua, 41°·72S, 171°·94E. Magnitude 7·0. Large landslides. Serious damage to wooden houses, bridges, railway lines, and underground pipes. Fault breakage. Three deaths.

1972 Jan. 8: Te Aroha, 37°·58S, 175°·69E. Magnitude 5·1. Minor damage to chimneys, furniture, and goods.

1974 Apr. 9: Dunedin, 45°·97S, 170°·52E. Magnitude 5·0. Damage to chimneys and goods valued at $250 000. The largest known shock in eastern Otago.

## A short book-list

Although seismology finds a place in several recent books intended to present the earth-sciences to the man in the street, few of them have earthquakes as a main concern, and many of those that do cannot be recommended without serious reservations. It is better for the reader who would like to know more to go straight to the experts. First on any list must come C. F. Richter's *Elementary Seismology* (W. H. Freeman and Co., San Francisco, 1958) which deals further with many of the topics discussed in this book, and contains a detailed and critical bibliography. It should make clear that although plate tectonics and what has been hailed as 'the new global seismology' provide a framework within which seismicity and tectonic processes can be viewed advantageously, they have destroyed less of the previously accepted picture than their more enthusiastic advocates sometimes imply.

Markus Båth's *Introduction to Seismology* (Birkhauser Verlag, Basel and Stuttgart, 1973) has a more physical and less geological approach and demonstrates that a very balanced picture of the rest of the world is to be obtained from its author's base in Uppsala. Elementary mathematics are used to very good effect without interrupting the flow of a very readable book. At a more elementary level J. H. Hodgson's *Earthquakes and Earth Structure* (Prentice-Hall Inc., New York, 1964) covers its author's special interests very well, but falls short of covering the ground implied by its title. Readers who find that the lack of formal studies in physics is an obstacle to understanding may find O. M. Phillips's *The Heart of the Earth* (Freeman Cooper, San Francisco, 1968) a help. Bruce Bolt's *Earthquakes: a Primer* (W. H. Freeman and Co., San Francisco, 1978) has some excellent descriptions of recent earthquakes and treats problems of current research interest.

Of geology texts that adopt an up-to-date standpoint *Understanding the Earth* edited by Gass, Smith, and Wilson for the Open University Press (Artemis Press, Sussex, 1971) and Press and Seivers's *Earth* (W. H. Freeman and Co., San Francisco, 1974) are recommended. The same publishers have collected a series of articles that appeared in the *Scientific American* between 1952 and 1973 under the title *Continents Adrift*. A standard text that has opened the door for several generations of students is Arthur Holmes's *Principles of Physical Geology* (Nelson, London, 3rd ed. 1978).

Engineers who would like more seismological background than is given in most books on structural design will find *Earthquake Engineering*, edited by Robert L. Wiegel (Prentice-Hall, Englewood Cliffs, New Jersey, 1970) of interest. Bolt, Horn, Macdonald, and Scott's *Geological Hazards* (Springer Verlag, Berlin, Heidelberg, New York, 1975) contains detailed case-histories of some recent disasters.

Many well-illustrated technical reports on particular earthquakes have appeared in the last few years, ranging from the many volumes dealing with the Alaskan earthquake in 1964 and the San Fernando earthquake in 1971, and the exhaustive Japanese reports on the Niigata and Tokachi-Oki shocks to the briefer summaries produced by UNESCO reconnaissance teams. Among good non-technical accounts of large earthquakes are Noel F. Busch's *Two Minutes to Noon* (Arthur Barker, London 1963) dealing with the Kwanto earthquake in 1923, and Monica Sutherland's *The San Francisco Disaster* (Barrie and Rockliff, London, 1959). With this should be perused William Bronson's extraordinary collection of photographs *The Earth Shook, The Sky Burned* (Doubleday and Co., New York, 1959). T. D. Kendrick's *The Lisbon Earthquake* (Methuen, London, 1956) is a scholarly work in the best sense, setting the disaster against the thought and social background of the times.

Two books that should appeal equally to the reader who likes to see for himself in the field and to the reader who expects books to save him the effort are *Earthquake Country* by Robert Iacopi (Lane Book Co., Menlo Park, 1964), which takes him on a conducted tour of the San Andreas Fault, and *Rugged Landscape* by Graeme Stevens (A. H. and A. W. Reed, Wellington, Sydney, London, 1974). This deals in fascinating detail with the structural history of central New Zealand and seems likely to become a geological classic. Both books are beautifully illustrated.

The standard work on world seismicity is still Gutenberg and Richter's *Seismicity of the Earth and Associated Phenomena*. A facsimile of the 1954 edition has been issued by the Hafner Publishing Co. (New York and London, 1965), and the data have been continued to 1965 by J. P. Rothé (*La séismicité du globe*, UNESCO, Paris, 1969. Parallel French and English texts). These contain detailed epicentre maps for the whole Earth, with the shocks classified by magnitude and focal depth.

Readers who would like to take a wider look at geophysics might begin with *Global Geophysics* by Tucker, Cook, Iyer, and Stacey (English Universities Press, London, 1970), and then proceed if their mathematics will allow it to F.D. Stacey's *Physics of the Earth* (John Wiley and Sons, New York, London, 1969). A seismological text on the same level is K. E. Bullen's *Introduction to Theoretical Seismology* (Cambridge University Press, 3rd ed. 1963). Those unable to follow Bullen's mathematics might still find interest in his excellent bibliography.

Three valuable books have appeared while this one was being written. *Geological Hazards* by Bolt, Horn, Macdonald and Scott (Springer Verlag, Berlin, 1975) has valuable chapters on earthquakes, tsunamis, and volcanoes together with interesting material on topics less closely related to earthquakes. B. A. Bolt's *Nuclear Explosions and Earthquakes: The Parted Veil* (Freeman, San Francisco, 1976) takes a commendably international view of both the technical and the political problems involved. *Earthquake Prediction and Public Policy*, the report of a commission of the U.S. National Research Council (U.S. National Academy of Science, Washington, 1975) for the most part avoids sociological and administrative jargon and sets out the issues clearly. Differences in public reaction and social values would prevent most countries from applying many of the conclusions, but the methods of enquiry will repay study.

Finally, a corner must be found to mention a few of the more important technical journals. Only two — the *Bulletin of the Seismological Society of America* and the *Journal of the Earthquake Research Institute,* Tokyo — are mainly seismology. Among those dealing more widely with geophysics are the *Geophysical Journal,* the *Journal of Geophysical Research, Izvestiya Akademii Nauk SSSR (Seriya Geofizicheskiya),* which is available in an English translation, and *Tectonophysics.* For engineers there are *Earthquake Engineering and Structural Dynamics,* the *Bulletin of the New Zealand National Society for Earthquake Engineering* (which in spite of its title has an international circle of contributors and readers), and the *Proceedings* of the triennial World Conferences on Earthquake Engineering.

# Index

Place-names that are used as the names of an *Earthquake* or a *Fault* are listed only under those headings unless other information is given. Seismic phases are grouped under *Phase*, but *P-wave*, *S-wave* and *L-wave* have separate entries.

Absorption of waves, 11
Acceleration, 116, 118, 120
Addison, Joseph, 165
Adobe, 70, 71, 113, 174, 176
Aerodrome, 176
Africa, 36, 56, 71, 172
African Rift Valley, 71
Aftershocks, 12, 27, 81-2, 97, 169, 171, 173
Ahuriri, N.Z., 106, 171
Alaska, 53, 85, 87, 174, 186
Aleutian Is, 75, 86, 87, 186
Algeria, 172
Allah Bund (= Kutch Fault), 60
Alluvium, 38, 121, 132, 174
Alpide Belt, 71
Amberley, N.Z., 169
Ambrayseys, N.N., vii, 174
America, 56, 66, 186
    See also North, Central, South, United States of
Amplifiers, 9-10, 12, 13, 33, 36, 136, 138, 139
Amplitude, 47, 69, 86,
    of microseisms, 83, 84,
    of volcanic tremor, 93
Analogues, electrical, 120
Anatolia, 63
Anchorage, Alaska, 116, 175, 179
Andes, 62, 179
Andesite, 75, 90, 94
Animals, 4, 103-4, 165, 169, 174
Antarctica, 28, 29, 50, 55, 56, 71, 85
Arauco Peninsula, Chile, 173
Archaeology, 37, 58
Arabian Plate, 75
Architects, vi, 1, 114
Archive, seismogram, 136
Arctic, 34, 58
Areoseisms, 145
Aristotle, 164
Array seismographs, 136-40
Artificial vibrations, 83-4, 121, 132-3
Ash, volcanic, 89, 91
Asia, 152, 164
Asthenosphere, 49-50, 72, 76,
    lunar, 144
Astronauts, 143
Astronomy, 44, 95, 144
Asymmetrical seismic regions, 72-5
    See also Continental margin, Island arc
Atlantic Ocean, 56, 58, 186
Atomic bombs, 134-40, 185
    triggering of earthquakes by, 140
Atomic reactor, 120
Attenuation, 11, 47, 76
Auckland, N.Z., 118, 151
Aurora, 57
Australia, 4, 40, 56, 134
Awa Shima (off Honshu), 154

Awatere 'Earthquake Rent', 167
Azores, 58

Bacon, Sir Francis, 56
Ballore, Comte F. de Montessus de, 70
Barometric pressure,
    See Earthquake triggers, Meteorology
Basalt, 38, 59, 75, 90,
    lunar, 144
Basaltic layer, 45, 46
Båth, Markus, 183, 185, 186, 197
Båth's Law, 82
Bay of Islands, N.Z., 151
Bay of Plenty, N.Z., 148
Bedrock, 121, 132
Beloussov, V. V., 50
Ben-Menahem, Ari, 69
Benioff, Hugo, 12, 74, 81
Benioff zone, 74, 148
Bikini, 134, 185
Billings, Montana, 136, 137, 140
Birds, 103
Blot, Claude, 94
Body waves, 17-23, 79, 93, 140
Bolt, B. A., viii, 198
Bonin Is, 152
Boskabad, Iran, 63
Boso Peninsula, Japan, 159
Boston, Mass., 166
Bracing of buildings, inadequate, 106, 108, 113, 114, 115, 116,
Bricks, 108, 109, 111, 112, 167,
    and palaeomagnetism, 58
Bridges, 107, 115, 119, 123, 125, 127, 158, 174, 176,
    approaches to, 127
British Association for the Advancement of Science, 13, 26
Büchner, Georg, 44
Building codes, 96, 105, 111, 118, 121, 129, 173, 174, 181
Building vibrator, 118-20
Buildings
    adobe, 70, 71, 113, 114, 115, 174, 176
    brick, 108, 109, 111, 112, 167
    concrete block, 114
    damage to, 3, 5, 78, 106, 108, 109, 112-7, 167-9, 171, 172
    decorative features of, 108, 114, 125, 175
    deterioration of, 107, 125
    earthquake resistant, 30, 95, 106-28, 132
    high-rise = tall, *q.v.*
    historic, 123, 125
    Japanese domestic, 158
    masonry, 172, 173
    native, 113, 114
    pre-stressed concrete, 175
    reinforced concrete, 114, 176
    rubble, 70, 71
    steel-framed, 114
    strengthening of, 123, 125, 132
    tall, 118-9
    wooden, 106, 107, 109, 116, 167, 169, 175

Bullen, K. E., 134, 198
Buller River, N. Z., 169
Bulletins, seismological, 26, 27, 193,
        of N.Z. National Society for Earthquake Engineering, 198
        of the Seismological Society of America, 198
Bureau Central International de Séismologie, 25
Burma, 71

Calcium, 51
California, 10, 62, 66, 78, 79, 94, 95, 97, 98, 100, 103, 105,
        112, 130, 133, 134, 146-7, 148, 159-63
California Institute of Technology, 78
California State Earthquake Investigation Commission, 159,
        163
Caloi, P., 49
Cambrian,
        *See* Geological periods
Cambridge, England, 12
Cambridge University, 58
Campbell Plateau, 88
Canada, 12, 69, 87, 136, 166
Canterbury, N.Z., 156, 168
Cape Kidnappers, N.Z., 39
Cape Lopatka, Kamchatka, 87
Caribbean Plate, 75
Caribbean Sea, 83
Catalogues, earthquake, 70, 71, 154, 187, 189, 193
Cavendish, Henry, 45
Central America, 70
Central Asia, 26, 84, 99, 130, 186
Chalk, 40
Chang Heng, 164
Change of shape, 68, 102
Charles II, 41
Charleston, S. Carolina, 123
Charters Towers, Queensland, 85
Chatham Is, 88
Cheviot, N.Z., 169
Chieng Mai, Thailand, 85
Chile, 53, 88, 173
Chimbote, Peru, 176
Chimneys, 3, 78, 107, 109, 110, 111, 169
China, 100, 107, 136, 154, 164
Christchurch, N.Z., 84, 168, 169
Circum-Pacific Belt, 71, 148, 150, 186
Civil defence, 104
Clay, 58, 175
Cocos Plate, 75
Coda, 48
Coimbra, Portugal, 165
Collapse earthquakes, 38, 68
Compensation, isostatic, 54-6
Compression
        faulting, 61
        first motions, 67-9
        of rocks, 39, 42, 43, 50, 81-2, 101-3, 138
Compressional waves
        *See* Longitudinal waves, P-waves
Computer, electronic, 2, 18, 35, 48, 119, 136, 137, 138
        *See also* Analogue
Concepción, Chile, 173
Conrad discontinuity, 46
Constantinople (= Istanbul), 164
Construction, 105, 106-28
        *See also* Bridges, Buildings, Structures
Continental drift, 56-9, 72
        *See also* Pangaea, Plate Tectonics, Sea-floor spreading
Continental margins, 72, 73, 75, 76, 89, 90, 146-7, 150

Continental shields, 56, 71
Continents, 45, 48, 54, 56-9
Convection, 48-9, 59, 73, 76, 89
Cook, Captain James, 167
Core, 20, 21, 44, 45, 51, 52, 57, 183,
        of Moon, 144
        *See also* Inner core
Core phases, 22, 23
Cotton, Sir Charles, 41
Crater lakes, 91, 92
Creep
        elastic, 81-2
        Fault, 66-7, 81-2, 104
        in metal, 15
        soil, 128
Cretaceous
        *See* Geological periods
Croatia, 30
Crust, 30-2, 45, 46, 48, 49-51, 54, 59, 72, 134,
        lunar, 144
Crustal phases, 30-2
Crustal structure, 32, 45-6, 48, 50, 79, 134
Damping
        of buildings, 111, 119,
        of pendulums, 8, 13
        of seismographs, 13, 15
        of violin-string vibration, 13
Damage,
        assessment of, 183
        secondary, 110, 111, 114
        *See also* Buildings
Dams, 35, 69, 107, 114, 125, 129
Deaths
        *See* Earthquake casualties
Deccan Plateau, India, 90
Deep-focus earthquakes, 6, 19, 24, 49, 68, 71, 73-7, 94, 147,
        148, 152, 157
Degrees, distance measurement in, 20
Depth of focus
        *See* Focal depth
Depth phases, 24-5
Denham Bay, Raoul I., 93
Denmark, 83
Density
        and velocity of seismic waves, 49, 51, 52
        of Earth's interior, 51-3
        of Moon, 144
        of rocks, 45, 55
        units, 182
Denver, Colorado, 25, 69
Design, anti-seismic, 116, 118-9
Dextral faulting, defined, 60
Dickinson, W. R., 94
Dietz, R. S., 58
Dilatancy, vi, 101-3
Dilatation, 67, 68, 138
Dispersion, 47-8
Distance
        epicentral and focal, 19
        measurement of, in seismology, 17, 20
Docks, 85, 174, 181
Drill-holes
        crustal exploration, 44, 50-1
        foundation testing, 121
        seismic control, 105
        seismographs in, 136-7, 139
        temperature in, 44, 73, 94
        *See also* Wells

Drownings, 88, 155
Duda, S. J., 186
Dunedin, N.Z., 150
Dunite, 51
Dykes, volcanic, 89

Earth
  astronomical motions of, 44
  density of, 45, 51-3, 183
  dimensions of, 44, 182-3
  fundamental vibrations, 53
  gravitational field, 45, 55
  internal structure of, 1, 21, 30, 44-53, 67, 134
  internal temperature of, 44-5, 48-9, 51, 66, 89
  magnetic field, 48, 57-9
  mass, of, 44-5, 54, 183
  origin of, 44-5, 54
  pressure inside the, 49, 66
  surface of, 55, 66
  thermal history of, 44-5
  *See also* Core, Crust, Inner Core, Mantle, Seismicity
Earth currents, 48, 57, 103
Earth tides, 97-8
Earthquake
  Agadir (1960), 107, 172-3, 174, 181, 185
  Alaska (1958), 87
  Alaska (1964), 53, 78, 85, 104, 116, 156, 173, 174-6
  Ancash (1946), 62
  Assam (1950), 86
  Buller (1929) = Murchison, *q.v.*
  Buyin-Zara (1962), 174, 181
  California (1906) = San Francisco, *q.v.*
  Constantinople (A. D. 640), 164
  Charleston (1886), 123, 166
  Cheviot (1901), 168-9, 195
  Cheviot (1951), 82
  Chilean, (1868), 88
  Chilean (1906), 159
  Chilean (1960), 53, 172
  Chimbote (1970), 107, 113, 176, 178-9
  Colombia-Equador (1906), 78, 154, 159
  Cook Strait (1950), 97
  Dasht-e-Bayaz (1968), 62, 63
  Dunedin (1974), 185, 196
  Fort Tejon (1852), 159
  Gediz (1970), 63
  Gisborne (1966), 100, 196
  *Hao-whenua* (1460), 151, 166, 167, 194
  Hawke's Bay (1931), 5, 52, 78, 95, 98, 106, 107, 117, 169, 171, 185, 195
  Imperial Valley (1940), 62
  Inangahua (1968), 5, 104, 108, 124, 133, 171, 185, 196
  Kutch (1819), 60
  Kwanto (1923), 107, 155, 157, 159, 161
  Lar (1960), 172, 174
  Liaoning (1975), 100, 115, 128, 176
  Lisbon (1755), 78, 86, 164-5
  London (1750), 70
  Marlborough (1848), 167, 168, 194
  Masterton (1942) = Wairarapa, *q.v.*
  Melousa (1960), 172, 174
  Mino-Owari (1891), 61
  Moroccan (1731), 172
  Mudurunu (1967), 63
  Murchison (1929), 51, 98, 132, 169-71, 185, 195
  Nan Shan (1927), 107

  Nankaido (A.D. 684), 154
  Napier (1931) = Hawke's Bay, *q.v.*
  Neapolitan (1857), 3, 166
  New Madrid (1811), 165
  Niigata (1964), 87, 117, 121, 122, 125, 128, 130, 155, 175-6, 181
  Northland (1963), 151, 196
  Owens Valley (1872), 159
  Quizvan (1962), 107
  San Fernando (1971), 100, 115, 116, 127, 185
  San Francisco (1836), 159
  San Francisco (1838), 159
  San Francisco (1906), 60, 78, 107, 111, 158, 159, 161-3
  Sanriku (1933), 78, 154, 159
  Shansi, (1556), 107, 164
  Skoplje (A.D. 518), 174
  Skoplje (1555), 174
  Skoplje (1963), 112, 174, 185
  South West Wairarapa (1855), 3, 78, 88, 104, 151, 166, 167, 195
  Southern England (1580), 164
  Tang Shan (1976), 106, 154
  Tango (1927), 65
  Taupo (1922), 93-4, 195
  Tokyo (1923) = Kwanto, *q.v.*
  Wanganui (1843), 167, 194
  Wellington (1840), 167
  Wellington (1848) = Marlborough, *q.v.*
  Wellington (1855) = South West Wairarapa, *q.v.*
  Wairarapa (1942), 109, 133, 168, 196
Earthquake casualties, 60, 71, 78, 95, 100, 106, 107, 108, 109, 125, 154, 155, 158, 161, 164, 165, 167, 169, 171, 172, 174, 176
Earthquake catalogues
  *See* Catalogues
Earthquake damage, 5, 78, 93, 133, 159, 161-3, 166-81
  *See also* Buildings
Earthquake engineering
  *See* Engineering seismology
Earthquake Engineering N.Z. National Society for, 133, 198
Earthquake Fault
  *See* Faults, geological
Earthquake geography, 70-7, 129-33
  *See also* Seismicity
Earthquake history, 129-30, 164-71, 187-9
Earthquake insurance
  *See* Insurance
Earthquake Investigation Commission, California State, 159, 163
Earthquake, largest, 78, 80, 107, 154, 159, 164
Earthquake lights, 173, 174
  preceeding tsunami, 88
Earthquake line, 132
Earthquake mechanism, 60-9, 81-2, 96, 101-3, 184
  historic views of, 164-5, 167
Earthquake origin
  *See* Epicentre, Focus, Hypocentre, Source volume
Earthquake prediction, vi, 30, 95-105
Earthquake recording
  *See* Recording
Earthquake Research Institute, Tokyo, 104, 159, 198
Earthquake risk, 2, 129, 131
  *See also* Zoning
Earthquake sounds, 3, 20, 91-2, 103-4, 171
Earthquake swarms, 82, 93-4, 97
Earthquake statistics, 76-82, 96, 98, 106-7, 130, 184-6
Earthquake warnings, 103, 104
Earthquake weather, 97, 98

Earthquakes, 1, 2, 3, 20, 25, 38, 59, 60, 64, 70, 76-80, 89, 129, 140, 143, 164, 186, 187-96
   and nuclear tests, 134, 135
   behaviour during, 108, 174
   collapse, 38, 68
   control of, 105
   distribution with depth, 76
   effect of, upon sinners, 70
   felt, 3-6, 78-80
   historical, 2, 3, 164-71, 187-9
   induced by fluid injection, 69
   intermediate, 73
   large, since 1903, 189-93
   numbers having given magnitude, 80
   periodicity of, 81, 96
   principal New Zealand, 193-6
   shallow, 72, 75, 76, 150-1
   submarine, 67, 87, 98
   tectonic, 91
   triggering of, 96-8, 140
   volcanic, 38, 91, 92, 98
   *See also* Aftershocks, Areoseisms, Deep-focus earthquakes, Foreshocks, Moonquakes, Sea-quakes, Seismicity
East Cape, N.Z., 88
Eclipses, 95
Economics, 1, 37, 95, 100, 104, 111, 131, 133, 136, 165
   *See also* Insurance
Eddy currents 13
Eiby, G.A., 183, 193
Elastic afterworking, 81
Elastic rebound theory, 61, 64-7, 81-2, 96, 102, 138, 147, 184
Electricity supply, 176
   equivalent earthquake energy, 185
Energy, 66, 78, 80, 81, 96, 185-6
Energy absorbers as safety devices, 119
Engineering seismology, 5, 11, 96, 106-28, 133, 181, 198
   *See also* Buildings, Design
England, 26, 86, 95
Epicentre, 5, 6, 17-9, 24, 71, 72-4, 135, 147, 148, 163, 168
   of Kwanto earthquake, 159
   of moonquakes, 141-2
Epicentre location, 5, 17-9, 25
Erosion, 38, 42, 55, 60, 62
   of volcanic spine, 91
Eruptions, volcanic, 89-94, 173
   false reports of, 169
   of Krakatoa, 91
   of Tarawera, 195
Eskdalemuir, 136
Ether, 101
Eurasian Plate, 73, 74, 152
Europe, 25, 66, 82, 187
Evison, F.F., 71, 103
Explosions, 32, 37, 46, 49, 50, 68, 134, 135, 138, 140, 166
   nuclear, triggering of earthquakes by, 140
   volcanic, 90, 91, 93

Farewell Spit, N.Z., 36
Fault
   Alpine, 130, 147, 149, 150, 161
   Awatere, 167
   Buena Vista, 66
   Imperial Valley, 62
   Neo Valley, 61
   Nukumaru, 60
   Kutch, 60
   Quiches, 62
   San Andreas, 60, 105, 130, 146, 147, 161

Wellington, 96
   Wairau, 167
   West Wairarapa, 167
   White Creek, 132, 170
Fault break, 60-3, 156, 170, 171, 184
Fault creep, 66-7, 81-2, 104
Fault movement, 60-4, 156
Fault scarp, 60, 61, 62
Fault zone, 130, 131
Faulting, 60-4, 65, 66, 67, 81, 93, 96, 98, 130, 156, 167, 170, 173, 174, 175
   and stress-drop, 80-1
   and topography, 63
   and zoning, 130-1
   of sea-bed, 85
   transcurrent, 60, 62, 64-5, 98, 132, 147, 156, 161
   vertical, 61, 62, 64, 98, 156, 170
Faults, geological, 5, 60-9, 130, 148, 154, 167, 170, 173
   and earthquake risk, 131
   Californian, 148, 159-61
   New Zealand, 147, 149, 154
   normal, 60
   reverse, 60
   strike-slip = transcurrent, *q.v.*
   transcurrent, 60, 62, 146, 149, 156
   transform, 161
Felt earthquakes, 3-6
   *See* Intensity, Sea-quakes
Fiji, 29
Filters, electrical, 34, 35, 36, 136
Fiordland, N.Z., 148, 150
Fire, 110-1, 114, 117, 155, 157, 158, 161, 165, 167, 171, 174, 180
First-motion studies, 67-9, 138-40
Fish, 104
Flexures, geological, 131
Flooding, 107, 111, 129, 133, 169, 176
Flores Sea, 77
Focal depth, 19, 29, 66, 80, 134
   and epicentral distance, 19
   and nuclear detection, 138
   determination of, 19, 24-5
   effect of upon felt intensity 6, 147
   greatest observed, 77
   of Agadir earthquake, 172
   of moonquakes, 143
   shallow limit to, 66
   *See also* Deep-focus earthquakes
Focal sphere, 67, 68
Focus, 5, 17, 19, 24, 30, 50, 64, 65, 66, 67, 167
Folding, 42, 43, 59, 73, 131
Foreshocks, 98, 104
Fossa Magna, 152, 157
Fossils, 1, 38, 40, 41
Foundations, building, 111, 114, 120, 121, 128, 129, 169, 175-6
Foveaux Strait, N.Z., 151
Fracture, 66
   *See also* Elastic rebound, Faults, Faulting
France, 41, 86
Franco-Prussian War, 30
Frank, F.C., 101
Franklin, Benjamin, 165
Franz-Josef Glacier, N.Z., 149
Free oscillations of the Earth, 53
Frequency, 47, 55, 86
Friction, 8, 9, 10, 66, 96, 111
Fujiyama, 90, 152
Furniture, 111
Fyfe, H. E., 170

Galitzin, Prince B. B., 15
    *See also* Seismograph
Galvanometers, 9, 13, 15, 34
Garm, U.S.S.R., 99, 101
Gases, Volcanic, 89
Gediz, Turkey, 63
Geodetic surveying, 96-7, 159, 160, 182
Geodimeter, 97
Geography, seismic
    *See* Earthquake geography
Geological column, 39, 40-3, 183
Geological periods, 40-1, 183
    Cambrian, 40
    Cretaceous, 58, 75
    Jurassic, 40
    Mesozoic, 56
    Pleistocene, 166
    Pre-Cambrian, 56
    Recent, 132
    Tertiary, 75, 174
    Triassic, 40
Geology, 1, 5, 33, 38-43, 54, 55, 58, 94, 130, 132
Geomorphology, 131
Geophones, 33, 34, 37
Geophysics, 1, 13, 37, 44
    *See also* Earth currents, Gravity, Heat-flow, Magnetism,
    Prospecting, Seismology
George IV, 41
Geosyncline, 42-3
Geothermal gradient, 44
    *See also* Heat-flow
Geothermal power, 35, 93, 94
Germany, 13, 134
Geysers, 94
Gibowicz, S. J., 81
Gibraltar, Straits of, 77
Gisborne, N.Z., 171
Glaciers, 38, 149
Glynn Wye, N.Z., 156
Golden Gate, Calif., 163
Golitsyn = Galitzin, *q.v.*
Granite, 38, 45, 57
Grantitic layer, 45, 46,
Gravimeter, 55
Gravity, 13, 37, 54-5, 97, 116
Gravity anomalies, 55, 72, 73, 75, 150, 152, 154
Gravity survey, 132
Grey River, N.Z., 149
Ground-water, 33, 102-3, 123, 169, 176
    temperature of, 184
Gutenberg, Beno, viii, 21, 44, 50, 71, 72, 79, 85, 134, 186,
    189, 197
Gutenberg discontinuity, 21
Gzovsky, M. V., 130

Hanning Bay, Alaska, 156
Haslach, Germany, 134
Hastings, N.Z., 95, 109, 171
Hatherton, Trevor, 94
Hawaii, 41, 86, 87, 90, 93, 174
Hawke Bay, N.Z., 39
Hayes, R. C., vi, 97
Health, risks to public, 111
Heat, 1, 44-5, 79, 184
    *See also* Convection, Temperature
Heat-flow, 45, 73
Heaton, T. H., 97

Heligoland, 134
Hertz, 47
Hess, H.S., 58
Hikurangi Trench, 150
Hiroshima, Japan, 134
Hodgson, J. H., 69
Hokkaido, Japan, 29, 152
Holland, 86
Hollster, Calif., 66
Honda, H., 69
Hong Kong, 83
Honshu, Japan, 152, 154, 176
Himalayas, 71, 73, 77, 97
Hindu Kush, 77
Huascarán, Peru, 176, 179
Hutt Valley, N.Z., 96, 109

Iceland, 58
Igneous rocks, 38, 41-2, 57, 89
    *See* Lava, Magma, Volcanoes
Imamura, Akitune, 154, 159
Inangahua, N.Z., 5, 27, 108
India, 56, 60, 167
Indian Ocean, 58, 186
Indian Plate, 73, 74, 150
Indonesia, 24, 41, 71, 91
Inertia, 7, 110, 111
Inner core, 51-3
    dimensions of, 183
Institute of Physics of the Earth, Moscow, 50
Insurance, 104, 110, 131, 133, 171
Intensity, 4-6, 78, 79, 129, 172
    damaging, 109, 114, 172
    factors modifying, 5-6, 129, 147
    near fault lines, 131
    relation to magnitude, 78-9, 114
Intensity scales, 3, 4-5, 79, 183-4
    *See also* Mercalli, MSK, Questionnaires,
    Rossi-Forel
Intermediate layer, 45
International Geophysical Year, 50, 58, 134
International Seismological Centre, 26, 189
International Seismological Summary, 24, 26
Intrusion, volcanic, 42, 89
Ionosphere, 57
Iran, 4, 62, 63, 107, 172, 174
Iron, 51, 57
    oxides of, 51
Island arcs, 75, 77, 90, 150, 154
Isle of Wight, 26
Isoseismals, 5, 6, 16, 74, 166, 167, 171
Isostasy, 54-6
    *See also* Gravity, Gravity anomalies
Italy, 3, 86
Iwafune, Honshu, 87

Japan, 25, 26, 67, 69, 82, 87, 93, 97, 98, 112, 118, 121, 129,
    130, 133, 146, 147, 152-5, 157-60, 174, 176, 186
Japan Trench, 157
Japanese Ministry of Construction, 120
Java, 90
Joules, 185
Jurassic
    *See* Geological periods

Kaitaia, N.Z., 151
Kamchatka, 77, 87, 152, 186
Karamea, N.Z., 170
Karapiro, N.Z., 76
Karník, Vit, 4
Kawasumi, H., 67
Keilis-Borok, V.I., 69
Kermadec Is, 88, 93, 150
*Kern,* 22
Kern County, Calif., 66
Kilimanjaro, Tanzania, 90
Knopoff, Leon, 69
Kondratenko, A.M., 99
Korea, 129
Krakatoa, eruption (1883), 91
Kulpa Valley, Croatia, 30
Kuril Is, 152, 186
Kyushu, Japan, 154

Laboratory studies of rocks, 69, 81-2, 132
Lahar, 91-2, 176, 178-9
Lake Brunner, N.Z., 149
Lake Eyre, S. Australia, 71
Lake Mapourika, N.Z., 149
Lake Taupo, N.Z., 91, 94
Lake Te Anau, N.Z., 148
Lamont (*now* Lamont-Doherty) Observatory, New York, 15
Land-bridges, 57
Landslides, 38, 106, 107, 131, 133, 169, 170, 176, 178-9
Large-Aperture Seismic Array (LASA), 136-40
Lava, 44, 48, 59, 75, 89, 90, 91, 93, 94
Leaning Tower, Pisa, 125
Lehmann, Inge, 51
Liaoning, China, 115
Lightning-rods, 165
Lights
    earthquake, 173, 174
    preceeding tsunami, 88
Lima, Peru, 25
Limestone, 38, 40, 41, 169
Linehan, Rev. Daniel, 37
Lipari Is. 91
Liquefaction of subsoil, 121, 123, 173, 176
Lithosphere, 50, 74
    lunar, 144
Lithospheric slab, 74, 76, 77, 148
Lituya Bay, Alaska, 87
Llanguanaco Valley, Peru, 179
Lodestone, 57
Long waves, 23
Longitudinal waves, 16
    *See also* P-waves, Sound waves
Los Angeles, Calif., 161
Love waves, 23, 24, 48
Low-velocity channel, 49-50, 84
Loyalty Is, 29
Lunar seismology, vi, 141-4
L-waves, 23-4, 28-9, 47-8
    *See also* Phases
Lyell, Sir Charles, 167
Lyttelton, N.Z., 88

Macedonia, 174
Magma, 89, 91, 93, 102
Magnesium, silicates of, 5
Magnetic reversals, 57, 58

Magnetic storms, 57
Magnetic striping of the sea-floor, 58-9, 73, 75
Magnetic tape, 35, 136
Magnetism, terrestrial, 48, 57-9
    *See also* Palaeomagnetism
Magnetometer, 58
Magnets, 9, 12, 13, 14, 15, 57
Magnification, 7, 8, 9, 11, 83, 136
Magnitude, 12, 27, 71, 78-80, 130, 184-5
    and energy, 78, 80, 184-6
    and intensity, 78-9
    body-wave, 79-80, 185
    local, 79-80, 185
    of Martian earthquake, 145
    of moonquakes, 143
    of nuclear explosions, 134, 140, 185
    Richter, 12, 78-80
    surface-wave, 79-80, 185
    unified, 79-80
    *Magnitudes of individual earthquakes are listed on*
        *pp.* 189-96
Mallet, Robert, 3, 4, 6, 166, 167
Manila, Philippines, 25, 95
Mantle, 20, 21, 30, 45, 49-51, 73, 134
    lunar, 144
    *See also* Upper Mantle Project
Maralinga, S. Australia, 134
Maria, lunar, 144
Marlborough, N.Z., 148, 194
Marlborough Sounds, N.Z., 167, 194
Mars, 145
Martinique, 91
Masonry, 37, 112, 172, 173
Masterton, N.Z., 95, 109
Mauna Loa, Hawaii, 90
Mayon, Philippines, 90
McKay, Alexander, 156, 168-9
Mediterranean Sea, 71, 77
Medvedev, S. V., 4
Melting
    at core boundary, 51
    of primitive Earth, 45
    of rocks, 41, 44, 94
Mentawai Is, 75
Merapi, Java, 90, 91,
Mercalli scale, 4, 79, 107, 183-4
    *See also* Intensity
Mesozoic
    *See* Geological periods
Metamorphic rocks, 38, 42, 57
Metamorphism, 184
Meteorites, 45, 143
Meteorology, 83-4, 95, 97, 98
Mexico, 89
Mexico, Gulf of, 36
Michell, John, 3
Micro-earthquakes, 130
Microns, 27
Microseisms, 11, 25, 26, 67, 83-5, 121, 136
Microtremor, 121, 133
Microzoning, 132-3
Mid-oceanic ridges, 58, 71, 72, 75, 90, 161
Middle East, 71
Milne, John, 26, 159, 187
Miramar Peninsula, N.Z., 167
Mississippi Basin, 97, 165
Mississippi River, 38
Modes of free vibration of the Earth, 53

Modified Mercalli scale
    *See* Mercalli scale
Mohole, 50-1
Mohorovičić, Andrija, 30, 32
Mohorovičić discontinuity, 30-2, 45, 46, 49, 50
Mole tracks, 63
Moment, 80-1
*Monotis,* 40
Mont Pelée, Martinique, 91
Montague I., 173
Montana, 136, 137, 138, 140
Montessus de Ballore, Comte de,
    *See* Ballore
Moon, 97, 141-5
    internal structure, 143-4
Moonquakes, 143-5
Moraines, 175
Morocco, 107, 172
Mortar, 109
Mortgages, 133
Moscow, U.S.S.R., 26, 50, 136
Mount Cookson, N.Z., 169
Mount Egmont, N.Z., 90
Mount Everest, 54
Mount Fuji = Fujiyama, *q.v.,*
Mountain-building, 42-3, 59, 73
Mountain roots, 45, 54
Mountains, 54, 55, 70, 73
MSK intensity scale, 4, 79, 183
    *See also* Intensity
Mudflow, volcanic = Lahar, *q.v.*
Murchison, N.Z., 169-71
Mururoa, 140

Nagasaki, Japan, 134
Nakano, H., 67
Napier, N.Z., 95, 117, 171
Nasca Plate, 75
Nelson, N.Z., 4, 148, 170
Nersesov, I.L., 99
Networks, recording, 1, 10, 12, 15, 25, 26, 33, 114, 130, 171
    *See also* Array seismographs
Nevado de Huascarán, 178-9
New Caledonia, 39
New England, 165
New Guinea, 40, 114, 127
New Mexico, 134
New Orleans, 166
New Zealand, vi, 1, 3, 5, 10, 12, 24, 25, 35, 36, 51, 66, 69, 77,
    78, 79, 82, 84, 87, 88, 92, 93, 95, 97, 99-100, 103, 107,
    112, 118, 119, 123, 129, 130, 131, 132, 133, 134, 136,
    146-54, 167-71, 174, 193-6
    Map showing principal place-names cited, 195
N.Z. Department of Scientific and Industrial Research, viii, 25
    Geophysics Division, vii, 36, 94
    Physics and Engineering Laboratory, 112, 114
    *See also* N.Z. Geological Survey; Seismological
    Observatory, Wellington.
N.Z. Earthquake and War Damage Commission, 133, 171
New Zealand earthquakes,
    deep, 148, 152-3
    principal, 193-6
    shallow, 150-1
N.Z. Geological Survey, vii, 170
N.Z. Ministry of Works and Development, 114, 170
N.Z. National Society for Earthquake Engineering, 133, 198
N.Z. Public Works Department, *Now* N.Z. Ministry of Works
    and Development, *q.v.*

New Zealand seismic regions, 148, 150, 153
New Zealand Sub-Crustal Rift, 148
Newbury, Berkshire, 26
Newspapers, 10, 79, 95, 169, 176
Newtons, 185
Ngauruhoe, N.Z., 90, 92
Nickel, 51, 57
Niigata, Japan, 176, 179
Nimbluk Valley, Iran, 63
North America, 84, 130
North American Plate, 75, 147
North Island, N.Z., 19, 90, 93, 148, 150
North Sea, 36
Northland, N.Z., 88, 151
Norway, 86
Nuclear bombs.  *See* Atomic bombs
Nuclear testing, 134
    detection of underground, 135, 136, 138-40
Nuée ardente, 91
Nur, Amos, 101
Nutation, 44

Observatories, 1, 2, 11, 25, 83, 134
    *See also* Networks, recording
Observers of felt earthquakes, 4-5
Ocean basins, 71
Oceanic trench. *See* Trench
Oceanography, 58
Oceans, 45-6, 48, 54
    *See also* Atlantic, *etc.*
Oil, 1, 8, 13, 33, 36, 66, 176
    *See also* Prospecting
Okarito, N.Z., 149
Oldham, R.D., 21, 44
Olivine, 51
Omori, F., 98
Ongley, M. L., 170
Origin. *See* Epicentre, Focus, Hypocentre, Source volume
Orogenesis = Mountain-building, *q.v.*
Orowan, E., 66
Osaka, Japan, 123
Oshima, Japan, 155
Otago Peninsula, N.Z., 150
Outcrops, 38
Overtones, 53

Pacific Ocean, vi, 58, 71, 77, 85, 87, 88, 131, 140, 150, 174,
    186
Pacific Plate, 75, 146, 147, 148, 150, 152
Pakistan, 60
Palaeomagnetism, 57-9
Pangaea, 56
Paricutin, Mexico, 89
Parnassus, N.Z., 169
Parthenon, 37
Pendulum,
    cross mounted as, 168
    damping of, 8, 13
    gravity, 13, 54-5
    horizontal, 10-1, 14
    inverted, 10, 111
    magnification of, 8-9
    period of, 8, 11
    simple, 7-8, 11
    types of, 10
    vertical, 10, 14

Period
  of buildings, 109, 111, 117, 118, 119
  of ground movements, 8, 11, 48, 53
  of microseisms, 11, 83-4
  of seiches, 86
  of seismographs, 8, 9, 11, 12, 13, 14, 15, 53, 136
  of simple pendulum, 7, 11
  geological, 40-1, 183
  relation to frequency and wavelength, 47
Periodicity of earthquakes 81, 96
  of moonquakes, 143
Permafrost, 175
Peru, 62, 107, 113, 176
Phases in seismograms, 22, 25, 27
  Body-wave phases
    *P*, 17, 18, 20, 23, 24, 25, 27, 28, 30, 79
    *S*, 17, 23, 24, 27, 30, 79, 140
  Core reflections
    *PcP, PcS*, 21
    *ScP, ScS*, 21, 22, 25, 27
  Core refractions
    *P′ = PKP, q.v.*
    *P′P′ = PKPPKP, q.v.*
    *PKP, PKS, SKP, SKS*, 22, 23, 25, 27
    *PKPPKP*, 22, 23
    *PKKP, SKKS*, 22, 23
    *PKIKP, PKJKP*, 52
  Crustal phases
    *Pg, Sg*, 31-2, 50
    *P\*, S\** = *Crustal phases refracted at the* Conrad
    discontinuity, *q.v.*
    *Pn, Sn*, 31-2, 50
  Depth phases
    *pP, sP, pS, sS*, 24, 25
    *sScS*, 25
  Impulsive and emergent
    *i* and *e*, 26, 67
  Surface reflections
    *PP, PS, SS*, 22, 24, 27, 79
    *PPP, PPS, PSP, PSS*, 22, 27
    *SSS, SSP, SPP, SPS*, 22
    *PPPP*, 22
  Surface-wave phases
    *L, L_Q, L_R*, 23-4, 27
    *See also* Travel-times
Philippines, 71, 186
Philippines Plate, 75, 154
Physics, 1, 43, 101
Plafker, George, vii, 173
Plains of Utopia, 145
Planetary seismology, 144-5
Planets, attraction of, 97
Plaster, 78, 108, 131, 173, 174, 184
Plate tectonics, vi, 72-7, 146-8, 150, 152, 154
  *See also* Continental drift, Sea-floor spreading,
  Transform faults
Platelets, 72
Plates, lithospheric, 72, 74-5, 76, 146-8, 150, 152, 154
Pleistocene
  *See* Geological periods
Pliny the Elder, 164
Plumb-line, deflection of the, 54, 55
  *See also* Isostasy
Poles, magnetic, 57
*Polflucht*, 57
Pore fluid, 102, 103
Pores, 69, 102
Port Ahuriri, N.Z., 106, 108

Potsdam, 13
Pre-Cambrian
  *See* Geological periods
Precursors, earthquake, 99-104
Prediction
  *See* Earthquake prediction
Premonitory gap, swarm, 103
Pressure, 1, 39, 42, 43, 50, 81, 102-3
  inside the Earth, 49, 66
Prince William Sound, Alaska, 85, 174
Prospecting, seismic, 30, 33-7, 58, 140
Pumice, 89
Puyehue, Chile, 173
*P*-waves, 17, 20-2, 24, 46, 49-52, 67, 69, 99, 100, 102, 103, 104,
  144 *See also* Phases
Pyramid, Great, 37

Quadrantal pattern of first motions, 67-8
Queensland, Australia, 85
Questionnaires, 4

Radar, 97
Radioactivity, 41, 45, 103
Radon, 103
Railways, 3, 123, 124, 175, 181
Raised beaches, 166
Randall, M.J., vi, 69
Rann of Kutch, 60, 167
Ranrahirca, Peru, 179
Raoul I., 88, 93
Rarefaction, 67, 69
Rayleigh waves. 23, 24, 25, 48
Rebeur-Paschwitz, E. von, 13
Recent
  *See* Geological periods
Recording,
  by radio telemetry, 10
  in strong-motion instruments, 2
  mechanical, 9
  photographic, 2, 9, 13, 136
  with heat-sensitive paper, 10
  with pen and amplifier, 13
Recording drums, 10
Records, earthquake
  *See* Seismograms
Reflection, 21, 45
Reflection prospecting, 36
Refraction, 21
Refraction shooting, 36
  *See also* Prospecting
Refugees, 157, 158, 170, 180, 181
Regional centres, 25, 26
Regionalization, seismic, 130
  *See also* Zoning
Reid, H. F., 60, 64, 159
Resistivity, electrical, 103
Resonance, 15, 111, 119
Reykjanes Ridge, 58
Reynolds, Osborne, 101
Richter, C. F., viii, 12, 67, 71, 72, 78, 98, 134, 154, 165, 183,
  186, 189, 196, 197
Richter scale
  *See* Magnitude
Ridges, submarine, 58, 71, 72, 75, 90, 161
Rifts, 71, 75, 148
Rigidity, 20, 49
Rikitake, T., 104

Rimutaka Mts, N.Z., 167
Roads, 107, 113, 123, 124, 127, 170, 181
Roche Percée, New Caledonia, 39
Rock 38, 48, 49, 55, 56, 57, 64, 99
    deformation and flow, 66
    dilatancy of, 101-3
    laboratory tests upon, 69
    melting of, 90, 94
    strength of, 80, 91, 96, 102, 140
Rocks,
    *See* Igneous, Metamorphic, Sedimentary
Romania, 77
Rome, Italy, 37, 49
Roofs, 108, 113, 116, 169, 174
Rossi-Forel scale, 4, 79
    *See also* Intensity scales
Rothé, J.P., 189, 198
Royal Observatory, Hong Kong, 83
Royal Society, 3, 70
Royal Society of New Zealand, vi
Ruapehu, N.Z., 91, 92
Rudak, Iran, 174
Rubble, 70, 71, 113, 176


Safety, public, 30, 104, 106-7, 125, 129
Saint Helena, 58
Saint Peter, tomb of, 37
Saint Pierre, Martinique, 91
Sakhalin, 87
Saltwater, Lagoons, N.Z., 149
Sampazari, Anatolia, 63
San Juan Capistrano, Calif., 159
San Francisco, Calif., 4, 60, 161
Sand craters, 123, 127, 128, 169, 176
Sandstone, 39, 40, 41
Santa Cruz Is, 28
Scandinavia, 86
Scoria, 89
Scotland, 41, 136
Scott Base, Antarctica, 28, 29, 85
Sea floor, 38, 42, 58-9
Sea-floor spreading, 72-7, 161
Sea-level, changes in, 131
Sea-quakes, 6
Secondary damage, 110, 111, 114
Sediment, 36, 38-40, 42, 43, 58
Sedimentary rocks, 38, 39, 40, 42, 57-8
Seers, 95
Seiches, 86, 165, 174
Seismic sea-wave = Tsunami, *q.v.*
Seismic zoning, 129-33
    *See also* Microzoning, Regionalization
Seismicity, 70-7, 129
    lunar, 143-4
    of the Earth, 71, 72-4, 146-63
    of California, 146-8, 159-63
    of Mars, 145
    of New Zealand, 146-54
    of Japan, 152-5
    *See also* Earthquake statistics, Microzoning,
    Regionalization, Zoning
Seismograms, 16-29, 65, 73, 93
    of moonquakes, 143-4
    of nuclear explosions, 135
    of San Francisco earthquake, 163
    strong-motion, 143-4

Seismographs, 2, 7-15, 33, 53, 66, 68, 92, 111, 132, 135
    array, 136-40
    damping of, 8, 13, 15, 78
    electromagnetic, 9, 12-5, 33, 34, 142
    Galitzin, 10, 15, 84
    horizontal pendulum, 10, 11-4
    lunar, 141-3
    magnification of, 8-11, 78, 83, 111
    mechanical, 9, 13
    Milne-Shaw, 10
    Omori, 9, 13
    period of, 8, 9, 11, 12, 13, 14, 15, 78, 136
    simple pendulum, 7-8, 10, 11
    strong-motion, 11, 111-2, 114, 116, 120
    torsion, 10, 12, 13, 78
    ultra-long-period, 53
    vertical, 10, 14, 55
    World-Wide Standard, 12, 14, 15, 135-6
    Wiechert, 9
    *See also* Seismometer, Seismoscope
Seismological Observatory, Wellington, N.Z., vi, vii, 11, 17,
    26, 27, 28, 29
Seismology, 1, 21, 30, 167, 182
    *See also* Engineering, Lunar, Planetary seismology
Seismometer, 9, 10, 136, 137, 139
    Benioff, 10, 12, 13, 27, 136
    Press-Ewing, 10, 14, 15, 28, 29, 136
    Willmore, 12, 15
    Wilson-Lamison, 10
    Wood-Anderson, 10, 12, 13
    as magnitude standard, 78-9
    *See also* Geophones, Seismographs
Seismoscope, 164
Selenoseisms = Moonquakes, *q.v.*
Seneca, Lucius Annaeus, 164
Seward, Alaska, 175
Sewerage, 176, 181
Shadow-zone for *P,* 20-1
Shaking table, 120
Shear, 61, 69, 82, 140
Shear-waves, 17, 23, 24
    *See also* Love waves, *S*-waves
Shields, continental, 56, 71
Shikoku, Japan, 152
Shimozuru, D., 93
Shinano River, Japan, 176
Shot instant, 34, 36, 134-5
Silicates, 51
Sill, 89
Sine wave, 46-7
Sinistral faulting, defined, 60
Skoplje, Yugoslavia, 112
Slumping,
    superficial, 63, 169, 175
    submarine, 85
Sodium, 51
SOFAR channel, 49
Soil creep, 128
Soil mechanics, 101, 111
Solander, I., N.Z., 151
Solar flares, 57
Sound waves, 17, 20, 21, 49, 91-2, 171
Source volume, 67, 80-1, 96, 102-3, 163
South America, 70, 71, 77, 87, 130
South Carolina, 123, 166
South Island, N.Z., 18, 88, 151
South Sandwich Is, 28
Southern Alps, N.Z., 147, 149

Soviet Union
    *See* Union of Socialist Soviet Republics
Space-craft, 141, 143, 149
Specific gravity, 182
Spencer's Gulf, S. Australia, 71
Spheroidal oscillation, 53
Spine, volcanic, 91
Sponge Bay uplift, 171
Springs, (mechanical), 12, 15, 55, 64
Springs (water), 92, 94, 174, 184
Sri Lanka, 91
Stable regions, 56, 71
Stanford University, Calif., 101
Statistics, 76-80, 82, 94, 96, 98, 106-7, 182, 186
    *See also* Earthquake casualties
Stewart I. N.Z., 133
Storm damage, 111, 116, 133,
Strain,
    elastic, 66, 80, 97, 102, 184
    in rocks, 81-2, 99, 103
    regional, 81-2, 99
Strain-gauges, 114
Strasbourg, France, 25, 26
Strata, 33, 39-41, 60, 93
Stress,
    in lunar crust, 143
    tectonic, 97
Stress-drop, 80-1
Strike, 60, 61
Stromboli, Italy, 91
Strong-motion records, 111-2, 114, 116, 120
Structures
    crossing faults, 131
    damage to, 133
    safety of 106-28, 131
    *See also* Bridges, Buildings, Dams, *etc.*
Stukeley, Rev. Dr. William, 70
Subduction, 73-6, 77, 147, 150
Subsidence, 96, 116, 127, 131, 173, 174, 176
Subsoil, 111, 118
    effect on felt intensity, 5, 129, 131
    liquefaction of, 121
    mapping of, 123
Sugami Bay, Japan, 155
Sulawesi, Indonesia, 24
Sumatra, Indonesia, 75
Sumida-gawa, Japan, 158
Sun, 44, 45, 97, 143
Sunspots, 57
Surface-waves, 11, 23, 29, 46, 47, 48, 53, 69, 79, 84, 93
    *See also* Free vibrations of the Earth, Love waves,
    Rayleigh waves
Suyehiro, K., 97
Swarms, 82, 93-4, 97
    premonitory, 103
S-waves, 17, 23, 49-52, 69, 104, 138, 144
Sweden, 25, 86
Switzerland, 4, 86
Symmetrical seismic regions, 72-5


Taiwan, 28
Tadzhikstan, 98
Tanzania, 90
Taradale, N.Z., 18
Taranaki, N.Z., 92, 148
Tarata, N.Z., 17
Tarawera eruption (1886), 195
Tasman Basin, 150

Tasmania, 82
Taupo, N.Z., 91, 93
Tectonics, 38, 60-9, 72-7, 130, 166
    lunar, 144
    Martian, 145
    *See also* Continental drift, Faulting, Isostasy, Plate
    tectonics, Sea-floor spreading
Teheran, Iran, 174
Telemetry, 10, 137
Telephone, 158, 169
Temperature
    effects upon seismographs, 8, 15
    internal, of the Earth, 44-5, 48-9, 51, 66, 89
    of lava, 90
    of the primitive Earth, 44
Tension, 61
Tertiary
    *See* Geological periods
Texas, 86
Thailand, 85, 91
Thereon and Therea, 164
Thomson, Sir J.J., 30
Tibet, 45
Tidal wave = Tsunami, *q.v.*
Tides, 97, 176
    bodily, 97-8
    bodily, on Moon, 143
Tide-gauges, 87
Tiles, 108, 111, 174
Tilt, 9, 92, 98, 103, 131
Timing, 10-11, 34, 136
Tinemaha, Calif., 135
Tokyo, Japan, 26, 104, 107, 123, 155, 157, 158, 159
Tomales Bay, Calif., 163
Tonga, 150
Tonga-Kermadec Trench, 24
Tongariro, N.Z., 91
Tongariro National Park, N.Z., 89, 91, 92
Torsional vibrations, 53
Towers, 109, 111, 119, 168
Toxic gases, 69
Transducer, 12
Transverse waves, 16, 17, 23, 24, 48, 49-52, 69, 104, 138, 144
Transform faults, 161
Travel-time curve, 17, 22, 23, 26, 27, 31
Travel-times, 17-29, 49, 100, 134
    for moonquakes, 143
    of crustal phases, 30-2
Tremor, volcanic
    *See* Volcanic tremor
Trenches, ocean, 24, 54, 72, 73, 75, 89, 150, 157
Triangulation
    *See* Geodetic surveying
Triassic
    *See* Geological periods
Triggering
    by nuclear explosions, 140
    of earthquakes, 96-8
    of moonquakes, 143
Tripartite stations, 83
Tristan da Cunha, 58
Tsunamis, 6, 85-8, 106, 155, 165, 172, 173, 176
Tuai, N.Z., 76
Turakirae, N.Z., 166, 167
Turkey, 70, 186
Turner, F. J., 24
Twyne, Thomas, 164
Tyan Shan, 130
Typhoons, 84

Union of Socialist Soviet Republics, 26, 51, 69, 99-101, 136
United Kingdom Atomic Energy Authority, 136
United Nations Scientific, Educational, and Cultural
    Organisation (UNESCO), 25, 174, 198
United States of America, 41, 71, 100, 136, 166
U.S. Army, 69
U.S. Coast and Geodetic Survey, 25
U.S. Congress, 51
U.S. Geological Survey, 25, 136, 173
U.S. Government, 135
U.S. National Earthquake Information Service, 25, 80
Units, 182
University of Auckland, 118
University of Coimbra, 165
Uplift, 4, 85, 103, 131, 154, 155, 156, 159, 166, 171, 173, 174
Upper Mantle Project, 50, 51
Uppsala, Sweden, 185


Vacuum, 55
Valdez, Alaska, 175
Valdivia, Chile, 173
Vardar Basin, Yugoslavia, 174
Velocity of seismic waves, 20, 30-2, 45, 46, 49, 65
    Mallet's measurements of, 166-7
    precursory changes in, 99-103
    on Moon, 144
    *See also* Travel-times
Vertical, deflection of the, 54
Vibrations, artificial, 83-4, 121, 132-3
Vibrator, building, 118-20
Vine, F.J., 58, 59
Volcanic tremor, 12, 92-3
Volcano Is, 152
Volcanoes, 38, 41, 48, 71, 72, 75, 89-94, 150, 152, 154, 173
Volume changes, 68, 102
Vrancea, Romania, 77
Vulcano, Italy, 91


Wadati, K., 24, 99
Waiau River, N.Z., 169
Wairakei, N.Z., 35, 93
Wairarapa, N.Z., 43, 95
Wairoa, N.Z., 171
Wanganui, N.Z., 18
Water-closets, 109

Water-mains, damage to, 163, 171, 174, 176
Wave-form, 112
Wavelength, 47
Wave-motion, 16-7, 24-5, 46-7, 112, 131
Waves, 1, 3, 6, 10, 11, 12, 16, 22, 23, 31, 39, 46-8, 52, 65, 78,
    111, 112, 140, 184
    dispersion of, 47-8
    elastic, 3, 65, 140, 184
    paths of, 28-9, 31-2, 49-50
    period and frequency of, 11, 47-8
    *See also* P, S, Longitudinal, Sound, Transverse, Surface
    *etc.*, Microseisms, Tsunamis, Seiches, *etc.*; Reflection,
    Refraction, Velocity
Weather forecasting, 83-4, 95, 97, 98
Wegener, Alfred, 56-7, 58
Weight, dropping, as seismic source, 33, 34, 37
Wellington, N.Z., 11, 17, 25, 28, 29, 68, 69, 92, 109, 132, 134,
    166, 167, 168, 169
Wells, 38, 66, 69, 103, 184
Wesley, Rev. John, 70
Westport, N.Z., 170
Whakarewarewa, N.Z., 89
Whangaehu River, N.Z., 91
White Rock, N.Z., 43
Willis, Bailey, 108
Willmore, P.L., 12
Wilson, J. Tuzo, 161
Wind loading, 116, 119
World War II, 25, 83, 134
World-wide Standard Seismograph Network, 12, 14, 15, 26,
    135-6


X-rays, 30


Year of earthquakes, 159
Yokohama, Japan, 123, 155, 158
York Minster, 125
Yugoslavia, 174
Yungay, Peru, 178-9


Zöllner suspension, 10
Zone of silence, 92
Zone, shadow, 20-1
Zoning, seismic, 96, 118, 129-33, 151, 181
    *See also* Microzoning, regionalization